Letters to Lily

ON HOW THE WORLD WORKS

Alan Macfarlane

P

PROFILE BOOKS

This paperback edition published in 2006

First published in Great Britain in 2005 by
Profile Books Ltd
29 Cloth Fair
London EC1A 7JQ
www.profilebooks.com

1 3 5 7 9 10 8 6 4 2

Typeset in Palatino by MacGuru Ltd

Printed and bound in the USA

A CIP catalogue record for this book is available from the British Library.

ISBN 978 1 86197 780 9

For Lily and, with her agreement,
for Gerry Martin, a real friend

ontents

Power and order

Self and others

Life and death

Body and mind

What are these letters?

$\mathscr{W}$hy write to you?

Dear Lily,

Let's imagine what a visitor from some distant planet would think of human history. Let us look down on the museum of human history from afar, with you, Lily, as one of the exhibits.

The visitor would almost certainly conclude that humans are very topsy-turvy. They are obviously just animals, yet they seem to think that they are special. They cannot decide whether to prefer their minds or their bodies. They cannot decide whether to prefer their senses or their thoughts. They think of themselves as immortal, yet they die. They think of themselves as lords of creation, yet they are a prey to very many other species. They have excellent minds, but this just leads them into folly and unreason. They claim to be the sole judges of truth, but spend much of their time lying. They are loving, yet they spend much time hating and undermining each other.

Humans are co-operative creatures, yet they are also intensely selfish. They can create great art, but leave the world an ugly mess. With their amazing technologies they generate great wealth, yet most of them live in degrading poverty. They enjoy peace but constantly kill. They strive to be equal, yet invent and sustain endless inequalities between classes, religious groups, and men and women. They preach tolerance and understanding, yet they torture each other for their beliefs.

The distant observer might well be confused, agreeing that 'Man is an embodied paradox, a bundle of contradictions.' Especially puzzling is the huge gap between human potential, the ability to make a rich, lovely and fulfilling life on earth, and the actual miseries human beings create for themselves and other species.

...

As your grandfather I would like to help you to understand this confused and confusing world. Since I will not be here for ever, it is important to put something on paper for you now.

I have spent my life as a historian and anthropologist trying to understand how the world works. I have written many academic books. However, as I get older, I have become increasingly interested in trying to understand and explain the bigger picture in a simpler and more concise way.

I write from a particular viewpoint, that of an elderly, white, British, male academic. Yet I hope I have escaped enough from these limitations to say something that applies more widely. Furthermore I am writing to a specific person – you, my grand-daughter, an English girl. You are now only seven, but I imagine you in ten years' time. Yet although this is specially for you, I hope that people who are older and younger than you, and of other countries and backgrounds, will also be able to appre-ciate what I say. For I would like Spanish, French, Russians, as well as Chinese, Japanese, Indians, Americans and others to be able to compare their experience with yours.

I have deliberately written the letters quickly and without referring to lots of books. It seems best to speak as directly as

I can from my experience. So there are bound to be gaps and there are ideas that you will question. These are personal letters, written to tell you what I feel and think about certain issues. They are based on a lifetime of travel in Europe and Asia, of teaching several generations of students at Cambridge University, of reading and writing about the past and the present.

I can fit these thoughts into a set of short letters because, in the end, there are just two questions behind all of them. The first is: what are humans really like? Are they basically violent or kind, selfish or social, creative or dull? The second is: what are the origins, and what is the nature, of the world we live in?

...

We know from everyday experience that, while we cannot absolutely predict the future, we can make fairly useful guesses which usually turn out to be roughly accurate. If there were no patterns in the past that continued into the future, all of the existence of humans and other animals on earth would be impossible. It is on the basis of what we have established about human motivation and what we have seen in the pattern of past events that we make endless decisions, big and small. There are no invariable laws, but there are likelihoods and tendencies.

You and I expect to hear the fish-and-chip van on a Wednesday evening – and it almost always comes. You couldn't undertake the smallest action, from eating a meal to playing a game or riding a bicycle, if this predictability based on past patterns recurring could not be relied upon.

In these letters I would like to try to describe some of the patterns that I believe I have found. I hope that you will then be able to stand on my shoulders and see further than I have. This is not easy. It is undoubtedly true that, as the poet John Keats wrote, 'Nothing ever becomes real till it is experienced'. It is practically impossible to imagine what love or hunger is like until you have experienced it. Yet I hope that if you have this book beside you as the experiences occur, it may help to put them into context and to make you aware that you are not alone.

Since both you and I, Lily, are British, the focus is often on our particular experience and history. Some may think that there are times when I extol the virtues of British civilisation too highly. Yet because I sincerely believe that the story happened in the way in which I tell it, I have left the apparent bias as it is.

Furthermore I want you, Lily, to know something about your roots. These can be explained only by my drawing attention to some of the oddness of British history. And I believe this is important to others too. For, by chance, much of the modern world went through the funnel of British history. A great deal was contributed from all over the world, but by chance Britain became the largest empire on earth at just the time when the industrial and scientific revolutions were shaping our modern world. This has left its stamp not only on America, Africa, Australia and India, but on many other places.

...

We often take this present world, and our own lives, for granted because it is all around us. It is difficult to imagine any other. You may believe that the science you learnt at school, the tools you use in your house, the paintings you look at, the language you speak, the wealth, freedoms and rights you enjoy are 'natural' and 'universal'. It's difficult not to believe that our world was bound to end up like this and that it's the natural thing. Yet is this the case?

The visitor from the distant planet would certainly not think you were normal when set against people around the world in the past and present. You are not typical at all. If you were, you would be married and would very soon have several children. Your marriage would have been arranged; romantic love would not have been the basis for the choice of your husband. You would have spent your childhood from the age of five or six working in the fields.

Now you would be trying to cope with your pregnancy while also spending many hours slaving in the cold and wet or heat and dust. You would be sick almost all the time, suffering from worms in your stomach, septic sores, coughs, diarrhoea. Probably you would have had other more serious diseases such as malaria, or AIDS. Many of your close relatives would have died when you were a child.

You would lead a desperately insecure life. Powerful people would constantly be demanding things from your family. Marauding soldiers might often cause havoc in your village. The law would give you no protection. You would be malnourished and often very hungry. You would be uneducated and have no chance of bettering your life. You would be considered inferior to every male you met, including your younger relatives. You might well be shut away behind a wall or a veil, your feet broken when you were a child or your genitals mutilated. You get the picture.

Then think of yourself. You have education, lovely clothes, good food, doctors, dentists and hospitals freely available, loving parents, political and religious freedom. You do not have to slave with your body and you can choose what you want to do in your life, when and whom you will marry, whether to have children. You believe you are equal to any man and that you will live to a ripe old age, benefiting from a pension in a country where there are no secret police and no extortionate landlords to live off you. Above all, you live in peace and free from serious violence and fear.

Yet even with all this, you are often anxious, lonely, confused, undecided about what to do. I hope these letters will give you a new understanding of the ever-so-human animal that you are, quite special but with all the fears and uncertainties that are part of being us, the people of one smallish planet circling a dying sun.

...

I was always taught to read books from the start to the end, and with equal attention to all parts. I was therefore very surprised to come across a remark by the philosopher Francis Bacon who suggested that 'Some books are to be tasted, others to be swallowed, and some few to be chewed and digested'. This applies equally well to the individual letters here.

Some you will find are already largely familiar or seem simple, and can be skimmed through. Others are deceptive: I've tried to keep the expression of the ideas as clear as possible, yet beneath the surface there are often concepts that are quite complex and may be totally unfamiliar. They take time to absorb. Some letters you'll need to read slowly, and just one at a time and no more. The ideas are very condensed; like powder or liquid, let them mix in your mind and expand outwards.

There is no need to read the letters in the order in which they appear in the book. Start with whatever question most interests you and dot around. As a new puzzle or query occurs to you, see if I've written about it. You may also sometimes find it helpful to read a letter, then read other things or talk round the subject with friends, and then reread the letter later when it will have a different meaning.

Although this may look like just another book summarising things, I hope it will be more than that for you. I want it to be a companion on future mental walks. Together we can explore the world in a continuing conversation long after I am old or dead. I walked and talked to you and to Gerry, with whom I went for many such walks and to whom the book is dedicated. I would like to continue our walks through the woods, over the hills, along the rivers and through gardens and museums.

2

*W*ho are you?

Dear Lily,

Who are you? Where did you come from? What has made you what you are?

You may be surprised by these questions and reply that I know perfectly well who you are. 'I am Lily Bee; I am a girl who was born in Australia, but my parents are English and I now live in England and think of myself as British.'

It all seems very simple, but let us investigate a little further.

When I was at school I used to write pretend letters to myself as follows:

Alan
Macfarlane,
Field Head,
Hawkshead,
Lancashire,
England,
Europe,

The World,
The Universe.

From this you can see already that I thought of myself as many people crammed into one. A named person, a member of the Macfarlane family, an inhabitant of a house, of a village, a county, a country, a region, a world, a universe. Let's look at who you are by following this same movement from the individual to the world level.

Are you a separate person?

You take it for granted that you are 'Lily' and that Lily is a person who is different and distinct from other people. You have a very strong concept of yourself as an individual. You probably assume that this is how all people think of themselves. Yet while it is true that most people have some sense of their separateness, being English you belong to perhaps the most individualistic society in history. So your concepts of your separateness and individuality are especially strong.

In most societies the family comes first, and the individual is submerged within that group. This means that it is really impossible to think of yourself without thinking of others. There is little meaning to the words 'I' and 'me'. This is shown in the very restricted use of such words in some languages. You would in many societies have a meaning only *in relation* to others. Your identity would come from being a daughter in relation to parents, a mother in relation to children, a wife in relation to a husband, a serf or servant in relation to a lord, a living person in relation to the ancestors.

This is why in a Nepalese village where I have spent a lot of time you would not be called or addressed as Lily, but as 'eldest daughter', or, when you had your first child, as 'mother of so-and-so'. In many other societies your name would change many times in your life. Imagine being called Lily until you were ten, then Jane for a few years, then Alice and so on, with your second name also changing frequently.

You, on the other hand, feel free and float around as a complete person with all kinds of inner powers and potentials. You may be a daughter or a mother, but these are not the things that make you who you are. You are Lily, and the other things are just aspects of yourself. The first basic assumption that you have, of your strong individual identity, with special and personal feelings, rights and freedoms, is very unusual.

Are you a woman?

You describe yourself as a 'girl' or 'woman'. You probably mean that you are not a man, that you have certain physical characteristics (breasts, womb) which give you certain potentials (nursing and childbearing) that are different from those of a man. This is all true. Yet as well as the physical differences you have characteristics that you have absorbed, largely unconsciously, from the day you were born, which we may call 'gender'. This is what the feminist Simone de Beauvoir was referring to when she wrote that 'One is not born a woman, one becomes one.'

You may let your hair grow longer than most men, wear make-up or perfume, carry a handbag, prefer particular colours, wear certain clothes, read girls' magazines, play only some games (hockey rather than football, for example), think of specific careers (media, education) rather than others (the army, the stock exchange). Yet the selection of all these as feminine ways and goals is a matter of chance and teaching. There is nothing 'natural' or genetic about it.

In some societies it is men who grow their hair long, while women shave their heads; it is men who wear perfume or make-up, and dresses (I was teased at school for wearing a 'skirt', i.e.

a kilt), and who sit around gossiping while the women do all the hard physical labour. Nowadays ideas of the female gender are changing very fast, and women are becoming soldiers in the front line, taking on many of the roles and attributes of men.

In particular if you add 'English' to 'woman', you become even more unusual. An English woman is the heir to a Christian society, living in a certain country and fitting in with its laws and customs. Most of your 'womanhood' is a construct of a particular history.

For example, 'being' a woman in England today entitles you to equality before the law, control over your own body, the right to own property, the right to vote, the right to choose your own husband, equal respect and an equal chance of going to heaven, if you believe in such a place. Yet 'being' a woman in almost all civilisations in history has automatically denied a woman all these things from birth.

You speak a language that has fewer gender differences built into it than most other languages. For instance, all nouns in languages such as French or Italian have to have their gender specified, while in traditional Japanese the notion of the superiority of men and inferiority of women was built into the language.

So you are not just a woman, but a very particular and historically unusual kind of woman, who has been constructed by millions of random decisions and accidents over thousands of years. You are not an artificial robot, but you are certainly the product of huge random variations. This process occurs in every interaction you have with every living person, in every moment you spend reading, watching television, in every sentence you speak and every thought you have.

What race are you?

You say that you are an *English* girl, but what does that mean? You may think that it means that if you went back through your ancestors you would find only Angles and Saxons. But in fact your great-grandfather's family was probably Viking (Danish) and a number of your ancestors were Celts (Scots and Irish). A DNA test on you would probably reveal all sorts of traces of interbreeding. We are discovering how mixed up our ancestry is.

Yet even before DNA testing, anyone who understood English history would know what a particularly mixed or mongrel race the 'English' are, with Celts, Romans, Angles, Saxons, Danes, Norwegians, French, Dutch mixtures up to the seventeenth century, and since then all sorts of peoples from the Empire and post-Empire. So the idea of being 'English' is just a constructed identity. It defines you in relation to others, the French or Germans or even Scots, for example. Yet it really means very little.

Are you British?

You might describe yourself as not only 'English', but also 'British', that is to say that on your passport and in your own feeling of yourself your nationality is British. Behind this is the idea of the nation, that is a bounded political, linguistic, cultural and territorial unit. You might assume that your idea of belonging to a nation-state is common, indeed universal, and has long been the situation of most people on earth. This can be questioned.

Many people now argue that, in most of the world, the nation-state is really an invention of the last two hundred years. There were no nations in India or Africa, or in the Near or Far East, in 1800. There were states and empires, but if you asked people 'What nation do you belong to?' they would not have understood your question. If you had changed the question to 'What is your people?' or 'What do you call yourself?', you would have got surprising answers. Even in France, Italy, Germany or Spain, people did not think of themselves as French, Italians, Germans or Spanish, but rather as Bretons, Gascons, Lombards, Basques, Andalusians and so on.

Most of the inhabitants of France didn't begin to think of themselves as primarily French until after about 1870, and the same is true of all the countries of continental Europe. The change occurred even later in other regions of the world such as Eastern Europe or the Middle East. In many parts of the globe it is only just happening. When I went to the Himalayas in the late 1960s the people I worked with in the central hills referred to the Kathmandu Valley alone as 'Nepal'. They thought they lived outside Nepal, in their own village and group and region, though on the map it was all 'Nepal'.

Nations are invented or imagined communities, where people who do not know each other and often have little in common come to think of themselves as 'the British' or 'the French'. Some say this is the result of the spread of printing and hence of newspapers and books in the national language. They also argue that the spread of an economic system which binds people together through a common currency and set of money exchanges is behind this – relatively new – way of thinking. Others see it as the result of factories and cities, or of new educational systems. Whatever the cause, it is true that nation-states have dominated the world only during the last two hundred years.

Yet, by chance, you happen to live in a somewhat older nation. Because we live on a small island that early adopted a common language, law, economy and set of political institutions, the English have been becoming a nation from as early as King Alfred in the eighth century. Five hundred years ago, if you had asked someone what nation he belonged to he might well have said 'England'. Then the English became British when the King of Scotland also became the King of England in 1603, and Scots and English people settled in Ireland from the seventeenth century. Now they are becoming English, Scottish, Welsh or Irish again.

We fight wars and discriminate against outsiders and immigrants as if there were such things as nations, but they are just lines on a map. Nations are constructed and deconstructed. There is nothing natural or given about them. They are imagined, invented concepts and there is no British nation, no English nation, except in our imagination. Some even say that they are short-lived fictions and that the age of the nation-state will soon be over as we merge in a global world. And not before time, according to many of those who have suffered the vicious effects of nationalism, like the refugee Albert Einstein who wrote that 'Nationalism is an infantile disease. It is the measles of mankind.'

Certainly what it means to be 'English' and 'British', as you will find, will fluctuate over your lifetime and your feelings of national identity will alter enormously. As it shifts back and forth, is aroused by war cries or lulled by talk of European integration, it is good to remember what a constructed thing it is. The same is true of those who live in most of the nations of the world, whether in Cyprus, Israel, Japan, North Korea, Vietnam or elsewhere. The pulse of national identity slows and quickens, and the very meaning of 'being' of a certain nation changes deeply as the world changes around a group of people.

Where do you come from?

We also invent our origins. We easily slip into the idea that the things around us were discovered, or at least basically adapted, by our own society. Yet if you think for a moment you will find that almost everything was invented in other civilisations.

The anthropologist Ralph Linton described the average American as follows:

he awakens in a bed built on a pattern which originated in the Near East ... He throws back covers made from cotton, domesticated in India, or linen, domesticated in the Near East ... He takes off his pyjamas, a garment invented in India, and washes with soap invented by the ancient Gauls ... Before going out for breakfast he glances through the window, made of glass invented in Egypt, and if it is raining puts on overshoes made of rubber discovered by the Central American Indians and takes an umbrella, invented in south-eastern Asia ... On his way to breakfast he stops to buy a paper, paying for it with coins, an ancient Lydian invention ... His plate is of steel, an alloy first made in southern India, his fork a medieval Italian invention, and his spoon a derivative of a Roman original.

We have reached only as far as breakfast – and through the day the assemblage of world cultures continues. Nevertheless, at the end, 'As he absorbs the accounts of foreign troubles he will, if he is a good conservative citizen, thank a Hebrew deity in an Indo-European language that he is 100 per cent American.'

So we are all composites of history, built up from our past. England is a particularly obvious example of this because, being part of a small island near a great continent, and being a trading and imperial nation, it has sucked in almost all of its culture from abroad. There is scarcely anything, in music, painting, architecture, science and knowledge, up to the eighteenth century at least, that was not largely the result of borrowings.

A particularly obvious instance is the effect of the imperial phase on British life, and above all the influence of India. In many ways a Martian might well regard England today as just an extension of India. It is not merely that more people are involved in making curries in England than in any other form of manufacture. Nor that much of the wealth that built parts of England, including many of its great houses, gardens, art collections and libraries, came from India. It is something more.

Many phrases and ideas have Indian roots: veranda, gymkhana, pyjama, kedgeree, bungalow and polo. Many items of furniture, food, architecture and botany flow from India and the Himalayas. And it is not just India. If we look at the underlying patterns of consumption in Britain they form a mirror image of Empire. We can see this in food and taste.

If we move down the west coast of Britain, wherever there is a great port, there sugar poured in from the West Indies and where it did so it sweetened the tooth of the British. So in Glasgow and much of Scotland there is a love for sugary foods, particularly sugar mixed with flour and baked into cakes and biscuits. As a boy I always used to feel proud when I saw lorries bearing the words 'Macfarlane Lang, biscuit makers', but I never asked myself why the Scots should be so famous for their sugary shortbreads.

Further south, sugar came into the Lancashire ports and found its way to Kendal, where the almost pure sugar lumps known as Kendal Mint Cake are manufactured. Bristol became a great West Indian port and Bristol sweet sherry was developed. It happened all over Britain, with what we ate, drank or wore. Many other things, including garden plants and those great staples rubber, tea, coffee and cotton, became part of the 'British' way.

The same would be true if we went to any other part of the world, where many of the characteristically 'local' things were imported from elsewhere. Much of modern India is of British origin, just as Britain is of Indian origin. Much of modern Japan was imported from China, just as much of present China was 'made in Japan'. Australia, just like North America, is a basket of foreign imports. We borrow, imitate, trade and steal and then conveniently forget.

How do you invent your life?

Since nations are invented and there is no actual thing out there that is essentially English, it is worth thinking about how we construct these categories and come to accept them. Nations are built by the use of political symbols to make us believe in their unity: national flags, anthems, myths of origin and heroes or saints. They are also the result of playing with history.

The art of creating a nation is the art of forgetting, that is to say, forgetting the many things that divide us and concentrating on those that unite. The wounds in many parts of the world such as the Balkans or Ireland will be healed only when people learn to forget, or at least put to one side, past bitterness and memories. This is not just a negative process of amnesia. There is also a positive building up of unifying symbols, what is known as the invention of tradition.

Humans are very good at accepting common traditions, shared histories and ways of doing things, which after a very short time appear to have been there for ever. This is universal. For example, the famous horse-race in Siena called the Palio, which many people think has been held continually for six hundred years, was, in fact, abandoned centuries ago and has been invented, or reinvented, recently.

Or many people think that the Indian curry restaurant is an old tradition, brought to this country. In fact, there were no curry restaurants of the kind we now go to in England until they were invented in the 1950s. They were invented in England and later exported to India. Even curry itself is a moderately recent invention: it could not have developed until after Europeans began to import its mainly South American ingredients (potatoes, tomatoes, chillies) to India from the sixteenth century. Likewise, in India, tea has been commercially grown since the 1840s, but it was drunk seriously by Indians only from the 1920s.

In England there are new 'traditions' being invented all the time. In Cambridge, for example, the very 'traditional' festival of Nine Lessons in King's College, which has become an icon of Englishness and is beamed all over the world on Christmas Eve, was invented in the early twentieth century. Admittedly it has bits and pieces of older words and music in it, but the form and structure are twentieth-century.

In fact, almost always if you look at some royal ceremonial such as a coronation service or wedding, most of it has been invented or heavily adapted for the present purpose. The same is true abroad. The tradition of clapping after a lecture or performance was unknown in Japan in 1870. The first recorded clap was made by a missionary in the speech hall at Keio University. Thereafter the Japanese learnt to clap and thought of it as the normal way to express approval.

Very much of what we think of as old and unchangeable and 'natural' in our own culture is a deliberate invention of only a few years ago. Even in the family or school we see this. We invent traditions about Christmas celebrations in one year and then the next year feel as if we have always done them. And it is not just actions. Few people who go on tours round Cambridge realise that almost all the buildings they see are quite recent, less than two hundred years old. The city feels ancient, but it is constantly evolving and being reinvented.

Is the world a village?

Any lingering feeling that you may have about being part of a separate culture will soon vanish if you think about the increasing pace of what has been called globalisation.

Of course globalisation is an ancient phenomenon. Ever since humans moved out of Africa about a hundred thousand years ago, there have been strong contacts between different parts of the world. Every day we are learning more about the strength of these exchanges and how humans have wandered and spread their languages, genes and cultures. Certainly since Alexander the Great penetrated down into India, or the time when huge numbers of goods and ideas travelled back and forth along the Silk Road between China and the West, worlds have met.

A further, even firmer, integration of the world was achieved by the Portuguese and Spanish in their sea-borne empires of the fifteenth and sixteenth centuries. It was fully completed by the British in their empire upon which 'the sun never set'. From the eighteenth century at the latest, humans lived in a truly global world.

Yet we do feel that we are more closely united in the twenty-first century as a result of electronic communications. The twentieth-century development of television, the internet and the mobile phone, building on the earlier integration achieved by the land-line telephone, the telegraph and radio, weaves us all together ever more tightly. When our English banking is handled in India, our goods come mainly from the Far East, and our television images from America, it is difficult to retain a sense of great separateness. No man (or woman) is an island now.

So you are growing up in an extraordinary world where fashions, diseases or financial turbulence spread from country to country in a few hours. The flow of money on the world market in one day is larger than the value of the whole American economy.

You can weave virtual networks of friends through the internet and navigate in cyberspace. You may one day be able to reach Australia or China as quickly as we can now reach

Edinburgh or Dublin. The 'law' whereby computer power doubles every eighteen months is altering everything. You will live in a world of genetic manipulation, nanotechnology (microscopic machines) and cyber-reality which it is impossible to imagine.

How can you survive?

In all this onrush of technologies and shifting politics you have to live with a double knowledge. On the one hand it is important that you distance yourself from your own history and culture sufficiently to be able to realise that the old racist, gendered, nationalist stereotypes are largely based on misunderstanding. You are a world citizen and you share your beginnings with everyone else on the planet.

Yet, on the other hand, while we are battered by all our new knowledge and have the sense that we are pawns in a huge world game, we should not resign ourselves to being shifted around the board. We could easily become cynical. We might come to believe that there is no such thing as truth, that impartiality is a fiction, that reality does not exist, that all observation is deeply biased, that all theories are based on political prejudice.

All these doubts are half right. We have to be wary of those who tell us that they have found the truth, the right way, the overarching purpose. Yet without a belief that truth, rightness and purpose can be found, or at least pursued, much of our life becomes pointless.

After all is said and done, you remain the unique, never-anticipated, utterly amazing and extraordinary Lily to whom I am writing these letters. There has never been anyone like you on earth before, nor will there ever be again. That this is true of every other person on the planet does not diminish the wonder.

So, through knowledge of how much around you is just an invention, a creation, you should be in a better position to enjoy the world. In particular you can unmask the ignorance that lies behind so much savagery and prejudice. You can interpret and may even change the world if you realise how much of it is not 'natural', in the sense of being given and unalterable, but 'cultural', in the sense that it has been invented and imagined into existence by humans.

When you read the rest of these letters, please remember that what I shall be explaining is how our particular, English, world was invented. This English world is not intrinsically better than any other invention or path through history. I explain it to you because it is our world. Many people in other places have been born into equally valid but very different circumstances. They will read this account with surprise, and not necessarily envy us in every respect.

Love and friendship

$\mathcal{W}$hy are families often difficult?

Dear Lily,

You will not have found the last five years easy. You will have argued with your parents, quarrelled with your sister, felt despair, anger, self-loathing, insecurity. You will have felt both intense love and possibly hate for those who brought you up. You may well be beginning to see the point of Oscar Wilde's remark that 'Children begin by loving their parents; after a time they judge them; rarely, if ever, do they forgive them.' On the other hand, your parents may have sympathy with Lillian Carter, the mother of the American President Jimmy Carter, who commented, 'I love all my children, but some of them I don't like.' Why is there this ambivalence on both sides?

There are particular strains in our family system. As soon as a baby is born it is implicitly being encouraged to be a separate and self-sufficient individual. It is usually put in a separate bed or cot away from its parents, fed regularly but not always on demand, left to cry unless it is a serious matter. It is encouraged to stand, in more ways than one, on its own two feet. The final outcome is known to be that one day he or she will leave

home. In the past people left early on, as a servant or appren-
tice; today they may leave to go to school, university, a job in
another town.

From that time, and in anticipation well before, he or she
will become a separate economic, religious, political and social
entity. He or she will emerge finally as a fully 'grown-up'
person who will make all the major decisions over their own
life; get a job, marry, travel, buy things on their own.

This is unusual. In almost all societies, as soon as children
are born they are encouraged to be part of a group. They will
be expected to be deferential and obedient to their parents and
older relatives for life. Important decisions will be taken by
relatives. An individual is not a separate entity.

Each way of imagining the family has advantages and
disadvantages. The Western system gives individual freedom.
Yet this freedom can be a great weight. It often leads to a potentially damaging struggle between the generations as the child
grows up.

A child has to grow separate from his or her parents and
other relatives including siblings, but this must be done neither
too fast nor too slowly. Parents (alongside schools) must nurture,
protect, advise, teach and discipline their children. However,
they must do so without exerting too much pressure and in the
knowledge that the aim of all this is ultimately to turn out a free
and separate being. Parents must not smother, spoil or swamp
their children with a love that makes them over-dependent.
Yet also they must give them security and support. It's a hard
balancing act.

Likewise the child needs to learn to operate freely, but also to
accept that in any structured group, including the small family,
there will inevitably be situations where a decision cannot
be shared. If it comes to a final battle of wills, the child must
either accept the authority of the parents, or leave. It is a painful
process in which both sides are likely to feel hurt and at times

let down. The novelist Anthony Powell caught the sadness by inverting the usual comment when he wrote, 'Parents are sometimes a bit of a disappointment to their children. They don't fulfil the promise of their early years.'

Why do parents and children argue?

This tension colours all our lives. It has led to the development of various techniques to make things easier. Long ago, much to the surprise of Italian and French visitors, it was noticed that many of the English sent their children off very young (from as early as age seven) to be brought up in another household. If they were rich, they were pages or ladies-in-waiting; if poor, servants or apprentices. The English said they did this because unrelated strangers or friends could exercise good discipline in a way that parents found very difficult.

Later this developed into the sort of education that I had: boarding schools from the age of eight to eighteen with parents abroad in India whom I hardly saw. My grandparents, with whom I lived, disciplined me. Meanwhile my parents were like grandparents who could show an uncomplicated and high level of affection.

The other way of proceeding, followed in most societies, has long been to keep a member of the family effectively as a 'child' until his parents die. Thus in parts of Ireland in the nine-teenth century a grown man in his fifties might in the presence of his parents be referred to as 'the boy'. Such a system has the advantage that there is no doubt about where authority lies. A father is like a king. On the other hand, it makes it difficult for people to break free into becoming fully responsible adults and mature citizens. Often the only way to achieve this is to leave home as soon as possible, as many Irish, people in India, Chinese and other migrants have done, when they have experienced the separateness (and loneliness) of 'escaping' from their families.

These clashes and tensions vary with the times. A rise in the cost of housing can mean that instead of leaving home and setting up separately, children are forced to stay in their parents' houses into their twenties or thirties. Or again, the rising costs of old-age provision in a separate home mean that children may have to bring their elderly parents to live with them, or move into their parents' home.

Both these situations can cause exhausting tensions. For they produce a direct clash between the fundamental ideal of the individualistic and egalitarian relations of modern society, and the need for some kind of hierarchy and discipline within an organisation. They can foment a deadly struggle between love for parents or children and self-love and self-esteem. Old age is a country that cannot be understood until it is reached.

How do families work?

Very few of us understand how our family works. Yet if we have some wider knowledge of this, it will put the conflicts and tensions I have discussed into context. It may make it easier to sort out the tangles if you realise that most of the difficulties do not have anything to do with our own particular personalities, but are generated by what turns out to be the particularly odd family system in which we live in modern individualistic societies.

In most human societies, it is believed that blood relationship can be traced only through the male line. In a few societies it is believed to flow only through the female line, and in a very few, including Western Europe and the United States, it is believed to flow through both males and females.

If you had belonged to a society where people were convinced that you were related only through females, for example among the Trobriand islanders of the Pacific, your father would not be a relative, just a person who lived with your mother. When a woman became pregnant, this was believed to be the result of the action of a ghost or spirit.

The belief that you are related only through males or through females makes it easy to form into large, exclusive clans, like the Chinese or people in India. But if you trace your links through both of your parents you will find that there is no distinct family group. The 'Bee' clan does not exist. You just have a network of relations, cousins, nephews and nieces, uncles and aunts.

This is the flexible and rather hazy system in which you live. Without research, you will find it impossible to draw a diagram of your relatives, or family tree, going back more than a couple of generations and which includes more than about fifty people with all their names and relationships to you. Yet in many other societies, people can name hundreds of relations and tell you of ancestors of some five generations or more back.

How do we name our relatives?

Our way of referring to or addressing our relatives does not help us to remember more distant relations. The system forms linguistic rings like the layers of an onion. In the innermost ring is our close family. We call people our mother (mummy), father (daddy), brothers and sisters, sons and daughters. They are our close relatives and we think of them as special. We cannot marry or have sex with them.

Then there are various other categories. Our parents' sisters we call aunts; their brothers are uncles. Our aunts and uncles' children we call cousins and our siblings' (brothers' and sisters') children we call nephews and nieces. There are elaborations like 'first, second, third' cousins – referring back up the genera-tions – or 'once or twice removed', which refers to the level of generation.

To this system we have to add a few terms to fit in the

non-blood relations acquired as a result of marriage. A person with whom we have a relationship created through marriage is called a relation in law, in other words an 'in-law'. So our sister's husband is our brother-in-law, our husband's mother is our mother-in-law, and so on. If a marriage has occurred and then been disturbed by a remarriage or divorce, we use the word 'step'. I married your mother's mother and so I am your step-grandfather. I am not related to you by blood, but through a step relationship. The wicked stepmother, who married a man after a child's biological mother had died, is famous in fairy stories and legends because it can be such a difficult relationship.

All of this, even if only half familiar, may seem natural to you, but it is in fact unusual. Normally the terms you use to refer to and address relatives are much more precise and elaborate, describing each separate relative by a special word. This helps people to know exactly whom they are trying to address when they have hundreds of relatives living nearby.

In a Nepalese village your father's oldest brother is called 'biggest father', his younger brother 'younger father'. Your mother's brother is called by a special term. This mother's brother is the most important relative of the senior generation apart from your parents. Your cousins are individually called by terms that sharply differentiate those you can marry from those you cannot (because they are thought of as close blood relatives).

Our systems of descent and the names we give our relatives have worked quite well since they were introduced by the Anglo-Saxons in the sixth century. However, in the last two generations there have been several major changes which have put great strains on this system.

What is a mother?

Until recently it all seemed quite simple. A man and woman had sex, a child was conceived and later born. The parents were the biological parents. If they were married to each other or lived in some legal relationship of that kind, they were also the child's social parents.

Now, however, with test-tube babies, artificial insemination, surrogate mothers and soon, possibly, cloning, it is getting very complicated. What is my relationship to the stranger who donated the sperm from which I was conceived, or to the woman who nurtured the foetus in her womb for a payment and then handed the baby over to another, or to the family who paid for and adopted me?

In this relatively simple case there are just four people involved, each of whom can claim to be a 'father' or a 'mother' in a certain sense. But the cases can get more complicated, and the law is having great difficulty in sorting out all the rights and obligations. Likewise, with little formal guidance, individuals are having to adapt and invent new relationships, categories and terminologies to deal with this.

In facing these apparently new problems we can take some comfort from the fact that even before artificial insemination, humans had developed some ingenious ways of dealing with similar patterns. A classic example was found in North Africa.

Among the Nuer people it is essential to have children. Blood-relatedness flows only through the male line. So what happens if there are no sons in the family? A rich daughter will be provided with the wealth to pay for a 'marriage' to another woman. The new 'bride' will be impregnated by another man. By paying for the bride, the rich daughter has become a social father to any children that are born. So a child when asked who is his or her 'father' may point to a woman. In other words, biological and social fatherhood are split and one can have a 'female' father, or a 'male' mother.

Another variant is 'ghost' marriage, where a dead male's ghost is married off to a woman after his death. She has children (by another biological partner) to this 'ghost', whose family have paid for the bride. So the line is continued even though the father is dead at the time of conception. This gives models for what is now happening with frozen semen.

What do we call our father?

Nowadays, around a third of the marriages in Britain end in divorce and remarriage. Many people have a succession of 'partners' with whom they have children but whom they do not marry. This leads to a simple difficulty: what do you call all those people who are important in your life?

When I came to live with your granny, your mother was eight years old. She already had someone she called 'Dad'. So what was she to call me? 'Alan' sounded a bit serious, so she called me 'Ali'. That sounded a bit too short, so she modified it to 'Ali Bali'. When you were starting to speak she suggested you too call me 'Ali Bali'. You changed this to 'Aya Baya', which was easier to say, but because it was a little long-winded you shortened it to 'Baya', which is what I have remained. My being your 'Baya' distinguishes me from your mother's father.

If you were from a different social class background you might do it differently. In many parts of England now, the man who is currently living with a child's mother is called 'Dad', while whoever conceived the child, the biological father now living elsewhere, is called by his Christian name. This is the opposite of what your mum did.

Could we marry our pets?

Until recently the definition of a Christian marriage was roughly 'the voluntary union, for life, of one man and one woman'. This began to collapse about a hundred years ago when it became possible, at least outside the Catholic Church, to have a full divorce from someone and then legally marry another person. This change undermined 'for life', though that is still preserved in the 'until death us do part' phrase in the wedding service. Furthermore, same-sex marriages of a man to a man or a woman to a woman are becoming widely accepted. So what is left of marriage?

As anthropologists analysed marriage in different societies, they soon realised that the Western Christian concept did not work well outside a particular area of the world. An obvious weakness was that marriage elsewhere was sometimes between one man and several women, or one woman and several men. Furthermore, marriage was often not for life or even for a long time at all, for it was very easy to divorce and remarry.

Some surprising types of 'marriage' emerged. People were found to be marrying someone of the same sex or even someone dead, as in the case of the Nuer people. Others were marrying someone (a high-status person who gave them a position in society) and then never seeing him again, but living and having children by someone else. People even 'married' parts of another person – a friend's arm or little finger – a rock or a tree, as a way of establishing property and other rights.

So the definition of marriage became longer and longer to try and encompass all these variations until it finally became just too complicated. It was better to look at marriage as a bundle of rights and obligations people establish in each other; as sexual partners, as bearers of children, as co-workers in the home, as earners of money outside the home.

Once these rights are considered as distinct, it is easy to see how they might be held either as a clump by one person, or by different people. Among the Yoruba of Nigeria, a woman has long been traditionally parcelled out between various people. Her sexuality, the children she bears and partial rights to her domestic services belong to her husband and his wider family. Some of her domestic services in certain circumstances belong to the family group she was born into. Her economic power and resources belong to her. The famous trading women of West African markets reflect this division since they keep their own earnings.

If we look at marriage in this way, we can see that same-sex marriage makes sense. Recently I read of a case in India where a young man married his ancient grandmother so that he could look after her more easily. Some people might even think it would be a cunning strategy to ensure the happiness of their beloved cat or dog, and evade inheritance tax, if they married the little creature.

Is the family weak?

Organising life around the ties created through blood and marriage is extremely efficient. In the majority of societies the whole of political life is based on family groups, the members of whom support each other in their feuds and vendettas. Many tribal societies, such as the Yanomamo of the Amazon forest or the Nuer of the Sudan, are examples of this, but it is also the case in many parts of China – and was in India in the past. The state is relatively unimportant. Marriage is arranged as a political alliance. Likewise, all property flows through the family, most jobs are found through family contacts, who you work with is organised on the basis of family relationships. The impersonal world of money, businesses and market exchanges just exists on the margins.

In such societies, all of religion revolves around the family. People venerate their ancestors, conduct rituals with their family, need children to help send them to a happy afterlife. Furthermore, most of social life is family-based. Only family are really to be trusted; they are one's closest friends, comrades, partners in leisure and work. The family welcomes the new members, who then pass into sexual maturity, get married and are looked after in old age and finally buried.

This is very far from our world, where the family can remain quite important, but mostly at the level of the individual. It is important for our emotions, for our first fifteen years of nurturing and perhaps in our old age. It often gives some satisfaction and pattern in the rest of life. Yet our political allegiances, our religious beliefs, our jobs, our friendships and those we trust are largely separated off. The family is only one element in all of this.

This is such a relatively unusual situation, and so obviously fits with a highly mobile industrial and capitalist society, that many people used to think that it was a recent phenomenon. They believed that it must be the result of the way society had been broken apart by the industrial and urban revolutions of the nineteenth century.

Yet historians have now shown that what we might call the individualistic and flexible family system which you experience goes back hundreds of years. This can be seen in the various ways we use to calculate who we are related to, the terminology, the inheritance systems, and evidence about who lived with whom and what their rights were. For a thousand years in England the family has not provided the foundation for the rest of society. Throughout that period it has contained that inner tension between desiring to be close and dependent and the desire to be free and adult.

This is very different from the situation in the majority of societies in both the past and the present. The contrast is described in the words of an old North American Pomo Indian of California:

> *What is a man? A man is nothing. Without his family he*
> *is of less importance than that bug crossing the trail ... A*

man must be with his family to amount to anything with us. If he had nobody else to help him, the first trouble he got into he would be killed by his enemies … No woman would marry him … He would be poorer than a new-born child, he would be poorer than a worm … In the White way of doing things the family is not so important. The police and soldiers take care of protecting you, the courts give you justice, the post office carries messages for you, the school teaches you. Everything is taken care of, even your children, if you die; but with us the family must do all of that.

In the modern West, our relations with our family change over our lifetime. Parents start as authority figures who are also the source of all good things. They then become objects of antagonism and perhaps derision. Hopefully they end up as loved grandparents to our children. Likewise children start as exhausting delights, before turning into rebellious monsters and then again, with luck, into the loved parents of our grand-children.

What is certain is that in the Western system parents cannot demand their children's unconditional love and obedience. Nor can children demand that their parents show them endless love and support. Love comes from self-sacrifice and tolerance. It comes from not expecting too much, not reliving in our children our failures and insufficiencies. And on the children's part it depends on an understanding of ageing and the loneliness this brings. Only thus can we avoid the danger pointed out by the old Pomo Indian:

With us the family was everything. Now it is nothing. We are getting like the White people and it is bad for the old people. We had no old people's home like you. The old people were important. They were wise. Your old people must be fools.

... 4 ...

What is love?

Dear Lily,

As an English teenager, you will have been bombarded with images of romantic love – at the cinema, in magazines and on television. You will be encouraged to think that the way to happiness lies in finding Mr Right.

Much of your life will be a quest for love. What is particularly unusual about the world of passionate love which we idealise is not that we feel such emotions, but that we make them a precondition for marriage.

Romantic attachments, an overwhelming love and desire for another, can be found in all societies. Often this is between members of the opposite sex and often the feelings are strongest in the period around the arrival of sexual maturity. So 'love' is not confined to what we would call 'love marriage' societies.

Yet in most societies, as in India, China and much of Africa and the Near East, where marriage and the bearing of children is the basic political, economic and social mechanism for the future, marriage is too important a matter to leave to the individual. Self-centred and irrational emotions should not dictate who should have children with whom.

While teenagers may sing love-songs and even, in some societies, have sexual relationships, marriage and child-bearing have to be arranged by older members of the family or professional matchmakers. Elaborate economic exchanges are organised and individuals are exchanged between groups. Marriage is arranged on the basis of relationships between the older generations on each side. Individual feelings have nothing to do with marital strategies. Someone does not choose when or who to marry. This choice is made by others.

I remember my shock when, even after knowing all this in theory, I went into a friend's house in a Nepalese village and asked him what he was doing the next day. He said he was getting married. I congratulated him, but commented that he had not mentioned this the day before. He replied that this was because his parents had only that morning told him that it had been arranged. I asked him whether his bride was pretty and nice. He said he had no idea as he had never met her.

Where did love come from?

Contrast this with the long literary and legal tradition in England. From Anglo-Saxon poetry, through medieval love poetry, to Chaucer, Shakespeare and the great later poets and novelists, English literature is awash with love, and its relationship to marriage. It is the single most important theme. This is not just glimpses of the flirtation of youngsters. It is endless reflection on this strange, irrational, overpowering feeling that can sweep one human being into a lifelong, unbreakable commitment to another. Endless advice, letters and sermons revolve around the theme of how to recognise and react to love, and how, without love, a marriage cannot work.

Nor is this just a literary phenomenon, some idealistic

and airy-fairy convention unrelated to real life. We can look at village records, court cases and legal treatises from the past. These show that a boy of fourteen and a girl of twelve could get married without a priest and without the parents' presence for much of the period up to the sixteenth century. The decision as to when and whom a person married was not a family or community one. It was an individual choice. A close emotional partnership with a 'married friend', a companionship to provide mutual help and to overcome loneliness, was too important a matter to be left to the decision of others.

Of course there were exceptions. At the level of the aristocracy there were often battles between parents and children. No doubt this happened at a lower level as well. And of course many people routinely look for shared interests, social compatibility and financial potential in their future partner. Yet behind all of this is a system that is concerned about the weighing up of emotion and practical advantages, of choices between various desirable goals.

Why marry at all?

In the past it was very difficult to stay single. Even today, the Yanomamo people of Venezuela always know when a man is a bachelor because he is dirty, his hair is uncut, he is badly fed, often sick. Without a wife he is hardly a person. Likewise in many societies unmarried women over the age of twenty are almost unthinkable; they are poverty-stricken, unprotected, a shame to their family. Basically, in order to obtain the pleasures of life, including the blessing of children, people used to have to marry. Most people in the past saw no alternative to marriage, even if this often condemned women in particular in many societies to a life of drudgery, perpetual childbearing and physical and verbal abuse.

England has long been exceptional in tolerating, even

encouraging, non-marriage. My forebears, four hundred years of Fellows of King's College, Cambridge University, were not allowed to marry (on pain of losing their Fellowship) but were looked after by servants. Up to a quarter of men and women in the seventeenth and eighteenth centuries in England never married. Marriage was an option. For the English, on the whole, children's marriage plans could be embarrassing, annoying, disappointing or heartening. Yet, in the end, it was up to them. It was their life.

Now there is a widespread move away from permanent relationships and marriage, particularly among women. In Japan, India, Europe, America, even China, many young women are reaching their thirties and forties without marrying or having children. They live comfortably, have good jobs and are quite affluent. They realise that marriage, childbearing and subservience to a man would threaten this, and such options seem like a form of imprisonment or sacrifice. The question for many women nowadays is not why one should stay single, but why one should marry and have children. Even though most of us dream of that soul mate who will love us above all the world, if no one absolutely special comes along we are not prepared to settle for second-best.

Many marriages of my parents' generation and earlier occurred and were maintained under parental and wider social pressures. Better marriage than ostracism and a slight feeling of failure, of being the last 'unbought tin on the shelf'. But it is different now. It is quite possible that, beautiful though you are, you will not move beyond boyfriends to a lifelong partnership. In this you will be one of the wave of new, independent, ambitious women who stand alongside men as equal but somewhat alone in the world. Your motto may well be 'Who needs a man?'.

You may think that this is something new. Yet when we visited an ethnic group in south-western China recently we found a society that for some centuries had given up marriage entirely. The men were away for up to half the year carrying goods to India. The women were left in charge.

Out of this arose a situation where marriage, if it had earlier existed, totally disappeared. When a boy reached puberty at between thirteen and sixteen he would be encouraged to find a female partner in another house. He would then start a pattern, which would continue until old age, whereby he went off in the evening to sleep in his partner's house.

Each courtyard house was planned so that there was a main area where the older women and the young children, that is all the children born of the women of the family, lived. Along another side were the animals – pigs and cows. The third side had enough bedrooms so that each adult female who was in a relationship with an outside partner could have a room. They were visited at night by these partners, who left at dawn to return to their own female relatives' house where they ate and worked.

There were no problems of property or inheritance since the land and house belonged to the whole female-headed group and all children born within it. If a partnership ended, the children stayed with the women and the biological father was not expected to contribute to his children's upbringing. There was no marriage ceremony, no word for marriage, no words for relatives through marriage like brother-in-law or sister-in-law.

Not very dissimilar are the West Indian and other patterns of mother-centred households found in the Caribbean and many other parts of the world. Here the woman stays in a house and brings up the children, living temporarily with a succession of men who beget one or more children and then move on. Some have ascribed this to the weak economic position of unemployed men, others to the legacy of slavery or of an earlier African family system tracing relations through the women. Whatever the reason, the pattern of temporary unions and children who live together, though they do not share the same parents, is increasingly widespread.

What has love got to do with marriage?

One important component of the development of our own marriage pattern was Christianity. The distinctive nature of Christian marriage was early established, the basic features being present by the ninth century. This was a religion that encouraged non-marriage (celibacy), one-to-one marriage (monogamy), a freedom of choice and a severe sexual code prohibiting sexual relations before and outside marriage.

The ideals of celibacy, the late age at which people married, the battle between biological desire and religious injunctions are clearly a part of the pattern of romantic love. Passion was herded into marriage; sex and marriage were synonymous in a way that is unusual in world civilisations. Biological urges were channelled into art and fantasy. These special features were present in Western Europe for many centuries before the Protestant Reformation of the sixteenth century.

In closely-knit, family-based societies any obvious display of emotion between husband and wife can clash with other family relations. Many of us have noticed that we become inhibited if we are with our relatives. When wider family links are strong, marriages are arranged and affection between husband and wife is a secondary force.

The rise of love marriage is linked to the degree of involvement of the small family in wider family ties. We now know that the family system based on a close partnership between the husband and wife was present in England from Anglo-Saxon times onwards. There is little evidence that wider family groupings were important in everyday life among the mass of the population. Romantic love was a system that could both flourish and hold together this individualistic society.

If family groups do not arrange marriages, why marry at all? One reason was that to have sexual relations outside marriage was considered a serious offence in the Christian world. Linked to this is the idea that the 'passion of romantic love' binds people together in long-term associations which would otherwise not occur. Rational, profit-seeking individuals might not settle down into fixed relationships at all were it not for the 'institutionalised irrationality' of romantic love. We might see this as a necessary drive to ensure the nurturing of children by a couple. It encouraged longer-term bonding, rather than just a brief sexual coupling.

Is love blind?

Choice, whether in the market of marriage or more tangible goods, is always difficult. The information is always insufficient, the variables too complex. It is bad enough buying a new computer or television, when one often has to trust the salesman and a hunch – but at least if such a purchase goes wrong it is disposable. Choosing a partner for life is infinitely more complex and the guesswork involved is immense.

Some external force of desire is needed to help the individual to choose. Hence passionate 'love' overwhelms, justifies and provides an apparently external and compulsive authority. On the other hand, love within marriage is not necessarily as passionate or 'irrational'. It can be calm, calculating, very like any other 'work'. Yet if a decision is made to sever a relationship, the loss of that mysterious 'love' is often given as the justification.

Love thus seems to be at its most intense when uncertainty and risk are greatest, in that phase when humans have to choose. When they make the most momentous decision of their lives, which will turn a contractual, arbitrary relationship into the deepest and most binding in life, love steps in as though from outside, blind and compelling. The heart has its reasons, even if the mind is perplexed.

So we might suggest that the pattern of romantic love, both before marriage and within marriage, is the result of a number of forces. The biological urge to mate, based on a deep attraction between males and females, is universal. But the way in which cultures encourage, use, or discourage it varies enormously. In the majority of societies, romantic feelings have not been encouraged, marriage and love are not connected, and marriages have been arranged. This has made it possible to knit people together by family links.

How does love fit into our lives?

It is certainly ironic that as societies become more bureaucratic and 'rational', so at the heart of the system there grows an impulsive, irrational emotion which has nothing to do with making money. There is a desire for the totally overwhelming, irrational escape into romantic love.

Romantic love gives meaning in an otherwise dead and cold world. It promises that fusion with another human being which is so conspicuously lacking in the lonely crowds of autonomous individuals. It overcomes separation and gives the endlessly choice-making individual a rest, a categorical imperative which, momentarily at least, resolves all the doubts and indecisions.

The desire to have, own, possess fits well with those similarly irrational desires to accumulate, possess and own that are the basic drive in the economic world. In the modern world it is obvious that consumer society has harnessed the romantic passions to sell goods. The marketing of love has raised this emotion to a high cultural pinnacle. Love provides the promise of freedom, of a deeper meaning in life, perhaps even of a return to the innocence of the lost paradise of Eden.

$\mathcal{W}$ho are our friends?

Dear Lily,

Many of your thoughts and emotions throughout life will revolve round friends. Why is friendship so important in our lives? In most societies, the people we interact with are largely a matter of luck; they are family, neighbours, members of the same caste. They are not chosen. They are, furthermore, not our equals. If they are relations, they are senior (parents, older siblings) or junior. Likewise if they are members of another caste or of the opposite sex they are by birth superior or inferior. The idea of meeting many of our equals is out of the question. If friendship of a kind develops it is likely to be lopsided.

What is lopsided friendship?

Patronage is lopsided friendship, that is to say where the two sides maintain their relationship because of their differences. One person provides certain assets, the superior may provide political protection, the client flatters or supports him in his schemes. The relationship is general and long-term, not like the specific and limited transaction with a bureaucrat or a shop-keeper. It has some warmth and a hope that it will last.

This system of patron–client relations is very widespread in the world. It is the main way of getting things done outside the family. It is particularly prevalent in places like Spain, Portugal, Italy and the Middle East and in regions such as South America that were colonised by the Mediterranean powers. It even spreads into the relationship with God or the gods: in certain branches of Christianity and Buddhism there are patron saints or gods to whom people pray when they are trying to get benefits.

Each patron usually has a number of clients. People try to have several patrons in useful places to help them obtain favours and to protect them against other powerful individ-uals. The patron is often encouraged to take an honorary family position by being made a spiritual relative, a godmother or godfather.

Do you have patrons?

Having a real friend, on the other hand, whom we must not exploit or use to further our own ends, is a curious phenom-enon. It tends to be found in societies where there are a lot of roughly equal people and where there is so much movement that we constantly meet potential new friends. It is predomi-nant where most of the important things in life do not come through the manipulation of personal relationships. Almost all we need in life is provided through an impersonal bureaucracy, the relationship between buyer and seller, underpinned by the legal system. Only in such a situation, where we do not have to manipulate contacts in order to survive, can we afford the luxury of disinterested friendship.

What is peculiar about Britain is that for a long period patronage has been relatively unimportant as a way of organ-ising personal relationships. There have been what we call 'patrons' of art or learning, and others who control jobs and other benefits. But if I asked you who your patrons were and who your clients, you would be puzzled, just as many of your predecessors for hundreds of years would have been surprised at such a question.

Just as patron–client relations are weakly developed in the white, Anglo-Saxon, Protestant parts of the United States, so they have been relatively weak in England for many centuries. With the exception of some ethnic groups and a few branches of politics, the arts and the professions, or in some criminal organisations, the system of patronage is just a pale shadow of the world of the *Godfather* and the Mafia.

So if family and patronage do not hold people together in England, and romantic love can glue us to only one other person at a time, what can provide the link between us? The short answer is friendship. This is why so much of your time at school was devoted to the making and unmaking of friends. Throughout your life, much of your happiness and success, or loneliness and failure, will depend on your ability to make 'friends', momentary or long-term. So what is this peculiar thing which is described by this Anglo-Saxon word?

What is friendship?

The essence of friendship is equality. It must not develop into that inequality of power and gifts that is the essence of patronage. If it does, it will be destroyed. It must also be based on liking, mutual interest and shared feelings and thoughts. To 'like' someone is very different from 'loving' someone. I have heard people say that they love their parents (or their brothers and sisters), but do not really like them much. This is quite possible and, in the end, both are important. What is certain is that pretended friendship, where there is nothing in common and nothing to share, does not work.

Friendship is not a static thing. It is like a river, meaningful only if it is heading in some direction. It must always be developing, changing and expanding, absorbing new experiences. As someone once put it, 'The English do not have friends; they have friends *about things.*' A shared activity or need is behind friendship. There are so many people in the world. Why spend time with just this one? Because one enjoys their company, they are 'good fun', amusing, supportive, kind. As we shall see, this often finds its strongest expression in playing games with them.

Friends must not be manipulative and calculating. Friendship abides by a central rule of ethics, namely that 'We should treat people as ends in themselves and not as a means to an end.' If you feel a friend is 'using you', then the friendship ends. Just as true love and beauty cannot be bought or sold, so friendship cannot be purchased. You cannot go to an agency and buy or hire a friend, while you certainly can hire a person's mind or body for a particular task.

So friendship is about the long-term liking of two equal people for each other. In England this can be between people of the opposite sex or of different ages. Men can be friends with women, adults with children. Even husband and wife can be 'friends' as well as companions and sexual partners. This is a very old pattern. The historian Eileen Power described how medieval life was 'full of married friends'. To a certain extent, the English can even be friends with their pets. As the novelist George Eliot put it, 'Animals are such agreeable friends – they ask no questions, they pass no criticisms.' Pets are the only kind of friend we can buy, but even they have to be respected.

We have to work at friendship; it neither comes naturally nor remains without constant attention. Friends can be likened to an orchard: they have to be carefully planted, pruned and protected. They cannot, however, be turned into private and exclusive property. You will find throughout your life that one of the most difficult things is to share friends – and sometimes to lose them.

Friendship often clashes with other ties, especially to our family and particularly our love partner. Yet when it works, it can be one of the deepest of all relationships. As a little girl you used to listen with me to Handel's famous aria based on the biblical story of the lament of King David over his murdered friend Jonathan. Handel's music captures the depth of their love.

How do friends communicate?

Often the best form of communication with friends is, surprisingly, silence. Friendship is not only about what we do say, but even more importantly about what we do not. True friendship occurs when 'information' is conveyed by absences of words. The striving is to convey as much as possible indirectly, 'between the lines'.

The reason such 'negative' communication is important is that it requires a greater closeness than positive communication. The greater the distance between sender and receiver, the more the need for explicitness and directness. Only when two or more people share an enormous amount can the much more economical negative communication take place.

All speech is an exercise of power because there is a speaker and a listener. So the more blatant and explicit the message, the more difficult it is to exercise discrimination, that is free will, in receiving the message. An explicit order, as in the army, is the worst: it is flatly coercive, binding, demanding obedience.

On the other hand, the kind of indirect, negative, allusive communication that is a peculiar characteristic of friendship allows ideas to flow and feelings not to be bruised. Someone who is a friend is presented with an opportunity to draw conclusions: 'Perhaps you would like to consider ...' This approach has several advantages. It avoids infringing the integrity of the other person; acts are apparently entered into with free will, as the contracts of rational individuals. Thus we do not say 'You must do this' when asking a friend for a favour, but 'I wonder if you could possibly ...'

This strategy is necessary where free and independent individuals are interacting. In an advanced, open and balanced society where fear is minimal, cajoling, requesting, persuading are all that can be done. People are not slaves, or even clients. They have to be enticed very gently and indirectly into proper friendship, and they cannot be forced to remain. They can refuse friendship or take their friendship elsewhere.

What is respect for other people?

Friendship is based on respect and courtesy. Courtesy and politeness mean putting ourselves into the place of the other person, to 'see ourselves as others see us'. We practise a form of empathy or sympathy which is impossible except between people who believe themselves to be, in essence, close enough or equal enough to have some sense of the other's feelings or predicament.

Yet courtesy and politeness are also distancing mechanisms, for while they establish a certain common closeness, they then keep people at arm's length. They can be used to emphasise the other's separate needs and wants, their personal social space. This can be a form of honouring of the other's individual identity. The Chinese philosopher Confucius alluded to the difficulty of the balance when he said, 'The most difficult people are women and servants. Getting too intimate with them costs you your dignity, while distancing them causes complaints.'

This idea of the social space surrounding an individual is

an important one. It is central to our individualistic concepts of who we are. The trampling on the social space of those weaker than ourselves – making another forgo his own time, space or desires to accommodate our own – is one of the chief devices, in most societies, for gaining power. Wasting another's time, as in the many occasions where people are made to hang around for hours, can be just as effective as physical abuse. Yet true courtesy is just the opposite of this; it is respecting that social space, keeping our distance while showing concern.

When should we touch others?

The social space is partly symbolic and invisible and hence dealt with through gestures, postures, language. But it is also partly physical, and hence can be observed in body distances. The range of acceptable body distance varies with the degree of intimacy and equality that is thought to exist in the relationship.

At one extreme is 'untouchability', whether literally (as in the caste system) or through keeping one's distance, as when a nobleman finds it distasteful to be close to a commoner. Neither of these two extreme situations is what we commonly associate with life in Britain, though there are some exceptions.

At the other extreme are what we find in certain tribal and peasant societies. Here there is, within the group, very little social and physical distance. So people will often stand or sit disconcertingly close for a Westerner's tastes – while some Africans find that Westerners appear aloof and stand too far away.

In some societies there seems to be little appreciation of privacy, separateness, the need for a protected zone of intimacy into which no one intrudes. I remember vividly the shock of living in a village in Nepal where the door was open and people dropped in constantly and commented on everything

I was doing. They followed us on our trips out of the village when we were trying to create a little personal space, and even going to the toilet out in the fields in private was a difficult exercise.

It is therefore interesting that many of the English effect a compromise; more or less the same physical distance is maintained for everybody, whether they are intimate or distant from us. Everyone stands under one law, the law of compromise, not too far apart, nor too close. They should be close enough to show engagement and involvement, but not so close as to cause embarrassment and intrusion. And, on the whole, we consider an intrusion into our personal space without an invitation odd and possibly threatening.

The questions of personal space are a delicate compromise, and as times and influences change they become confused. Twenty years ago I would have considered it very strange to kiss female friends or acquaintances on the cheek or to hug men, but now these continental customs have spread widely. I constantly find myself wondering how to behave.

It used to be so easy – a handshake at the start and end of a meeting with a friend. Now I often wonder when and how we should kiss or hug. The problem is even greater across cultures. In Japan, to kiss on the lips in public is an obscene gesture, even when the couple are married, and even touching another in public until recently was considered rather indecent. A bow and a name card on first meeting; thereafter just a bow or smile.

Yet even the simple handshake is a delicate art. It symbolises friendship, equality, mutual grasping, in other words involvement and the taking of a calculated risk (of being rejected) by stretching out one's hand. At the same time, however, the arm is extended and fends off the other; this is not a drawing together as in the embrace. It is a stiff gesture: let us be friends, but let us also keep our distance and respect our mutual independence.

The handshake and an older form of rather restrained middle-class Englishness went together well.

Two friends are like magnets. They can be mutually attracted, yet if they get too close, there can be repulsion to a safer distance. Friendship is thus a balancing act, like a ballet or dance. It is both spontaneous and to be worked at, both natural and artificial. Like happiness it comes unexpectedly and cannot be forced. It is usually a side-effect of other interests.

Humans are very social animals and love to love and be loved. To be able to feel warmth in the company of good friends or mates is a special pleasure. It helps to overcome some of the loneliness of our rushed and individualistic lives. We are no longer islands, but part of a continent. We find mirrors for ourselves in others, support and help in difficulties, the pleasure of giving when we have too much. Some of the moments I shall always treasure are those when, as true friends, you and I have explored the world together, enjoying a new garden, a visit to the Natural History Museum, or discovering the fairy-tales of the Brothers Grimm, with a joy that could not have come if we had been on our own.

6

Why play games?

Dear Lily,

When you were small you particularly enjoyed treasure hunts and dressing up. Almost all the time you were playing elaborate games of 'make believe' with your younger sister. You lived for much of the time in a fantasy world.

Watching you, I was reminded that humans have been defined as *Homo ludens*, Latin for 'playful humans'. For while this playful characteristic does not distinguish us from all other species, it is particularly developed in humans. The evidence you can see all around you in the mania for competitive games, gambling and sports. It is also apparent in behaviour in many parts of our life that we do not normally think of as 'games' or 'sport'.

There are games of skill and those of chance, of single combatants against each other or of teams, involving different artefacts and different rules (balls, cards, dice). Each tends to work in a slightly different way and to appeal to a different part of our psychology.

Why play?

Humans are strongly motivated by curiosity and by a basic playfulness, a desire to compete, fantasise, imagine, struggle. This playfulness is very marked in children, but continues throughout life. The desire to win, to dominate, to outstrip the opponent, the delight in good performance, the satisfaction in co-ordinated muscular or social movements, the pleasure in the calculation of risk – all sorts of different elements are involved.

A game is a sort of experiment outside time and space. In a game, individuals or teams who start almost exactly equal and play according to the same rules, end up with one temporarily vanquishing the other. It creates difference out of uniformity. It is dynamic and progressive, creating variability out of simi-larity, artificially creating conflict. It divides and separates people who were previously joined and equal. One person has the top hat in Monopoly, buys up Park Lane and Mayfair and becomes a rapacious landlord for as long as the game lasts, while another person gets the boot and Old Kent Road.

Much of this is opposed to what happens in many civili-sations in India, Africa and China where people attempt to control and downplay open competition in social life. Rituals, that is orderly, standardised repetitive behaviour, are dedicated to *reducing* confrontation and variations. Thus rituals tend to create a temporary phase of equality and closeness in unequal civilisations; they join people and create unity.

We see a games-like process at work in many of the central institutions of a modern society – the Stock Exchange, the Houses of Parliament, the Law Courts – as well as on the actual games field. All of these take the form of bounded games, worked out in an arena that allows regulated conflict. This helps change to occur without disrupting the wider society.

Within the particular 'field' of the game, during a limited time span, people can behave in odd and often irresponsible ways. They can wear odd clothes (huge helmets, white trousers), they often hit each other (boxing) or tackle each other (rugby) or throw things at each other (cricket). Or they may shout at each other in an aggressive way across the floor of the House of Commons, or be very rude to each other in a court of law, or run around madly gesticulating as in the Stock Exchange. Yet such behaviour is limited. At the end people should shake hands and become friends again, for it is 'only a game'.

Who plays?

From at least the sixteenth century, the English became the leading inventors of competitive team games. If we think of the present games of the world, almost all were invented or modified in England; cricket, football and rugby are the most famous.

As well as games, England became a great country for sports, horse-racing, dog-racing, mountaineering, hunting, fishing and shooting. Likewise the English were, and still are, great hobby-mongers. George Orwell noted, 'We are a nation of flower-lovers, but also a nation of stamp-collectors, pigeon-fanciers, amateur carpenters, coupon-snippers, darts-players, cross-word puzzle fans.' Yet the English were only part of a European pattern, for the French, the Italians and the Dutch also form part of a 'playful' civilisation.

We might assume that this kind of enthusiasm for games is universal. Yet my first impression is that until a few years ago it was limited. I have been told that there were until recently no competitive team games in Japan. There were instead a number of activities that it is very difficult to classify. They are not exactly games, for they seem to have a solemn and ritual component. Hence they are often described with a term such as 'martial art'. Even the famous tea ceremony is neither a game nor a hobby, neither an entertainment nor a ritual, but a little of each.

These activities lie at an intersection between art, ritual and game in a way that makes them feel strange. They include a number that have the ending 'do' (*kendo, judo*) which means 'the path' or 'the way' and implies a semi-religious aspect, and others such as *sumo* wrestling or *pachinko* (a kind of bagatelle) which do not feel quite like a game. There were no ball games in which teams 'fought' each other.

It is only in the last hundred years or so that the competitive team games of the West have bounced, kicked and batted their way round the world, creating a universal addiction. So everyone is mad about football and many other people are crazy about cricket. The recentness of this change suggests that games work only under certain political, economic and social conditions. A degree of political and social equality is both a cause and consequence of the development of team games. They can be suppressed as leading to disorder and they can soon become a form of political activity. The Indians took up cricket with added zest when they realised that they could beat their white masters at it, and also legitimately stand around in a field for hours without being told they were being lazy.

When games spread they can also be radically altered. When the Trobriand islanders of New Guinea in the Pacific took up cricket, they changed almost all the rules so that each side had dozens of players, dressed in war dress, and hurled objects at each other. In another part of New Guinea they have learnt to play football, but they go on playing as many matches as are necessary for both sides to reach the same score.

Is science a game?

Playfulness often consists of trying out moves, making wild guesses, following intuition and hunches, leaving the logical path, taking risks, not becoming too solemn or wedded to a particular idea or strategy, innovating and experimenting.

Successful science often requires a good deal of playful, exaggerated, humorous, outrageous speculation and testing. By definition, the major advance will occur in unexpected areas and these are often reached by leaps of the mind. The overly serious, logical, thorough, highly disciplined mind often misses the significant, strange clue that gives a new insight.

A trained Confucian scholar or Buddhist monk may be less likely to make the breakthrough than an overgrown undergraduate full of fun, games and pranks. Francis Crick's book about the discovery of DNA is significantly called *What Mad Pursuit*. The ideas were so far-fetched and incredible that most people would have dismissed them as a joke.

One of the great problems in the pursuit of knowledge in most societies is that it threatens too many vested interests. Probing the mysteries of nature may bring power, a threat to the rulers; it may undermine previous knowledge, a threat to priests; it will alter status positions, a threat to the elders and higher social groups. When Galileo pointed out that the earth revolved round the sun rather than the other way round, he was forced to retract his statements publicly under threat of torture.

The boundedness that we find as a central aspect of games, and which we also find essential in law, politics and the economy, is equally important for science. Very often those engaged in strange pursuits are hounded out as magicians or sorcerers. But, particularly in the less controlled areas of Protestant Europe and America, scientists of past centuries could engage in their particular part-hobbies, part-games, without fear of angry mobs. They could pursue them in the hope that their skill and ingenuity in this particular 'game' against the greatest opponent (a cunning Creator who had concealed the clues in nature) would be recognised for their virtuosity.

Why do children play?

Playing games is usually strongly encouraged in schools. This is partly because it strengthens the muscles and uses up surplus physical energy. Yet team games are also believed to improve social skills. The essence of a team game is to balance selfishness, the desire to shine and triumph, with sociality, the desire to help one's team win. This balance is also one of the most difficult things to achieve in much of social life. When to keep the ball and when to pass it to another is an art that stretches out into many of our activities. The balance between co-operation and self-assertiveness is well taught within the structured environment of the rules of a game.

It is also believed that games enable people to learn how to demarcate their lives. While the game is on we abide by certain rules. Then the whistle blows and we no longer have to. Learning how to handle defeat (it took me some years not to weep bitterly after losing a game) and feel relaxed with someone who has outwitted or outplayed you is another important art.

Likewise the subtle art of playing within the rules, but using as much scope and skill within them as possible, is one that is handy in almost every branch of life. You have to learn the rules of your trade or occupation, but if you just stick to these without creative thought then you will end up as nothing special. If you break them and are caught the result is even worse. How can you keep to the rules and yet excel? Skill, personal tricks, long training and perceptive observation of others are among what's needed. The concept of 'spin', which makes the ball behave in odd ways in cricket and disguises the real motives of politicians when they deal with the public, is one example of this.

What is the fascination of games?

People enjoy playing games because they are animals who like to compete and dominate; to play, strive, outwit, win are all important survival tools. But there is more to games than this, particularly team games. Members of a cricket, football or bowls team play together and often socialise together, and either create or express their friendship in this way. Friendly rivalry over a game of chess or in the squash court may also cement friendship. Matching minds and bodies or depending and sharing with other members of the team, both give great satisfaction.

Friends play together, and the stress on learning games at school is also meant to be a lesson in friendship. Like friendship, play is not directed to a practical goal. It is 'just a game' – but to refuse to play is a rejection.

Equally intriguing is why people watch games and sport. The extraordinary growth of spectator sports, undoubtedly deeply influenced by television and by the way in which sport, alongside sex, is the main way of selling goods, is one of the marks of our world.

The historian of technology Lewis Mumford suggests that modern sports may be defined as 'those forms of organised play in which the spectator is more important than the player'. They are a spectacle, in many ways closer to drama or ritual than to playing a game.

The crowd become part of a chorus, emotionally and psychologically blending together, taken for a moment out of their ordinary lives and worries. Like spectators at the contests of gladiators and wild animals in Rome, or its modern equivalent the bullfight, or even the circus, the crowd cheers and boos. Even in the privacy of their home, people dress up in their team's colours, drink lager and pretend that they are part of the crowd as they watch the television.

Being in a crowd makes us brave. We can shout and say things we would normally be too timid to express. It is often the time when we can make our prejudices and passions known, whether for our country, our political opinions, or our hatreds, in a way that as single individuals we find impossible. It is not surprising that all dictatorships love assembling partisan crowds and setting them marching and singing and shouting.

Mass sport and private play are forms of conspicuous consumption. Many modern societies have a great deal of leisure, and people fill up their spare time – and often demonstrate their new-found affluence – through games. Often they do this publicly, but equally often privately, in the world of computer games and internet rivalries.

The increasing amount of leisure time often created by machines must be filled. Playing in various ways is what humans like to do in their spare time. So if anything is the new 'religion' of the world, it is football. More money, emotion and activity are now generated by sport, games and hobbies than anything else on earth, except war. Indeed war, to some of its proponents, is the sublimest form of game. It adds the spice of the risk of death to the usual thrills of other contests. On the other hand, for many people it is better to fight in the World Cup than in the trenches.

Violence and fear

7

*I*s violence necessary?

Dear Lily,

In English, the word violence has a relatively narrow meaning, referring mainly to violent physical actions. It means using an unnecessary and unwanted amount of physical force against another. The 'unwanted' is important, since much of life consists of the use of force. When a child is lifted off the ground, when a doctor or dentist does their work, when we play many games, force is involved. Yet we do not call this violence. If we punch a face, knock out someone's tooth or embrace a person against their will, then we call it a violent act. Always physical force is involved.

The French word *violence* embraces a much wider set of meanings. Here both physical and what is called symbolic violence are included. For example we can talk of the symbolic violence contained in language, architecture, gestures, painting, government directives, class or gender. The very grand building I inhabit next to King's College Chapel is designed in a way that instils awe into visitors, just as the lofty chapel itself compels some feeling of reverence on to all those who enter. Many of these instances do not directly involve the use of physical force, yet they exert pressures on an individual which may go against her will and interests. In this letter I will use the broader, French, meaning of the word.

Do we have to hurt each other?

There are very few human relationships in which there is no violence. Even if they do not control their children with physical force, parents almost always use symbolic violence to discipline them. They tell them to shut up, to obey what they say or else. They exercise control by using presents and gifts and even by the indirect violence of excessive love or guilt inducement. There are threats and encouragements; force is below the surface all the time. It is part of the inequality built into parent–child relations and it can easily move from what is considered justified control to 'abuse', that is the over-use or inappropriate use of power. It is a delicate balance.

In many societies the relations between parents and children are so unequal that the use of both symbolic and physical violence is often not considered 'abuse'. In traditional Roman or Chinese society, the power of the father was such that he could kill his children if they were disobedient, or torture his wife if she was insubordinate. In some societies a brother may be duty-bound to kill his sister if she threatens the family honour by having an affair. The levels of what we consider to be abuse are often very high indeed. In some places violence is almost an obligatory form of male behaviour, showing that someone is a 'true man'.

Yet it would be wrong to think that there has been a steady movement from the early stages of society, when violence in the family was common, to modern societies where it is frowned on. A number of hunter-gatherer societies have almost no inter-personal violence, while levels in many places in the so-called 'civilised' world are extremely high. In the three years I have spent in a Nepalese village, I have seen physical violence in only one family over a short period of time. Otherwise I have not seen a single person hit a child, or a wife beat a husband, or the reverse. There is very little symbolic violence; little threatening, shouting, bribing. From infancy onwards, people are nudged into certain actions or thoughts by gentle, if consistent, pressures and suggestions.

In England a fairly radical change has been occurring over the last two generations. The inequalities within the family are being challenged. There is talk of laws being introduced to ban all corporal punishment whether in school or in the home.

Yet elsewhere the amount of interpersonal violence seems to grow. Crimes of violence, including robbery, murder and rape, appear to be on the increase. The media is full of violent images, both in fiction and in the news. So people have a sense of anxiety about the threat of attack, even if their fears often bear little relationship to actual trends or crime statistics. In Japan and in England the hundreds of thousands of people who are killed or maimed in road accidents are hardly noticed, but if one little boy kills another, or two schoolgirls are murdered, the whole nation is traumatised.

Why are we cruel to other animals?

Humans are just one species of animal. They share over 98 per cent of their DNA with chimpanzees. Yet they often imagine themselves to be a different sort of creature, in some way superior – a view upheld by Christian theology. There is thus an ambivalence in humans' treatment of other animals.

It is difficult to see a single developing pattern in the attitude of humans towards other animals. In many early societies there seems to have been a belief in a good deal of overlap. Humans could turn into animals and vice versa; myths told of these changes, and animals had human spirits. Then, with the domestication of animals some thousands of years ago, other species became both closer to and further from humans. As the cats and dogs were brought in, and the sheep, cows, goats and buffaloes were penned, so animals paradoxically became separated off from humans. Often a threefold classification developed.

Pets, that is companions of humans such as cats and dogs, as well as animals they rode such as horses, were the inner circle. They were like children or very close relatives, dependent and submissive. Physical incorporation of pets through eating was forbidden. A second ring was formed by domesticated animals: sheep, cows, yaks, buffaloes and pigs. They were like cousins – close, but not family. They could be, and usually were, brought close into one's life by being eaten. Finally there were wild animals, which were like enemies or non-kin. These were again divided into the edible – deer and wild game of various kinds – and the normally inedible meat-eaters such as leopards, tigers, bears and wolves.

So for thousands of years humans and animals were both interdependent and yet also separate. In particular, certain religions assumed that a human-like god had created different species. In the Christian myth, God had created the animals on one day and humans on another. He had made Eden and filled it with animals and placed a man as its ruler. Animals were at the disposal of humans and they were created as formed and separate species.

The whole idea of a vast gulf between humans and animals collapsed in the middle of the nineteenth century when Charles Darwin outlined the long-term evolution of species and showed that humans were but one late, and minor, branch of a tree which included all the other species. Ever since then we have become increasingly aware of how much we overlap. Almost all the things that were supposed to divide humans from animals have vanished. Some animals use tools, have a sense of humour, use simple forms of language, have self-awareness and perhaps even a sense of their own mortality. They feel, think, hope and fear.

As it becomes daily more obvious that animals suffer and think much as we do, it might have been expected that there would be a growing sensitivity and care towards them. There are signs of this in organisations to promote vegetarianism or to prevent cruelty. Yet they just touch the edge of the problem. For it would not be difficult to argue that, as we witness the extinction of many species and the factory farming of animals and fish, there is more exploitation and systematic cruelty in the world now than there has ever been. We still manage to suppress our affinities to whales, pigs, cows and chickens and continue to torture, slaughter and eat them.

As we consume our steaks, sausages, hamburgers and fried chickens, millions of us have little idea of (or interest in) the conditions of our fellow creatures. Perhaps it will not be until some new and superior species emerges on earth, some computerised android, which breeds humans in tiny cages, force-feeds them, drains their bile, eats them, that we will seriously begin to crusade for the abolition of animal-on-animal cannibalism. Meanwhile the greatest predators on earth munch their way through the animal kingdom. We are caught in a dilemma. For we are a meat-eating species, which gains much of its protein from consuming other animals. It is almost impossible to imagine that we will change, but we may, with sufficient will, find ways to minimise the pain we inflict on our fellow species.

Why do people join criminal gangs?

Criminal organisations exist because they serve a purpose. In the case of many of the Mafia-like organisations, criminal gangs run an informal or 'black' economy which enables the formal or 'white' economy to work. The normal market, in places like Russia and India or traditionally in southern Italy, does not operate properly. There is little trust in the legal institutions which are supposed to underpin the market. The police, bureaucracy and politicians are widely believed to be corrupt. There is often inefficiency and over-regulation. Nothing gets done without huge efforts and bribes.

In this situation the local mafia, through the bonds of loyalty and fear, through the concept of *omerta* (honour, keeping one's word) and the punishment of deviation, provide the assurances and the security that the state cannot provide.

If one loses a valuable object it is no good going to the police who are inefficient and corrupt. Far better to engage the 'brotherhood' of the mafia who will put out the word, and very soon the stolen object will be hastily returned and the thief punished. Or again, if one wants to do a deal, make a contract with an unrelated person, whether it is just to buy or sell a cow, or to build a new road or airport, it is essential that the other party be under some pressure to honour the deal. So the mafia is used as a general guarantee.

To avoid time-wasting and money-wasting obstacles, licences, customs obstructions and regulations of various kinds, the mafia will smooth the way. The national and international reach of *cosa nostra*, 'our people', will overcome all difficulties.

The mafia ensure this by a blend of physical and symbolic violence. Occasionally the mafiosi are sent out to use the bullet, the knife or the fire-bomb, but most of the time the threat is enough. The dark glasses which stop human contact through the eyes, the large, dark, bullet-proof car, the prickly-pear leaf left as a calling card, the head of a favourite animal on the pillow, certain menacing tones and gestures, all these make offers of protection difficult to refuse.

The mafia tend to operate in the grey area between the

legal and the illegal. They inhabit the land of debased human desires, of gambling, drink, sex, illegal sports and drugs, which the state both tolerates and at the same time tries to eliminate.

Why do communities attack each other?

Of course ethnic and religious violence have been present in human societies for thousands of years. When we hear about the terrible Hutu–Tutsi massacres in Africa, the Muslim–Hindu violence which periodically erupts in India, the awful events in Kosovo and the Balkans, we seem to be living in a world where the tide of intercommunal violence is rising. Yet when we remember the massacre of up to a million Armenians in the early twentieth century, or of millions of Jews in the genocide of the middle of the century, it seems likely that we could go back through history and find endless examples of such violence.

It appears that whenever people are held together by a sense of 'we', through notions of religion or race, then these concepts can suddenly become a dividing line. 'We' are humans, 'they' are subhumans, no different from the animals which we torture and slaughter at our will.

What is perhaps most distressing and perplexing is that people who previously seemed to get on very well and be tolerant of each other's differences can so quickly become deep enemies and commit terrible atrocities on each other. One week there is chat and coffee with a neighbouring family, the next they are demonised, so that to rape their daughter or chop off their son's hand seems a reasonable thing to do.

Humans are clearly very malleable and suggestible. There does not seem to be an innate and ever present enmity that suddenly 'erupts'. There are differences that normally do not matter or cause strong feeling. Yet when feelings are manip-ulated by a Hitler, Stalin or Milosevic, or through a wider changing political context, fear is whipped up and sane, tolerant people become fanatical. The instincts to protect the family and community, and for vengeance at perceived wrongs, are mobilised, and in a few hours your friends become your foes.

It is not unlike the psychology of witchcraft, where someone's smile can very easily seemingly change from friendly to sinister if you suspect them of being a witch or an outsider. It would be a great service if someone could design an 'ethnic and religious hatred-defusing kit' which could be applied as these terrible situations begin to catch fire.

What is state violence?

A state is the organisation that has the monopoly on the use of violence. There are two major forms of this. One is against other states, which we call war. The other is the organised violence against its citizens practised by almost all states. There is the symbolic kind – the fascist architecture, thought control through propaganda, giant parades and nationalist music. There is also the development of penal and legal institutions, which often divides up the population into the free and the imprisoned.

In relation to imprisonment by the state, it is worth remembering that this punishment has varied over time. In most traditional civilisations it was too expensive to keep people locked up for 23 hours a day in a cell. So they were punished in other ways: mutilated, sent to be galley slaves, put in treadmills, dispatched to plantations and labour camps. Some were enslaved. Only affluent civilisations have been able to imprison large numbers of their citizens or to keep hundreds waiting on death row. That the Americans can afford to keep one in every two hundred of their citizens in prison suggests a very rich and, some would say, unimaginative and cruel society.

Given the wealth and attitudes in many modern states, there is a tendency for prison populations to grow rapidly as time passes. It is less bother to lock people away than to try either to deal with the roots of crime or to rehabilitate. So the British prison population inexorably creeps upwards and the profits of the increasingly privatised prison service grow. The reputation of politicians who are 'tough on crime' is enhanced.

The waste of human potential, and the basic unfairness of creating an environment of hopeless degradation and then blaming the criminals, are ignored. The state tends to become a prison machine. It can easily become a surveillance state, its public places filled with closed-circuit cameras, its wealthy private citizens living in guarded and walled estates, its police increasingly heavily armed. To fight violence, violence of a slightly different kind is used.

So we end up with the grim fact that like all species on earth, humans are necessarily violent. They cannot survive without predating on nature and on each other. Some religions such as Buddhism and some sects such as the Quakers exhort their followers to renounce all violence and live in peace. This is a worthy ideal. Yet the moment we breathe or walk we destroy other creatures.

It is all a matter of degree and of intentions. Quakers, and members of the Jain religion (who wish to avoid causing all suffering, even to small insects), try to avoid inflicting pain. They are clearly different from those who deliberately practise violence. Next time you eat some meat or kill a slug, it is worth considering what you are doing and whether it can be called violence.

$\mathscr{W}$hat is war and why do we fight?

Dear Lily,

Many people have wondered whether human beings are naturally aggressive. If they are, does this explain why warfare has played such a large part in human history? For anyone looking at the whole history of human beings would conclude that after eating, sex and playing games, killing or maiming other humans is the most common of our pastimes.

Like other animals, humans have an instinct to survive. If this suggests to them that fighting and killing will help, then they will usually do so. Many also fight for pleasure, a rough game of excitement and competition which appeal to most of us. You know this well enough, Lily, if you remember the fighting games we played when you were young, and pretended to be a tiger, raptor or other sharp-toothed beast.

Some very peaceful hunter-gatherer societies have been found in South America, Malaysia and elsewhere. They do not know of war and are peaceful within the group. Periodically mighty civilisations such as China and Japan have experienced several hundred years of almost complete peace.

Yet, if we survey the whole of human history, we find that the use of physical force against other animals (including other humans) is a practically universal feature. Now that women have begun to be recruited into the front line of armies, you might find that you yourself are killing people in a war.

Yet simple aggression, or love of fighting, or desire to survive cannot be seen as the main reason most individuals have been caught up in warfare in the past. Most wars for many centuries have involved unwilling combatants. The politicians and generals decide; the troops, through fear, need, loyalty or hope for booty, apply themselves to capturing or killing the enemy.

Individual aggression has little to do with it. The pilot who released the atom bomb over Hiroshima was not, in all probability, feeling aggressive. He was just doing his job, no more 'aggressive' than the driver of a car changing gear or a farmer planting seed. Clearly wars would not happen if humans were actively programmed against the use of all physical violence. On the other hand, no animal would survive for long in this competitive world if they were so programmed.

What is war?

We need to distinguish between active and passive war. Active war is a period of armed conflict, with acts of direct physical violence, 'hot war' as we might call it. Passive, or as we call it 'cold' war, is the use of threat and counter-threat, with little actual fighting. This is a period of constant anxiety, fear and threat, something the world witnessed between 1945 and 1989 and which it has reinvented for itself with the 'war against terrorism'.

A second major distinction is between permanent and limited war. Another name for permanent war is 'feud'. In feuds, every act of violence automatically generates the conditions for counter-violence, 'eye for eye' as the Bible puts it. It is like a see-saw. Every killing alters the balance, which has to be redressed, but when violence is answered with violence, the situation is again unbalanced. This kind of unceasing warfare or feud is the characteristic form in tribal societies. It is from one such society, the Highland Scots, that the term 'feud' or 'deadly feud' was taken.

Such feuding is to be found among the Bedouin, the tribes of Afghanistan and central Asia, or famously in Albania and the Balkans. Mountains, deserts and other rough country where people keep animals and there is little central political control are the classic areas for feuds.

The other form is that found among forest-dwelling tribesmen – the head-hunters of the Assam-Burma border, of the Philippines, of Amazonia or elsewhere. Here there is a pattern of constant raiding and inter-village war, often accompanied by head-hunting. 'Blood for blood' and the taking of human heads as powerful trophies are the signs of this perpetual warfare.

Why is there this ceaseless fighting? In trying to understand it, it is important to distinguish between the 'functions' of such warfare, for example that it may keep the population density down to an appropriate level for the available resources, and the reasons given for the warfare by the people themselves.

These reasons nearly always involve concepts of honour and shame, the lust for glory, manliness, the need to defend one's own group and its status, the need to avenge insults. This is a world of constant, intermittent but unresolvable feuds because there is no mechanism for concluding the quarrels, no central authority accepted by all, just a world of shifting alliances and distrust.

People engaged in most of these feuds have limited aims. Usually they are not concerned to conquer territory or eliminate the enemy, but rather are content to burn down some houses, steal some food or heads or women or whatever is valuable.

It is an elaborate, violent game, often with its own intricate rules and forms of honour. Many see analogies with the kind of activity in places such as Israel and Palestine today.

Why do countries fight?

Another major type of war is the pitched battle, with winners and losers, a beginning, a middle, an end. While such conflicts are limited in time, they are often far less limited in the destruction they cause. These are the wars of what we half-ironically call 'civilised' societies. That is to say they emerged some five thousand or so years ago with the rise of territorial states.

These are the wars of the Macedonians, Greeks, Romans, Turks, Mongols, French, British, Americans and so on. They have starting and ending dates, such as 1914–1918, 1939–1945. They begin on one day and end on another. Within the war period the fighting is often far more 'total' than in tribal wars. They are fought to defeat or conquer another bounded state, and this often involves huge-scale slaughter and destruction. It is not uncommon for millions to die in such a war, both from the fighting and from the famine and disease that they bring with them.

These wars are fought for rather different reasons from the feuding ones. There may be symbolic reasons of hurt pride, jealousy or revenge as in feuds. Yet the two main reasons are fear and greed.

Fear is indeed a powerful force. The enemy pose a threat, so one should attack before they do. This was a widespread motive and justification for almost all 'civilisational' wars until recently. During the second half of the twentieth century, a new principle of international law was established which banned pre-emptive strikes on sovereign nations. Recently some powerful Western leaders have revised the oldest justification for war by declaring that if it is in a country's self-interest to attack another which it feels might one day become a threat, this is justified. It is a move that takes us back to a world based on fear, arms races and pre-emptive strikes.

The second main motive is greed, that is to say the almost universal fact that while there are many losers, there are always some winners. These are the arms manufacturers, some bankers, the successful warriors, some politicians. There is greed for power; a good war bolsters political power and deflects one's critics. There is greed for land and other resources that can be seized through conquest.

The constant wars of aggression of empires, from the ancient Babylonians and Chinese, through the Romans, the Habsburgs and the British, up to the current Americans, are well known. This tendency of states to engage in almost constant warfare is strengthened by what one might call the 'reverse domino effect'.

In the normal 'domino effect', as in the 'war against communism', it was argued that to lose one country, for example Vietnam, could cause all the dominoes standing in a row nearby (such as Cambodia, Laos, Thailand) to 'collapse' into communism. In the reverse effect, as soon as one territory has been annexed, it puts great pressure on the successful conqueror to consider taking over the next.

One example comes from the history of the Roman Empire, which, in order to protect its ever widening territories, was drawn into annexing ever more. The British Empire was the same. In order to 'protect' India, the British felt they had to take control directly or indirectly of its borders – Afghanistan, Kashmir, Nepal, Assam, Burma. Soon British eyes were upon China and even Japan.

There is no standing still with empires. Either they push outwards or they sink beneath the onset of the 'barbarians' on the frontiers. America has increasingly been caught in this trap. Past failures can somehow be overlooked, as in the case of Vietnam, and the people aroused again to further attempts to wipe out the threatening hordes.

How do weapons change warfare?

Another difference between 'unlimited' or feuding warfare and limited but total war is technological and organisational. Feuding wars are fought seasonally, part time, by an amateur subset of the male population. Civilisational wars tend to be fought all year round (except when the climate prevents this), often by professional (conscript or mercenary) armies. The amount of training, the nature of the discipline and the internal hierarchies differ.

Furthermore, over time the weapons have changed. Most wars in history have been fought with simple weapons – bows, spears, swords. But in due course the evolution of state systems led to the development of a new order of weapons. Then the scene changed.

Gunpowder weapons transformed warfare in Western Europe from the fourteenth century. Through a strange quirk, in the country where they had been invented many centuries earlier, namely China, they were in effect soon banned or not used. Indeed, four-fifths of the great civilisations on the earth up to the eighteenth century – the Islamic States, China and Japan – all banned the use of gunpowder weapons. Only in Western Europe did cannon and small arms using gunpowder develop. It was partly this divergence that finally gave Europe the destructive advantage with which it colonised almost all of the planet between the fifteenth and nineteenth centuries.

Can war be good?

War has been almost universal in human history over the last fifty thousand years. The constant feuding wars probably inhibited the growth of civilisations in various ways. Minor gains were destroyed, populations remained relatively sparse and spread out, the ecology was protected but few major innovations could occur. As soon as a group became prosperous and relaxed its warlike discipline it was destroyed by the warriors from poorer but more warlike neighbouring groups.

For many thousands of years the world saw the warlike, feuding societies on the margins fight the settled, agrarian civilisations at the centre. The greatest contest of all was between the pastoral nomads of central Asia, the Mongols, and the settled agrarian peoples whom they overran in China, India, Russia, Eastern Europe and the Middle East.

In this vast, thousand-year clash of two forms of human organisation, the Mongols destroyed vast civilisations and ruled three-quarters of the Asian landmass up to the eighteenth century. Their technologies of destruction, principally the horse and the Mongolian bow, were superior to the war technologies of settled states until about 1700. It was only the development of more sophisticated gunpowder weapons that gave the West the final advantage.

So, for a very long period, apart from honing male physique, encouraging heroic poetry, adding some footnotes to the art of war, improving horse-breeding, and giving certain peoples a sense of purpose and heroic glory, war probably did little for human development. In the balance, the losses far outweighed the gains.

In one area of the world, however, war led to technical progress. The small kingdoms of Western Europe were constantly at war from the Middle Ages on, and a form of political 'survival of the fittest' swiftly developed. Very rapid developments in architecture, boat construction, navigation, metalworking and some branches of physics and geometry emerged out of this desperate competition.

If Europe between about 1400 and 1800 had been as peaceful

as China or Japan, it is likely that much of the rapid increase in reliable knowledge and technical efficiency would not have occurred.

Without the advances in cannon-boring made through these centuries, the steam-engine cylinder could not have been made and no industrial revolution based on steam could have occurred. If we measure human progress by man's capacity to control the physical world, then war of the Western European kind did lead to a sort of progress. Yet this has to be placed against the horrors and miseries.

What are the disasters of war?

War is the first of the three great checks to population growth. It was not chiefly the slaughter on the battlefield that inhibited this, but the almost inevitable side-effects. As foreign armies marched to and fro across northern Europe during the Thirty Years War, about a third of the population died, mainly from starvation and disease. Armies needed to live off the land: soldiers seized the stored grain and seed-corn, destroyed the ripening crops, killed the livestock, burned the tools.

It is also in such times that disease multiplies. With body resistance reduced by undernourishment, and with large hordes of soldiers and camp followers coming in from outside carrying new germs, the peasants died in their thousands or sometimes millions. Epidemic diseases, in particular typhoid, cholera, plague and typhus, spread. Endemic diseases such as dysentery and malaria increased hugely. The most vulnerable – the old, women and children – will usually be the first to die, but almost everyone is vulnerable.

Tribal groups that have previously had no contact with the outside world are most at risk. Nineteen out of twenty million of the native population died when the Spanish conquered what is now Mexico. Most did not die at the end of a sword, but through famine and disease. Likewise hundreds of thousands died in North and South America and the Pacific of smallpox, influenza, measles and other diseases against which they had no immunity.

It is very doubtful that the wars of 'civilisation' have done anything to improve either human intelligence or human physique in a selective way over the last five thousand years. They have caused horror piled on horror, a catalogue of atrocities and inhumanities which make any sensitive and informed person despair.

Does war enslave us?

Nowadays those who start wars are even more remote and isolated from its horrors than they were in the past. So they may feel that they do not share in the personal cost. Yet this is not true. For war has invisible costs, hidden injuries, less manifest than the rapes, mutilations, deaths, sickness and starvation, yet as deadly to the civilisations that engage in war as the physical scars.

The feuding wars of tribal societies tend to create equality by keeping groups in balance. If one group gains a temporary advantage, it attracts predatory attacks from neighbours, and is returned to the average position. On the other hand, the wars of civilisation have a strong tendency towards creating inequality, both between the contending groups and within them. The immediate effect of war is to make the conquered into slaves, prisoners, permanently in thrall to the conquering power.

Another effect in the past was that after the emergence of states, a caste of warriors, often armed knights who could afford expensive weapons, arose and dominated the rest. As a result a weak, unarmed mass of the population was crushed by the warriors with their superior weapons and castles. War both

justified their privilege and made any questioning of their right
to bear arms into an act of treason.

Furthermore the movement towards a centralised state is
made much more likely by war. War against outsiders justifies
higher taxes and the maintenance of a standing army. It encourages the development of a large bureaucracy to administer the
state's taxation, the suspension or elimination of civil liberties
and the destruction of all those who criticise the government.

The effects of war in turning Rome from a vibrant republic
into an autocratic empire have often been noted. Victory was
as disastrous as defeat. All opposition or questioning of the
state and its motives was banned. What was demanded was
unquestioning loyalty, unthinking patriotism, 'my country
right or wrong'. Thus the core of liberty and equality is quickly
undermined by war.

Are there exceptions?

This anti-democratic tendency applies most strongly in continental empires and states where a fear of invasion by one's
neighbours is ever present. The fact that England, Japan and
for several centuries the USA could be conceived of as separate
'islands', not threatened by neighbours, gave them a respite
from this fear.

In the case of England, the country was very often at war.
Yet much of the fighting was an optional activity, taking place
on other people's territory (for a long time in France). When
extra taxes were needed for such activity, it gave the moderately powerful subjects a chance to bargain for more rights
and freedom from their rulers (who had no standing army).
Hence wars tended to increase liberty. This is part of a wider
pressure; warfare from the time of Napoleon onwards has been
a powerful instrument in widening the franchise because of the
state's dependence on mass armies and conscription.

The USA in the nineteenth century did not need to be afraid, so its inhabitants could not be blackmailed into suspending their liberties. September 11th 2001 symbolised the start of an era when the United States became virtually joined to the continent of Eurasia. Or so it feels to many Americans. So America, used to peace, is now perpetually at war, even if that war is against a nebulous enemy.

In this new war, democracy is felt to be constantly under threat. America now has a huge and expanding standing army and navy. It feels it must make pre-emptive strikes against seemingly threatening neighbours, even if they are thousands of miles away. There is a temptation to dismantle the sets of checks and balances, the rights to freedom of speech and thought, the jury system and other processes that protect the rights of individuals. We are almost all the losers in this new perpetual war.

9

*W*hat is witchcraft?

Dear Lily,

Almost every day we are faced with problems of explaining why unpleasant things happen. Friends are injured, children are ill, we suffer accidents and pain or, despite our best plans, we fail to achieve what we set out to do. It is natural to search for causes of these misfortunes, both in order to help deal with the suffering and to avoid future difficulties. Why did the car skid and crash on this particular day? Why do I and not someone else contract a painful disease?

Usually we know the obvious cause. The road was slippery, the light was poor. Yet we have driven down this road many times and there has previously been no problem. We drank untreated water, or went to a new restaurant, or were bitten by an insect. Yet at other times we took the same risks and this did not lead to illness. So, very early on in life, we learn to distinguish between the 'how' questions, asking how something happened, and the 'why' questions.

There is a story of an African who got malaria and went to the doctor, claiming he had been bewitched. The doctor said that malaria was spread by mosquitoes, to which the sick man replied that he knew that, but who had sent the mosquito?

There are two levels of cause, the material one and another which we like to relate to human purpose. When a granary falls and crushes someone among the Azande of North Africa, everyone knows that the immediate cause is white ants which have eaten away the wooden pillars. But why was this person walking under it and not another? Who was the witch who turned chance into design?

Since most things that have happened to us from when we were very young seem to be the result of decisions made by others, it is quite natural that we should believe that the suffering that frequently afflicts us is caused by a human-like force, someone who consciously hurts us in some way. Once we have decided on such a cause we have various choices, depending on the culture we live in. We may choose to believe the cause to be evil spirits, ancestors, God or witches.

To choose witchcraft as the explanation – that is the bad intentions of another human being – has a number of advantages. Evil spirits are largely uncontrollable. We are uncomfortable (if we believe in them) to think that our ancestors are plotting against us. God is supposed to love and care for us, not kill or maim us. On the other hand, we know many people who are ambivalent towards us. They blow hot and cold. They may secretly be wishing us harm and be able to carry out their intentions because they are witches.

Why not believe in witches?

People in the majority of human societies today – as in the past – believe that much of the pain and trouble in the world is caused by witchcraft. The effects of the stars, of random chance or of God's punishment are less appealing as explanations largely because there is less we can do as a result of such beliefs. The stars are mindless and unapproachable, chance is uncontrollable and random, while God is inscrutable and acts on a plan which often runs counter to our wishes. Yet witches are detectable and can be fought. They think like us, but have evil intentions. To find them we can turn to diviners.

Divination, using various kinds of oracle or shamanic ritual, is a technique to discover the cause for a misfortune. A sign in a mirror or glass ball, the throwing of dice, bones or stones, footprints in ash or sand or the voice of a summoned spirit point us to the offending witch. We can then take action and eradicate him or her. We can set up anti-witchcraft devices such as special substances or sacrifices to ward off the evil or treat the afflicted. All such divination uses devices that prevent it from being shown to be false. If a cure fails, it is because the witch was too strong or the counter-magic used against her was wrongly performed. If the wrong person is accused of witchcraft it is because the real witch has laid a false trail.

Witchcraft is a closed world. It is impossible to challenge its basic premises from within. In the past, almost everyone believed in the power of witchcraft. A sceptic, if such existed, would be accused of being a witch or in the power of one. It is very like many other closed systems which you will have heard about, for example communism. It explains much of the suffering in the world. Every new event adds to its strength. It is very attractive to human beings who live a pain-filled existence.

Does witchcraft help us to feel less guilty?

All of us have ambivalent feelings to those around us, even towards our nearest and most loved friends and members of our family. Sometimes in a burst of rage we even want to hurt our parents or siblings. Witchcraft helps to explain and even justify many of these feelings. It helps to shift the blame for them on to the witch. It helps us to feel less guilty.

Many of us have experienced confusion when stopped by a hungry, poorly dressed beggar in the streets, particularly if it is a girl or woman with a baby. She asks for money. Sometimes we give, often we turn away. In our mind we justify our lack of charity: 'The money would only go on alcohol; it will only encourage further begging.' 'Anyway,' we tell ourselves, 'we are not going to give in to menacing or threatening behaviour.' Yet we still feel guilt, which often leads to a sense of impotence or even anger.

In many parts of the world, including England three centuries ago, this would be the typical witchcraft situation. A poor old woman comes to the door and asks for help. She is a neighbour or distant relative. We have helped her before, but this time we refuse. Our religion tells us that we ought to give, but our fear of encouraging dependency or of not being able to meet the demands of our family leads us to say no. We feel guilt.

As we turn her away we think we hear her muttering or see a scowl on her face. She looks a bit frightening, witch-like. We are apprehensive. A few days later our child is sick or an animal dies. We suspect that her malevolent anger has caused this. We go to a diviner or take a case to court and our inner suspicions are made external. Others support us and report similar incidents. She is shortly imprisoned and tried as a witch. This is a situation I have read about many times in English court records and seen in action in a Nepalese village.

So witchcraft beliefs can be seen to be both intellectually and socially attractive. It should not surprise us that they are so deep-rooted and almost universal. Rather, the surprise is the exception, the societies where witchcraft has, apparently, never been believed in (for example Japan for a thousand years). Even more curious are the places where witchcraft, having been an important belief system, then died away, as in England in the later seventeenth century or most of Europe from the middle of the eighteenth century.

Why did witchcraft decline?

Up to the later seventeenth century in Europe almost everybody believed in the reality of witchcraft and the courts tried many suspected witches. A hundred years later most intellectuals had rejected such a belief and the courts no longer accepted witchcraft as a subject for trial.

If the beliefs in witchcraft were circular and irrefutable, how were they undermined? If it is so logical, why give it up for the less emotionally satisfying world which we now inhabit, where we constantly ask 'why' questions and are given such answers as 'I don't know', 'It is all random', 'There is no meaning or pattern'? If witchcraft beliefs help us to overcome feelings of anger and ambivalence (which we continue to feel to this day) by projecting the guilt on to others, why abandon them and leave ourselves alone with both our suffering and our guilt? We seem to have chosen a dry and rather unsatisfactory option, even if in doing so we have saved many poor old people from torture and death.

Some say that the rise of experimental science in seventeenth-century Western Europe undermined the world of magic and witchcraft. This is part of the story, but we need to remember that many of the early scientists were believers in witchcraft. When I asked my 'adopted' niece, who had done biology and other sciences at school in a town in Nepal, whether she believed in witchcraft, she said that of course she did. Whenever a mysterious or incurable disease occurred, she would suspect witches.

This suggests that to a certain extent 'scientific' explanations in terms of atoms and germs answer only the 'how' questions, and so the need for a 'why' cause is still present. Indeed this blend of science and religion is what a number of distinguished modern scientists who argue for the need for religion often affirm. Albert Einstein caught this beautifully: 'Science without religion is lame, religion without science is blind.'

Another argument is that the levels of risk and suffering that were behind many of the accusations began to diminish in the later seventeenth century. It is suggested that magical and witchcraft beliefs bridge gaps in our control of the material world. When we lack technical, organisational or social solutions, we turn to magic.

Faced with rough seas in a fragile wooden boat, we use magical protections. Faced with the hazards of the road, we hang little charms and talismans in our cars. When we do not know why hundreds are dying of a mysterious disease, we use amulets and magical protections. When financial insecurity, crime or disastrous fires are widespread, beliefs in a magical universe, so the argument goes, tend to rise.

If, on the other hand, the risks from fire, flood, old-age poverty, crime or disease are diminished, confidence will rise. The 'swamps' of insecurity where witchcraft 'breeds' will be drained, so such beliefs will decline – or so it is argued.

There are many difficulties with this argument, although again there is probably something in it. Most of the insecurities continued largely unabated until several centuries after witch-craft accusations and beliefs had died away. People would have had to anticipate a more secure world some generations before it actually came about. It was not until the later nineteenth century that the causes of disease began to be properly under-stood, or that public sanitation and financial security for the old and sick improved significantly.

We can see that witchcraft beliefs fluctuate. My visits to a Nepalese village over thirty years gave me experience of a place that in 1970 was full of witches and counter-witchcraft rituals. Twenty years later the shamans were gone and open beliefs and accusations of witchcraft had greatly declined. There was far less interest in magical explanations. For even though the risks remained and the Western scientific and technological solutions – medicine, electricity, artificial fertiliser – were largely unobtainable at the village level, people *believed* in the new technologies as potentially more powerful than spirits or witches.

Certainly one reason for this was largely accidental. Just as some have argued that doctors 'manufacture' disease, lawyers encourage disputes, teachers generate ignorance and missionaries imbue a sin complex, so it is clear that having a resident diviner who earns his living by finding witches generates, or at least reinforces, the belief in witches. Once the shaman had left the village for more lucrative work in the town, witchcraft beliefs, or at least accusations, dried up.

Yet there are other parts of the world where the fear of witchcraft is increasing. It is reported that in many of the cities and shanty towns of Africa the consciousness of witchcraft and the desire to try to protect oneself from it are growing. There are new witch-finding cults, and diviners are doing a good trade.

Furthermore, the emotions and fears that lay behind the great witch purges of the past are still with us today. We still engage in 'witch hunts', though the subjects may now be suspected communists or terrorists. In this way we refuse to accept the blame. We feel less consumed by guilt when we turn from the hungry and hopeless and blame them for their own condition, whether on the streets of our own town or in the developing world. We still surround our risky endeavours with magic, whether setting out on a journey, taking an exam or going to hospital for an operation. We still read the stars and peer into the future with mixed hope and scepticism.

What do we learn from witchcraft?

We learn to distinguish between types of power. There is power to do good, which we approve of, and power to do harm, which, if directed at us, we dislike. So, using the association of black with night and evil, people call the latter 'black' and the former 'white' witchcraft.

We distinguish power that is internal, a matter of thought and emotion, which leads to prayers and curses, and we call this witchcraft or religion. Such power usually comes from requesting, addressing words of an imploring kind, to a larger power, Satan or God. We ask for diabolical or divine power.

On the other hand there are externalised actions, the making of images and sticking pins in them, burning of hair or finger-nails, making a potion and uttering a commanding spell aloud. Here by the manipulation of objects, often accompanied by words, we force or conjure nature to act. This is magic.

This famous distinction, first developed in the study of the Azande tribe, is somewhat similar to that between religion and science. Witchcraft is internal and invisible, like religion. Magic is external and visible, like science. Magic like science aims to control nature. Its goals are also very similar to those of science.

Are we free of magic?

Our modern lives, however apparently 'rational' and free of superstition, contain much magical thinking. We curse our politicians, half-hoping the curse will strike them down. We pray for delivery when we are frightened, we engage in a thousand minor protective rituals through our day. Just observe yourself and you will see how many magical acts there are, particularly when you are afraid or out of control. The world of witchcraft and magic is never far away.

One reason Harry Potter, the hobbits and even Alice in

Wonderland strike so many resonances is that because even as adults we are reluctant to relinquish magic. There are those who argue that the greatest art derives its power from enchantment, or magical beliefs. Certainly many great artists seem like magicians.

We may think that we now live in a 'disenchanted' world, that we have banished the witches, vampires, goblins. Yet five minutes in the 'real world' – in a bookshop, watching television or in a school playground – will show us how wrong such a presumption is. Magic is alive and well. Its capital is Disneyland.

$\mathscr{W}$ho are the terrorists?

Dear Lily,

There are many secret organisations dedicated to undermining the state. These are often classified as rebel or terrorist
movements. The main point here is the obvious one that
one person's freedom fighter is another's terrorist. To some
Chechens, Karens in Burma, Catholic Irish, Basques, Kurds,
Nagas, Palestinians, Tamil Tigers, their dreams and hopes for
independence seem attainable only through organised violence
against what they consider to be an overbearing state. They
believe they are fighting for their freedom and dignity. Yet to
those in power they are terrorists. It is mainly a question of
perspective.

We can see this easily enough by the way in which terrorists
become non-terrorists once they achieve their goals. When they
become the Israeli state, Maoist China, or ANC-led South Africa,
the terrorist label is discreetly forgotten. Nelson Mandela is
a good example of the transition from 'terrorist' to national
hero.

There seems to be a growing number of these organisations.

This partly reflects access to weapons and explosives, partly increasing wealth. They often centre on the lines that have been drawn across the world by colonial powers. The borders between states, mainly set out in the nineteenth century, which crosscut or ignore ethnic groups such as the Kurds, Basques, Nagas, Tamils and many African groups, are often felt to impose apparently arbitrary and alien rule upon them.

What seems to be at the root of this widespread problem is the lack of strategies to make people free but united. The idea of an international umbrella, under which *almost* sovereign states could carry on their lives according to their own wishes and customs, seems very difficult to achieve.

The bloody history of resistance and terrorism over the last century could have led to a two-tier model, in which certain functions necessary for co-working at a high level were done by an overarching state, but everything else was devolved. This is the model that, for example, some hope that the European Union will achieve. Yet it appears very difficult to manage. Almost every large nation faces the draining effects of local terrorism or resistance in the absence of a satisfactory legal solution.

What seems relatively new is the spread of these organisations round the world. The new type of terror is international, a coalescing of some of these groups and the emergence of others. This has led into the so-called 'war on terrorism'. In fact, however, there is nothing particularly new about such a supposed 'war'.

Why do people feel menaced?

Those in power usually feel under threat. At one time it was the Jews who were rumoured to form an international conspiracy to undermine Christian values. They were believed to eat Christian children, to engage in obscene rituals and generally to be subversive of all good values. In the twelfth and thirteenth centuries, certain beliefs coming in from Asia were declared to be heretical and the Cathars or Albigensians in the south of France were destroyed by sword and fire in a giant and ferocious crusade led by the Pope.

Then in the fifteenth century an even greater menace was thought to have arisen. Satan or the Devil emerged to lead a secret assault on civilisation with his army of witches. For two hundred years the international conspiracy of evil was thought to consist of witches. Since they were such a threat and could not be detected by normal means, special measures were needed. Manuals were written; legal codes were bent and amended to deal with the new threat. The previous tools to crush heresy, including the Holy Office of the Inquisition, were now used in the war against supposed witches. Thousands were rounded up, tried, convicted and burnt.

So extreme was the fear that even in countries without the Catholic Inquisition and with a different legal system, the laws were altered to deal with the new threat. In England in the sixteenth century, people who could not normally act as witnesses – children against their parents, a husband against his wife – were permitted to do so in these special circumstances. Previous evidence of behaviour, attitudes and crimes, not normally revealed, could be brought before the court. The individual could be placed under unusual physical and mental pressures in order for evidence to be wrung out. She (or he) could be deprived of sleep for long periods, supposedly to see whether her 'familiars' (small diabolical pets) came to visit her, but in effect breaking down her resistance. The presumption of innocence was greatly diminished, the necessity for direct proof was waived and circumstantial or 'spectral' (hazy spiritual) evidence was allowed.

In the end, faced with universal fear and loathing, shunned by their friends, told that they were part of a grand conspiracy of satanic covens or cells loosely joined to each other, the poor creatures confessed and implicated others. They then confirmed that an organisation existed whose totally irrational, unjustified and unprovoked aim was to undermine 'civilisation' as people knew it. So 'civilisation' responded by further abandoning the very justification for its existence: using the special techniques now allowed, it 'proved' the existence of witches and hanged or burnt thousands of them. Only much later did doubt set in. It emerged that the whole conspiracy was a delusion created by the legal methods used to attack it. Thousands had been slaughtered on the basis of an illusion.

Similar panics still occur. In the 1950s it was a panic about a secret conspiracy of 'communists' that led to the McCarthy trials in America and the destruction of the reputation of many innocent people.

Then in the 1980s in Britain a new threat came to light, the so-called paedophile rings. The details of their activities, and the widespread sexual abuse of children by their own parents, were often 'recalled' when children were 'counselled' by sympathetic experts. Satanic rituals in which children were sexually abused – and even human sacrifices were supposed to occur – were suddenly believed to be widespread. Hundreds were imprisoned; thousands of children were taken away from their parents in dawn raids. Only later, as the panic declined, was it discovered that most of the accusations were false, created by the very methods created to try to deal with them.

So there are plenty of precedents for the fear of a malevolent Other, and all of them tend to involve the shadowy presence of Evil, the Devil or Satan. Worldwide conspiracies against civilisation were thought to exist for thousands of years. Among them were Christianity and Islam themselves before they came to dominate.

What is the 'Axis of Evil'?

There has recently been a rise in the fear of what a president of the United States called the 'Axis of Evil'. This is a general umbrella term which, like 'the Empire of Evil' of an earlier president's remark about the Soviet Union, has wider implications once it circulates through the media.

The evil is envisaged as a threat to all civilised values. It is believed to threaten the state and all aspects of a society, just as in the past witches or Jews or heretics were thought to menace the foundations of Christian morality.

Some think the threat is sufficiently serious to justify the dismantling of the protections for 'terrorists'. A vast conspiracy is feared, and this fear tends to be fuelled by the moral panic that is whipped up. This movement appeals to those whose power and prestige are enhanced. They may, as with the great witch-hunters of the past, feel a glow of satisfaction and passionately believe that they are protecting their God and their country.

Looking back after the event, we may well come to feel the same about the current panic as we now do about witch-hunting: people may conclude that the action of the state in countering terrorism is undermining the very values it claims to protect.

Beliefs in Satan, witches and the 'Axis of Evil' are a perpetual, irrefutable justification for sweeping counter-measures. We are used to the temporary and drastic suspension of normal legal protections and processes during a limited war. In the Second World War, for example, suspected aliens were rounded up and imprisoned without trial, all citizens immediately lost many of their rights, freedom of speech was severely curtailed, loyalty to the state became paramount. Serious criticism was discouraged as being close to treason. If you are not fully for us, it was argued, you must be against us. The state was justified in bullying, lying, deceiving, swooping down, spying on anyone.

Truth is said to be the first casualty of war; the freedom and rights of individuals are the second.

Afterwards there may be apologies, as there were, for example, to the large numbers of innocent Japanese rounded up and locked away in America after Pearl Harbor. But that is afterwards. War itself usually spells an end to liberty and equality before the law.

Yet wars, at least the typical wars of the nineteenth and twentieth centuries, had one compensation. They tended to be bounded. There was a period of war, and civil liberties and the normal processes of law were suspended. But then there was peace, and the luxury of freedom could again be afforded by the state and was demanded by a citizenry who had not forgotten their earlier freedoms. People even persuaded themselves that this is what they had been fighting for, even if temporarily they had had to abandon their rights and freedoms.

The 'Axis of Evil', whether al-Qaida, or the satanic cults of witches, is rather different. This is a world linked to certain tendencies within Christianity and Islam. Those involved on both sides of the struggle believe that there is someone out there who is trying to undermine their way of life and whose motives they cannot fathom. These unseen folk are Evil, whether they are the feared Western capitalists or Islamic fundamentalists. They are believed by many to be in league with the Devil.

The defenders of 'our' way of life believe that Evil never sleeps, is always plotting, always invisible, irrationally consumed with a desire to destroy 'our' rational, sane, orderly, pleasant way of life. It lurks menacingly – 'reds under the beds' as the communists were once described, or, to use a more modern metaphor, the 'monster' hiding in the wardrobe of the frightened child in *Monsters Inc*.

Just as in the past witches were thought to hide behind the outward smiles of neighbours, terrorists are believed by some to conceal themselves as 'students' in our universities. Evil will use any weapons, of single or 'mass' destruction, curses, the poisoning of wells (a well-known technique ascribed to witches and Jews in the past), pestilences (biological warfare against animals and humans) and plagues of caterpillars or locusts.

There may be temporary victories, but there can be no truce or termination. We must fight continuously, for Evil is hydra-headed. Cut off one of its manifestations, for instance the Taliban in Afghanistan, and it will spring up again elsewhere. Worst of all, it is not just an external threat, as are the conventional enemies – the Germans, the French, the British or whoever we were fighting against in the wars between nation-states. The minions of the Evil One are in our midst, or so it is alleged.

We are told that terrorism feeds on envy: the envy of poor immigrants for their hosts, or of impoverished people in the developing world who cannot accept that the fact that they earn one-hundredth of what a Westerner in many affluent societies earns is perfectly fair. The poison lurks in the devious practices of people who eat strange foods (not, as was supposed with Jews and witches in the past, babies and other sacrificial victims, but highly spiced and strange substances, or rubbishy fast food), who go through strange rituals (not satanic ones, but worshipping Allah or other gods), who wear too few clothes (miniskirts) or too many (veils).

Of course there are differences between earlier panics and the present one. Witches, we know, could not actually harm people. A bomb, delivered by whichever side in the battle, kills and maims. The main point, however, is to realise from past experience that it is very easy to get into an almost unending vicious circle of fear. We would do well to remember a line from Edwin Muir's poem: 'We have seen Good men made evil wrangling with the evil,/Straight minds grown crooked fighting crooked minds.'

Can the struggle against Evil ever end?

The fight against 'Evil' continues; the 'elimination' of terrorism – as in the past, witchcraft – is the goal. We are told this is a war we must 'win'. Yet a moment's thought will show that such a goal forever recedes before us. In a world so blatantly unjust, where some consume three-quarters of the world's resources while the rest live indebted and enslaved, how can those who wish us ill be eliminated?

Witches in the past were blamed for the envy they understandably felt for those who denied them help. The guilt felt by the better-off was reflected back, and uncharitable behaviour became justified because it was against a 'witch'. So nowadays a rich Westerner or Asian can blame 'fanatics' for being potential suicide bombers. They can be angry at 'asylum-seekers' for foolishly getting themselves born in a country where no economic living can be made or where torture is widespread.

A 'war on terrorism', along with the endless battle, paranoia, aggression and undermining of civil liberties that it justifies, inevitably feeds the power of the state. It is easy to see how swiftly we can move towards the world portrayed by George Orwell in *Nineteen Eighty-Four*, with a seemingly benevolent 'Big Brother' telling us that 'one more effort', one more (temporary of course) erosion of our privacy, dignity, freedom or wealth, will finally eliminate the 'Evil One'. Just one more invasion to 'root out' the contagion, to 'drain the swamps', to eradicate the 'vermin', to crush and destroy.

All the metaphors are taken from the constant human battle to destroy – weeds, vermin, pests, wild animals – that has been classified as unworthy of respect or understanding. They are metaphors that were used in the medieval battle against Satan and his witches, and they are the ones used today.

If we make this last effort, the nightmare will be over, the 'foreign bodies' that infect our world will be eliminated, and Utopia will be ushered in. For some, this means eliminating the insidious poison of consumer capitalism; for others, the nightmare of closed and illiberal religious fanaticism.

Both dreams are unrealistic in our interconnected world. The masses will not want to give up the hope of living in a rich industrial society. Nor will we be able to stop them hating us, to persuade them to thank us for our civilised ability to soak up the world's wealth. The best we can do is to control our level of fear. I agree with the great American president Franklin D. Roosevelt: 'Let me assert my firm belief that the only thing we have to fear is fear itself.'

Belief and knowledge

$\mathcal{W}$ho is God?

Dear Lily,

Religion is usually defined as a belief in some entity or entities who exist(s) alongside but outside this material world. It can be one person, as in the monotheistic (one God) systems of Judaism, Christianity and Islam, or the many gods of Hinduism, Shinto, Taoism and certain forms of Buddhism.

In the West, where the prevailing belief is in one God, creator and sustainer of the world, lovingly concerned with His children, there are rituals to keep close contact with this father figure. At birth, marriage and death God joins His family, ratifying and consoling. At certain times of the year He is asked to bless and in times of trouble He is leant on for support.

Questions are put to Him. Why is there so much pain in the world? What happens when we die? And the answers are usually found in His holy word, the Bible. This gives rules of conduct in the Ten Commandments and in the Sermon on the Mount. Divided into a multitude of sects, often at war with one another, this religion shares enough common beliefs to give it one name, Christianity.

In this and other religions there are sacred spaces, godly areas set apart from the everyday concerns of our lives. In these, prayers are directed at the all-powerful One, who is pleaded with and cajoled – but not, as in magic, commanded.

In the West a set of beliefs defines Christianity, which is both its strength and its weakness, since it can be divisive and intolerant. In other parts of the world there is often a more relaxed attitude. Different beliefs and rituals can be blended together. In a Nepalese village, for example, a person may call in a Hindu brahmin to do a *puja* for success, bury an elderly relative with the help of a Buddhist lama and then try to cure a sick relation with a shamanic ritual.

In Japan, belief is partly dealt with by Western philosophy or by Buddhism, many rituals are performed by Shinto priests, and ethics are partly catered for by Confucianism. There is no single system. When I asked a group of Japanese schoolchildren what their 'religion' was, they were puzzled. They did not recognise the word or a special thing one could call 'religion'.

This often makes it very difficult for Japanese or Chinese visitors to understand Western societies. Even a relatively secular country like England seems to them to be highly 'superstitious', full of the assumptions of religion. There are traces of God in our philosophy, poetry, art and everyday life and nothing makes sense unless we see the ghost of Christianity behind it. Many foreigners think of us, whether we go to church or not, as religion-soaked.

Where is the sacred?

The distinction between the sacred and the profane is more complicated than it looks. If we go up to the altar in a church, we feel we are in a sacred space. Yet there are many other places and actions that feel special – a cremation, a prayer before a meal, a moment of national celebration or mourning. Are these sacred?

In much of the West, after the Protestant Reformation the division into sacred and profane was undermined. All of this world became a profane, secular sphere, and God was removed to another, distant, sacred space. So there is no obvious distinction of the kind felt in many religions whereby a particular day, place, relic or icon is sacred. Many Westerners lack a strong idea of 'sacredness' in their lives.

On the other hand, in many societies it is the opposite. Everything is to a certain extent sacred. In a Nepalese village, all of life is simultaneously and potentially sacred and profane at the same time. There is a little godling living in the fireplace, another in a basket in the corner of the living room, another in a bowl of water, others on the doorstep and round the eaves of the house. There are numerous godlings in large trees or rocks. Divinity lurks everywhere, and its power can be activated at any time by an appropriate ritual.

Religion is impossible to define precisely because it has so many features. Yet not all of them will be found in any specific society or in the same combination. This helps to explain the fact that, though there can be no societies without a code of right and wrong, there have been some where it has not been possible to find a sense of a particular God or gods.

Are right and wrong the same everywhere?

In many societies murder is immoral; in others it is, in certain circumstances, considered the highest of moral acts. In many, sexual intercourse between unmarried people is sinful, but in the majority there is nothing wrong with it. In many it is fine to lie to a stranger; in others one should never lie.

It is even more confusing because ethical systems seem to be blown about by the winds of change. In my life I have seen sexual ethics totally transformed from those prevailing when I was brought up. The concepts of right and wrong are being radically altered by genetic engineering, which affects our basic attitude to the borders between the natural and the artificial. If we look at the ethics of our own country in the past we can see that they were very different from our own.

Furthermore, in most societies, ethics are not universal but contextual. The morality or immorality of lying, killing or eating someone all depends on the circumstances. We know this in a mild way in that 'Thou shalt not kill' evaporates quickly in war, or similarly 'Thou shalt not steal' is forgotten in a famine, or exhortations not to lie by someone facing life in a concentration camp. Yet it is even more extreme than this. The ethical system usually varies for different castes or classes, for men and women, differs according to whether one is dealing with relatives or not, differs if one is treating members of one's own or another ethnic group.

One of the astonishing features of parts of Western society is that not only do we have a strong ethical system, which we pursue as an ideal, but the foundation of this, the idea of innate 'human rights', is now proclaimed as not only incontestable but universal. These rights are believed to apply everywhere on the planet, to men, women, rich, poor, old, young, irrespective of class or kinship. This is an extraordinary claim.

Furthermore, such rights are increasingly dissociated from God or a particular religion. Rather they are based on ideas about what is the ultimate nature of human beings – love, respect, 'do as you would be done by'.

So ethical codes have become more relative. We are aware of their limitations and the variations around the world. Certain old standards, for example in sexual behaviour, have been abandoned. Yet ethical standards have simultaneously become more universal. They are now increasingly based on the local traditions developed in Western Europe and America and are spread by a combination of military and technological supremacy. It is a truly confusing world.

Does religion mirror this world?

In most societies and over most of time, it was believed that God or the gods came first and then they created humankind, often in their own image. Increasingly this was questioned. In the nineteenth century many people described religion as something constructed by humans. People made the gods to be like themselves.

Indeed the idea that we construct God, rather than the other way round, is an old one reaching back to the ancient Greeks. Later, in the sixteenth century, Michel de Montaigne wrote, 'Man is quite insane. He wouldn't know how to create a maggot and he creates Gods by the dozen.' Two centuries later another French philosopher, the Baron de Montesquieu, referred to 'a very good saying that if triangles invented a god, they would make him three-sided.'

This seems to make sense the moment we look at a range of societies, since it becomes obvious that their ideas of God, heaven and hell vary enormously. Those who herded animals, like the people who created the religions of Judaism, Christianity and Islam, had a picture of God as the patriarch or father figure of a tribe of herdsmen who wanted animals as a gift. Those who grew grains and lived in settled villages often had a variety of smaller and larger gods who reflected their diversity, as in Hinduism, Taoism or Shinto.

It is even possible to find direct mirrors of this world in the ideas of heaven. In a Nepalese village, the dead spirits are believed to live in an exact copy of the ordinary village. In 'soul village', people keep similar animals, eat similar grains, dance in a similar way, and live in houses like those they occupied when alive. The only difference is that there is no disease, hard work or death. The whole idea of such a projection is described by the English poet Rupert Brooke, imagining the 'Heaven' of some fish:

> *Fish say, they have their stream and pond;*
> *But is there anything beyond?*

Fish conclude that

> *… somewhere, beyond space and time,*
> *Is wetter water, slimier slime!*

In such a world, all is perfect:

> *Oh! never fly conceals a hook,*
> *Fish say, in the Eternal Brook,*
> *But more than mundane weeds are there,*
> *And mud, celestially fair.*

> *Unfading moths, immortal flies,*
> *And the worm that never dies.*
> *And in that Heaven of all their wish,*
> *There shall be no more land, say fish.*

There is obviously something in this idea that heaven is often just a mirror-image of what is found on earth. When people live in a small-scale society, where everyone's experiences and values are roughly the same, it is possible to make a heaven which is like this life without the pain. Having made such a heaven, and a God who presides over it, the moral rules of the present society and the present arrangements seem to be endorsed by an apparently separate supernatural order. God and heaven mirror this world, and this world should mirror God and heaven.

Yet constructing a heaven is usually more complicated than this. People in most societies have for a long time become divided by class or caste, by gender and by occupation. If one group were designing heaven it would look like one thing;

another group would design it in another way. Hence feminists see God as a She, young people would prefer her young, and black people may not be too keen on her being white.

The only solution is to make God, heaven and the spiritual world as vague and abstract as possible, as in Anglican Christianity. In the Anglican heaven, I learnt when I pressed my teachers on the subject, there are clouds and a vague fatherly figure, but the rest is up to the believer to fill in. Dead friends and relatives can be placed in the context of one's choice.

You, Lily, as a child, invented your own heaven where, as you explained to me, an endless game of pass-the-parcel took place. Each person won a prize when they unwrapped a layer of the parcel, and the prizes were their heart's desire.

What is sin?

A society with a religion of rules imparts a strong sense of sin. To break the ethical rule is bound to displease God or the gods. In Christianity, masturbation, lying and cheating are widely thought to be sins that God will punish. On the other hand, in the majority of societies, where ethics are one thing, and religion and ritual another, it is different. In Japan, for instance, breaking rules of sexual behaviour might lead to social sanctions, but it does not upset God.

So when the Christian missionaries arrived in Japan in the sixteenth century they found one of their most difficult tasks was to persuade the Japanese that they were sinful. There was no such concept as 'sin'. Many Japanese could see little reason to adopt a religion that preached salvation from the consequences of sin through the sacrifice of Jesus Christ who had taken upon him the sins of the world. It was a big problem.

The same difficulty was faced by missionaries in other parts of the world. In many tribal societies people were believed to be good or bad human beings, moral or immoral, kind or unkind. Yet this had nothing to do with whether they would go to heaven or to hell. Indeed, in most of them there was a belief only in a heaven. There was no hell at all, just a rebirth into this world in another form, or a land where all the dead went. So again the missionaries had first to persuade people of their sinfulness and then to provide the remedy in their teaching, just as merchants had to persuade people they needed their goods before trying to sell them.

One way some people have tried to explain the difference between attitudes is to note that on the one hand, in the majority of societies, people feel shame when they do bad things, particularly if they are found out. The failure is in relation to other people. On the other hand there are those religions such as Christianity where people feel a sense of guilt. That is to say, people experience an inner feeling that they have betrayed something beyond this human society. Even if they are never found out in their lies or sexual misbehaviour, God will know, and they feel guilt. Robinson Crusoe on his island clearly felt guilt at certain times although there was no one else on the island. This was because he had a sense of an invisible God watching him.

The opposition between shame and guilt is a little over-simple, but it is a useful way to start to try to understand the difference. Too much sense of sin and guilt has weighed down and even destroyed many people. Equally, an absence of a sense of sin and guilt has turned others into 'amoral supermen', that is people with no real sense of good and bad. A little more sense of sin and guilt might not have been amiss in the case of Stalin or Chairman Mao, while perhaps a little less might benefit some of the anxious and guilt-ridden individuals you are bound to meet.

Does Evil really exist?

It is not widely recognised that Evil and the Devil are so closely linked as to be inseparable. In the Lord's Prayer 'deliver us from evil' used to be 'deliver us from the devil'. Yet the word 'Evil' with a capital 'E' has come back into fashion lately with a great deal of talk of this or that action being 'utterly Evil', of the 'Empire of Evil', the 'Axis of Evil'. So what is Evil and does it really exist?

There are clearly many wrong, immoral or criminal thoughts and actions and when we condemn them we call them evil. In this sense we refer to antisocial acts as evil. We consider rape, cruelty to animals, serious lying, incest and many other things to be 'evil', that is 'seriously not good'. No one would have difficulty with this. In this sense, almost all behaviour, if carried to extremes, or done for the wrong reason, can turn into evil. In the words of the poet William Blake, 'A truth that's told with bad intent/Beats all the lies you can invent.'

The problem comes when a bishop or politician condemns a barbaric murder or genocide or terrorist attack as 'Evil' with a capital 'E'. Sometimes the use of this word is an attempt to deal with the extreme feelings of revulsion and outrage people feel. To call something 'absolutely Evil' is the strongest condemnation we can make. Hitler or a suicide bomber who kills dozens of innocent civilians is condemned as 'pure Evil'.

The word gets its power from the often hidden connections with its history and the link with the Devil. An Evil person or act is completely unacceptable. People often feel that there is no purpose in trying to understand it, no way we should try to think whether we too might have done such a thing in the situation of the person we condemn. It is pure corruption, pure irrationality, pure evil intention. Evil comes from some dark force that hovers on the edge of our world, Satan, the Devil, the Antichrist, the opposite of God.

This absolute Evil is sustainable only in a world that believes in the radical opposition between Good (God) and Evil (Devil). Most civilisations do not have this opposition. Some Japanese may consider the dropping of atom bombs on their cities as 'evil'. Yet since they have no Satan or Devil – a concept absent in Hinduism, Buddhism, Shinto and Taoism – they cannot think of a conspiracy of Evil, or pure Evil.

Why does God allow so much pain?

One of the greatest puzzles facing all of those who seek meaning in this world is how to reconcile a loving, caring and all-powerful Creator with the horrors we find every day in the newspapers and on television, and in our personal lives.

It was a problem seriously examined by Shakespeare, whose character King Lear concludes that 'As flies to wanton boys, are we to the gods;/They kill us for their sport,' and by William Blake, who asks the tiger, 'Did he who made the Lamb make thee?' and by Tennyson, when he tried to understand why his dear friend had died but could see around him only 'Nature, red in tooth and claw'. And by Joseph Heller when he half-facetiously wrote, 'Good God, how much reverence can you have for a Supreme Being who finds it necessary to include such phenomena as phlegm and tooth decay in His divine system of Creation?'

We seem to be trapped. If God is what he is claimed to be, why does he allow all this suffering? Or, putting it another way, can I believe in a God who seems to preside over such mayhem? Where was God in the Rwanda genocide, where was he in the death trenches of the world wars or in Stalin's gulag or Hitler's concentration camps or Pol Pot's killing fields? Where was he in the floods, fires, volcanoes, earthquakes and tornadoes?

The conventional answers do not seem totally satisfactory. We are told that humans brought all this pain on themselves through an act of disobedience, that we are being punished for our 'original sin'. But surely God, being supremely wise and all-powerful, could have foreseen this outcome and killed the serpent or provided an alternative apple tree, or talked the overambitious angel out of rebelling?

Another suggestion is that God, like a loving parent who gives his children the exercise of free will, has to allow them to make mistakes and hence to suffer. If a small child were to be sheltered from all risks it would have to be locked up in a padded cell. God made us a wonderful world in which we can make good or bad choices, and the latter can lead us into dangerous situations, injury or death. This sounds vaguely plausible, but of little comfort.

An alternative solution in some religions is to treat the world as a painful illusion. There are a set of trials and apparent miseries, from which we can withdraw into our inner selves and await the bliss of Nirvana or extinction. Another alternative is to accept that biology, society and economics control our lives. We do appear to have some free will, and we will try to increase happiness for ourselves and others. Yet, in the end, pain is present from the moment we are born. It is part of being human and something that constantly asks us to wonder, with the philosopher Nietzsche, 'Is man one of God's blunders or is God one of man's blunders?'

12

*C*an we control the spiritual world?

Dear Lily,

Much of the effort to control supernatural spirits revolves around various rituals. There is ritual with a small 'r' which covers almost everything that humans do. This is standardised, repetitive, formalised, communicative behaviour. A handshake and a kiss of greeting are good examples. In much of the West, the bodily movements of greeting have taken a recognised form; to shake with the left hand, or kiss someone on the nose rather than the cheek, would be considered strange.

The handshake communicates friendship, trust, affection or the sealing of a bargain. It is a social ritual, and if you examine your life you will find it is full of such actions. Such a general use of the word 'ritual' would also cover a great deal of low-level repetitive obsessive behaviour associated with certain forms of mental illness (such as constantly washing one's hands or brushing one's hair).

Other people's rituals almost always seem odd. Here is part of the account of a visiting anthropologist who wrote an article 'Body Rituals Among the Nacirema' (worth spelling backwards):

> *The daily body ritual performed by everyone includes a mouth-rite … this rite involves a practice which strikes the uninitiated stranger as revolting. It was reported to me that the ritual consists of inserting a small bundle of hog hairs into the mouth, along with certain magical powders, and then moving the bundle in a highly formalized series of gestures.*
>
> *In addition to the private mouth-rite, the people seek out a holy-mouth man once or twice a year. These practitioners have an impressive set of paraphernalia, consisting of a variety of augers, awls, probes, and prods. The use of these objects in the exorcism of the evils of the mouth involves almost unbelievable ritual torture of the client … The extremely sacred and traditional character of the rite is evident in the fact that the natives return to the holy-mouth man year after year, despite the fact that their teeth continue to decay.*

What is real Ritual?

What turns these small-'r' rituals, including cleaning one's teeth, into Ritual with a capital 'R', can be seen by looking at the difference between the Protestant and the Catholic communion in Christianity. The Protestant communion is a ritual. The clergyman takes the bread and wine and gives it to a communicant who eats and drinks it 'in remembrance' of Christ's sacrifice for us. It is a gesture of communication between the present congregation and Christ. Yet nothing spiritual happens or is changed.

In the Catholic communion, when the priest blesses the bread and wine a small miracle occurs. The bread becomes the flesh of Christ, the wine His blood. This is not just a way of speaking. It is believed really to happen, and hence it is called 'transubstantiation', that is the changing of substance. Some Catholics believe that if we took the wine after the blessing and put it under a powerful microscope we would find that it was no longer grape juice, but had the DNA of Christ's blood.

So Ritual creates a bridge between this material world and a spiritual dimension which is always there but normally invisible. It is like plugging a device into an electric socket and then being able to tap the energy which is ever present, though concealed. Once one is plugged in, it is possible to use the energy to have effects at a distance in space or time and to change this material world.

A handshake or kiss symbolises or expresses friendship and equality. It may also inaugurate such friendship. So it can be both expressive and instrumental. Yet it has no particular link to God or the gods, except in certain special Rituals where, for example, a person kisses the Holy Cross or takes an oath of allegiance to an overlord, followed by a kiss or handshake.

What Ritual can do is to bring together special words and actions in a way that automatically changes this material world. So there are Rituals to bring the rain, to make the crops flourish, to prevent sickness in animals, to cure sick children, to take the spirits off to the land of the dead, to make a woman fertile or to bring success in battle.

Where has Ritual gone?

After the Protestant Reformation in Western Europe in the sixteenth century and the rise of a new scientific outlook around the same time, Ritual was supposedly banished. We have lots of ceremonies, processions and formalised behaviour. But the idea that spiritual power could automatically be released by people's saying words in a certain order or doing things in a formal way, for example beating a drum or lighting candles to bring rain, seemed to the reformers and rationalists both superstitious and unscientific. This scepticism has persisted among many Europeans and Americans.

So while there are many 'secular rituals' – public parades and much of what goes on in sport and entertainment – these are limited to this material world. This is the case even if they often give people the slightly 'out of this world' feeling of true Rituals, what has been called 'effervescence' or excitement.

These secular rituals may have great power over us. Mass parades, such as Hitler's rallies or the displays for Chairman Mao, when hundreds of thousands march and wave flags, obviously move people deeply. Fascism and communism and all strong political ideologies love secular rituals since they help to control hearts and minds. Yet while they may have the psychological power of Ritual, they are not religious. They do not ask God to interfere and change this material world.

Both ritual and Ritual are immensely powerful and they shape our lives. They obtain their power because humans are deeply affected by symbols and standardised actions. Put up certain symbols, colours, signs and shapes, play the right music, orchestrate a specific set of actions (a goose step or swinging of arms), and an individual, especially if he or she is in a large crowd, will quickly be deeply transfixed.

Drama and ritual are therefore very closely linked. The ancient Greeks knew this well when they talked about the purging, cathartic, transforming effects of plays. The same effects can be seen in many other forms of dance and drama around the world, for instance in Hindu societies or Japanese Noh performances. As humans we find ritual and drama deeply influence much of our waking life and even our dreams. We are constrained in what we can do and what we can think by rituals because they create paths through time which force us in a certain direction.

Even when we try to release ourselves from the power of ritual we are often trapped. The original Quakers were among the most extreme anti-ritualists among religious groups. They tried to expel all formal, standardised, repetitive, behaviour from their lives, in language, in gestures and in their worship. Their services have no music, no symbols, no apparent formality. Yet the stillness and simplicity become a sort of anti-Ritual ritual which is in some ways as compulsive and constraining as anything they were attacking. Anyone who tried to stand up and sell goods in a Quaker meeting would soon discover that there were ritual rules.

What are myths?

Most rituals include a mythical dimension for they are based on a myth, or mythical stories are recited during them. So myth and ritual are inextricably linked. Yet our common understanding of myths makes it difficult for most of us to understand what they are.

People often describe other people's beliefs as 'just myths'. This assumes that myths are untrue, as if myth and factual truth are contradictory, or that they are to be distinguished from *real* history: 'We know that Robin Hood never existed though there is a myth that he did.' In a fact-obsessed and scientific culture we use the word 'myth' in order to describe what people believe without foundation, or beliefs that we do not share.

Yet this strong opposition between 'truth' and 'fact' on the one hand and 'myth' on the other conceals something much more important. It fails to account for the strong hold that myth has in all our lives whether we are explicitly 'religious' or not. Myths are particular kinds of stories which cannot be judged by the simple criterion of scientific truth or falsehood. They are trying to say something beyond the level of ordinary truth.

The opposition between 'myth' and 'fact' or 'truth' disappears further when we consider modern science. Many cosmologists and astrophysicists now believe in the Big Bang theory of the origin of the universe, or its successor string theory. These concepts are so abstruse and the information so complex that the theories cannot be subjected to all or many scientific proofs. They cannot be shown to be factually true. They are just a guess, a working model. So it is a paradox that some of our most rationalistic and scientific thinkers have surrounded themselves with an explanation of the origin of our universe and world that is beyond proof and perhaps a 'myth' in the wider sense.

In doing this, they are demonstrating one of the major functions of myths, one large category of which are myths of origin. The story of the Garden of Eden in Christianity, or of the Sun Goddess who founded Japan, and many of the stories of the origins of drums or incest in a Nepalese village are like this. People do not usually ask whether they are literally *true*. They are ways of thinking about puzzling and unresolvable questions.

We still do not know how human life, or life at all, arose on this planet. We do not know why we have a sense of right and wrong. Myths give us complex accounts of such matters. Kipling's *Just So Stories*, such as 'How the Camel got his Hump' or 'How the Leopard got his Spots', are myths in this sense. When we read them we do not ask whether they are true or false; they just make sense at a different level.

Another function of myth is as a charter or explanation of how things are as they are. Some people say that women are inferior because they came from Adam's rib, that the Fascists are superior because they are descended from the ancient Teutons, that communism will finally triumph because humans in their original innocent beginnings had no property. We live by myths of many kinds and manufacture them every day to justify the inequalities and injustices, or the surprises and changes, of our lives.

Myths try to explain the contradictions and mentally insoluble, unresolvable tensions in our world. How is it that we seem to be both animals and non-animals? Many myths tell of the changing of humans into animals, of vampires and were-animals. How do we seem both to be mortal, born to die, yet immortal? The death and rebirth of Christ, of King Arthur, myths of birth and rebirth in Hinduism, many myths tell us stories to help us think through these problems. This is obviously like much great literature and drama which puts forward these mysteries and unresolvable contradictions and states the arguments on both sides, then leaves us to decide the truth.

So myths and mysteries are closely linked. We can believe in fairies, hobbits, Harry Potter's world, Father Christmas or the little spirits that steal children's souls in the forests around the village in Nepal. Yet if pressed as to whether they are literally true, we would be sceptical. The room for half-belief, poetic belief, 'as if' belief is immense and most humans spend much of their time thinking in this way. Myths, like poetry and drama, require only a 'willing suspension of disbelief' to exercise their power over us.

What are symbols?

Basically symbols are objects, physical or immaterial (such as a sound), that stand for something else. Supposing you wanted to send someone a message to tell them that you were happy. You could do this by a direct method such as sending them a photograph of yourself laughing. In this case what you send them, the representation of yourself, the photograph or thing that signifies what you felt, looks just the same as the thing it represents or signifies. A photograph is a wysiwyg – 'what you see is what you get'. When you look at the photo, the link between the signifier (the photograph) and the signified (your face) is very strong; the two are almost identical. The relationship is explicit, an exact matching. Some very elementary picture-writing or 'pictography' is like this. It is not symbolic.

Or you could show your friend a smiley face, not your own but a conventionalised one of the kind many people send as an e-mail. There is now some relationship between you, happiness and the smiling face, but the gap between what you want to represent and how you represent it is a little wider. There is room for interpretation, and your friend may need to be taught to recognise a couple of lines and a couple of dots as a smiley face and to realise that this stands for your happiness. Chinese writing is like this. For example, the word for 'house' is a picture of a house, but over the ages it has become distorted. We are still not in the land of real symbolism.

Or you could send a short note saying 'I am very happy'. Now, if you examine those letters, you can see they are absolutely arbitrary. There is no possible relationship between the letters 'h-a-p-p-y' and the human emotion of happiness. The letters are abstract and arbitrary symbols, which have been joined together. The reader, having been taught how to decode them, can interpret them as symbols pointing towards the idea of happiness.

So symbols get their power from their arbitrary and abstract nature. When we decipher them, they can affect us deeply. When a persecuted Christian saw the sign of a fish on a wall, he or she could read into it the Greek letters for the word 'fish', which could be read as the first letters of words in the phrase 'Jesus Christ, the Son of God and Saviour'. Yet others just saw a picture of a fish. When the police arrive to examine a murdered man in southern Italy and find a prickly pear lying in his lap as if by accident, they know it is a Mafia killing. Or when you see a blue poster in a window at election time in Britain you believe that the people inside will probably vote Conservative. Yet there is no intrinsic relationship between prickly pears and the Mafia, or between blue and the Conservatives.

Each culture has its symbols, and this is particularly true of colours. White is the symbol of death in Asia; black is that symbol in Europe. Red is the royal colour in China; in many parts of the world it is gold. Why the important colours in much of Africa should be brown, white and red has been widely discussed. Can it be related to their prominence in human life in the form of milk, blood and faeces? Whatever the reason, colours, sounds and shapes can all carry powerful meanings, as we all know too well with the swastikas of the Nazis, who perverted a benevolent Eastern symbol into one of power and hate.

Symbols are enormously powerful because, although there is a commonly understood element to them, each of us can also read our own meanings into them and respond in different ways. They gain even more power when placed together in a series. When they are carefully constructed into a ritual or work of art we are enchanted and overwhelmed.

Religion is largely about the use of these apparently arbitrary symbols which we usually interpret at a level below our consciousness. We are symbol-producing and symbol-consuming creatures. We are able both to explore and to communicate very deep truths, particularly in the most abstract symbolic forms such as music, art and mathematics. Yet we can also be trapped, confused and led astray by symbols and our minds seduced by their power.

What are taboos?

Symbols are often associated with boundaries, and these boundaries are in turn enforced by taboos. So what are taboos? The word 'taboo' came into our language from the Pacific island term *tapu* meaning a combination of secret and forbidden. It is a useful word for us since we find that much of our life seems to be broken up into things we can and can't do. It is good to have a shorthand term for apparently meaningless or unexplained prohibitions: we speak of them as taboos.

We classify certain things as safe, decent, acceptable and clean, while others are dangerous, indecent, unacceptable and dirty. Of course what we classify in these boxes is very culture-specific, as are our reactions to breaking taboos. In some societies to eat the brains of another human being would be taboo; in others, not to eat them when offered would be taboo. In some, for an older male to have sex with a young boy is taboo; in others, not to do so if he is in a position of initiating the youth would be shameful.

Many taboos seem to be centred on periods of ambiguity, ambivalence or in-between positions. So there are many taboos at the turning-points of life – at birth, at marriage and particularly at death. There are also taboos associated with the intersections between our body and the outside world. There are many taboos linked with menstruation, with faeces and urine, with breaking wind, burping and spitting.

Certain bounded groups, for example Indian castes, some Orthodox Jews, and gypsies, are particularly concerned with trying to keep certain categories apart. They are anxious about the ritual pollution or degrading danger that occurs for instance if we eat the flesh of certain animals, or mix milk and blood, or have sex with the wrong person or at the wrong time. These groups have taboos in the strong sense – Taboos with a capital letter. That is to say that if you break a Taboo, something serious will happen unless you purify yourself.

In my Nepalese village, if you come into contact with death, or touch an unclean (lower-caste) person, you have to go through a little purification ritual with water in which gold has been dipped. In *tapu*, even if you did not mean to offend, danger is there and you will be punished. The incest taboo is one of the most famous precisely for this reason. To commit incest is to break boundaries, to mix up blood. The gods will punish you, even if you are not aware that you are breaking a taboo, as in the case of Oedipus who unknowingly married his mother.

On the other hand, most of us use the word in a much looser sense, just meaning something that one should not do. I might tell you that it is taboo to walk on the grass in King's College, Cambridge, it is taboo to spit in the street, it is taboo to wander around naked in public. Yet if we do any of these things, though there may be social or even legal consequences, there is no particular spiritual danger.

We are not polluted by walking on the grass, nor is the grass polluted by our feet. Our children will not become sick, our animals will not die, if we do these things. Nor will we expect to be sent to hell for them. We have broken a rule which we do not necessarily agree with, or even see the point of. There is no particular moral or spiritual danger. Indeed, as a child, you and your sister Rosa particularly delighted in the breaking of taboo and insisted on walking over the grass with me (a Fellow, so above taboo) whenever you could.

This is because Taboo in the strong sense works only with people who have a particular idea of a world divided into strongly defined areas of purity and impurity, of safety and danger, even of the sacred and the profane. Many of us think of the world as being roughly level and uniform in spiritual terms. There are clean things and 'matter out of place' or dirty things. But the boundaries between things are not so rigid. When we come into contact with the pollution of death, we do not have to destroy everything associated with the dead person, as happens with gypsy caravans or in some Hindu funerals.

What is sacrifice?

It is not easy to communicate with God or the gods and it is even more difficult to spur the Divine into action. The most obvious way to try to compel them is to offer them a gift or bribe, which should prompt them to reciprocate.

Obviously this gift should be of something we really value. So in societies that herd animals, the sacrifice is usually one of these precious beasts – a cow, buffalo, sheep or cockerel. So Christianity, which came out of the nomadic herding societies of the Middle East, was built around the sacrifice of sheep, culminating in the gift of God's own son, the 'Lamb of God'. In rice-growing cultures such as Japan, the sacrifice is of rice or rice wine.

The sacrifice has two elements. There is the gift, the physical object which is placed on the altar, and there is the spirit which it contains. So in a Nepalese village a cock, sheep or buffalo is sacrificed and the blood placed on the shrine. The gods drink the blood, but what they really consume is the spirit of the gift, the essence or soul of the sacrificed object. When they receive this they are pleased and return a favour or protect the worshippers.

In Christianity the sacrifice was shifted from actual animals to a symbolic sacrifice of God's own son. Yet this began to be taken very literally, and the Protestant Reformers reacted to what was considered an overemphasis on the outward form. They said it was no good burning candles, burning incense or sacrificing money. What God really wanted was an internal offering. So the idea spread that the way to please God was to give up sinful behaviour. 'The sacrifices of [for] God are a broken spirit: a broken and a contrite heart, O God, thou wilt not despise.' Better an obedient and disciplined heart and strong intentions to be good than the smoke of burnt offerings and streams of blood.

So, over much of the world, religion has been internalised. Yet sacrifice has not gone away. Many people still give up things for Lent, or abstain from this or that because they feel that it will somehow do them not only physical but also spiritual good. Being a vegetarian, weight-watching, giving up time and money to charities, all these are forms of sacrifice. Even in a world of consumerism and pleasure-seeking, in many people there is a strong Puritan streak.

Furthermore, the notion of sacrifice and its value varies enormously from culture to culture. Many British war memorials to those who were killed in the two world wars speak of their sacrifice. Have a look at what is written on such memorials when you travel around elsewhere. In France it will be 'glory', and in Japan you will find no such memorials with lists of names at all.

Why does ritual matter?

Almost all of our life revolves around patterns and rhythms of repetitive, standardised behaviour. This feature of humanity has often been co-opted in the service of politics or religion. When the power of ritual is harnessed, whether it is in the formal language of prayers or political speeches, or in the compulsive movements of our bodies when we are praying or marching, our minds are constrained.

Rituals give us confidence, unite us with others, and help us through our most difficult times such as grieving or death. They help to rearrange social relations as at a wedding, or reorder our social networks as at a funeral. A life without ritual would be inconceivable. It would become patternless and meaningless. Yet we should remember that there is a price to pay for the power of ritual.

I have often wondered why no one has ever suddenly stood up in the middle of the famous Christmas Carol service at King's College, Cambridge, in order to proclaim their particular view of life, drawing the attention of the millions of listeners around the world to some cause. Yet as I sit through the service I feel the huge weight of solemnity and ritual which makes it difficult even to cough or shift in my seat. Rituals act on us through our body and senses so that they become entrenched in our way of life and leave us little control. We cannot easily escape from their power.

This is as true of secular rituals as it is of those clothed in formal religion. During the Cultural Revolution in China there were numerous 'rituals' to worship Chairman Mao. People conscientiously observed them, like the rituals of 'Asking for Instructions in the Morning' and 'Reporting Back in the Evening' during which millions recited quotations from Mao's works, holding the *Little Red Book* pressed to their breast. Chinese friends now say that at the time they were often embarrassed and sceptical, but could not resist the group pressure.

So all we can do is to celebrate rituals, but at the same time try to stand back and examine the ways in which we are constrained, brainwashed as it were, by ritual power. Freedom of a sort comes from understanding and controlling the rituals we perform and are involved in.

$\mathcal{H}$ow do we learn?

Dear Lily,

Being human, we ought to know more and more. Certain biological drives, if harnessed, will encourage inventiveness and effort. These are the ones that we share with other animals: the drive to sexual reproduction, the drive to satisfy hunger, the drive for warmth and shelter. The pursuit of these is undoubtedly a powerful background force in the evolution of ingenious solutions by humans. It also leads to a great deal of competition.

Almost all human societies develop inequality. Sometimes this is within games, art and knowledge; sometimes it is in material or symbolic goods (things that bring status and respect). The important thing is that competition, the desire to rise and the fear of falling, is the spur which drives many to attempt and perform difficult and often unpleasant things. This spur is not confined to modern Western societies. One of the major sources of creative and inventive energy is the desire to win the admiration or envy of people we want to impress.

On the other hand, equally important is the pleasure of

working successfully with people. Thus, with unique linguistic and co-operative tools, humans are above all social animals. Almost all significant advances in human culture involve mutual, co-operative effort. A single person can achieve little.

Why do we give?

One way of understanding this is to think of the pleasure we get not only from receiving, but also from giving, presents. The idea of a gift is that we offer it freely to another. Yet in practice it often means that the receiver must then return the compliment. In the wider sense, a gift is not just a present but can be many things done to please or impress another.

Whatever the gift it has several elements. There is the external, 'material' element, anything from food to a poem, from a victorious battle to a new theory in mathematics. Then behind this there is the 'spirit' of the gift, that is the social and symbolic relationship it represents. To give something and have it received, the way of giving and receiving, and the appreciation expressed in the counter-gift, all express a social relation. They allow the individual to show respect, express his or her personality, win esteem.

The pursuit of knowledge can be seen as a giant gift-giving network. What is presented to others in the network is more than mere material things. A scientist may discover a new fact or theory that she presents to her colleagues. Part of the scientist's spirit is invested in the theory. Furthermore, the gift tends to set up the obligation to reciprocate. Hence each scientific discovery is cumulative, not merely because it opens up diverse new understandings, but because it puts an obligation on others to give something back.

The gift should not be too precise, calculating or 'rational'. If scientists are constantly thinking of what would 'pay off' quickly, the kind of fundamental science that requires real risks and long-term effort would never be undertaken. Most significant science is fairly crazy – following hunches for years, struggling for very small rewards and forgoing short cuts and short-term gains. For whom does the scientist do this? For others, a small group of friends and colleagues, teachers and pupils, a society which will honour his name, for posterity or God, but always as a gift to the other.

Why are we puzzled?

Humans, like a number of higher animals, have a great deal of curiosity, love of pattern-making, ingenuity and playfulness. If these are encouraged, or just allowed to flourish over time, they will lead to experiments, creative solutions to problems, ways of avoiding obstacles and rational attempts to overcome difficulties.

The processes of wonder, surprise and admiration are obvious in the case of a young child. I remember filming you, Lily, in Australia when you were very young as you tried out foods, fitted shapes together and explored your world. I could see a very powerful survival instinct at work in your desire, from when you were just a few days old, to understand how things work and are connected. Just to look is to start asking those 'why' questions for which children are famous.

To answer these questions, the child uses all sorts of methods: comparison, deduction (working from general laws to particular cases), induction (working from particular cases to general laws) and experimental testing. Every child has to be a pretty good scientist in order to survive. Yet this sense of curiosity and wonder is very often dampened in later life, either by external pressures or by an inner feeling that the answers are already known.

A child, a painter, a poet, a scientist, all are filled with wonder and surprise and try to explore and solve puzzles.

The only difference between a child and a modern scientist is that as science becomes more effective it develops other tools and methods for this purpose. The child uses its natural intelligence, the musician draws on the accumulated heritage of music in his own society, and the natural scientist employs mathematical and other methods in pursuit of understanding. Science also tends to be *cumulative*, knowledge can be *tested*, and questions are *open* and never finally settled. These three characteristics combine to give the potential for the *development* of reliable knowledge.

How does technology help?

What is special about human beings is that, more than other animals, they can transfer what they learn from their individual brains to the external world. They can store and transmit ideas through an elaborate cultural system. This makes knowledge grow quickly. This essential skill of human beings, their 'culture', can be either immaterial (language, songs, myths, traditions) or material (writing, physical tools, rituals and ways of working). Part of this vast realm, the effect of which is most dramatically changing your life, is technology.

One way in which technology alters our world is through the storage and expansion of ideas. New ideas become embedded in tools, which then, in turn, help us to think better. It is a triangular movement.

There is an increase in theoretical understanding, reliable knowledge about the world. This first point of the triangle is vital. The repeatable and dependable information about how the world works is almost always obtained through disinterested research. This is then sometimes embedded in improved or new physical artefacts or tools, the second point on the triangle. These artefacts, if they are useful and in demand and relatively easy to produce, are disseminated in huge quantities.

This multiplication of objects and their mass dissemination is the third point of the triangle. This then changes the conditions of life and may well feed back into the possibilities of further theoretical exploration.

This triangular movement has occurred in many spheres of life. The speed of moving round this triangle and its repetition lies behind much of what we describe as human development.

It is a general principle that as each piece of reliable knowledge is added it leads to the possibility of doing dozens of new things. Just as adding a wheel to a Meccano or other construction set transforms the potentials of all the previous pieces, so it is with many technologies, including wheels, printing, clocks, glass, photography and computing.

Unless something gets in the way of this process, reliable knowledge about the world and effective action to improve life should expand ever faster. This has been the story of the vast growth of the last three hundred years. Human understanding and control of nature have grown amazingly.

What did glass do?

Glass has changed the world. That it has done so appears to be the result of a giant accident, the fortuitous side-product of other developments. The history of glass shows the way in which many of the increases in human knowledge through technology are the result of the unintended consequences of something else. It also shows that once the process of putting increased knowledge into artefacts becomes a conscious aim, it can lead to very rapid and impressive developments. It is an excellent illustration of the triangle of knowledge, leading through new artefacts and back to further knowledge by way of the multiplication of new tools. It also illustrates the Meccano effect because glass itself has not just been one added resource for humans, but allowed changes in so many other technologies.

It began to be obvious to Islamic scholars from the ninth century, and to Western European thinkers from the twelfth, that glass was more than just a marvellous substance for holding cool liquid and enhancing its beauty. It let in light but not cold. It could be manipulated to alter vision.

The idea of examining microscopic objects through glass and of bending and testing the properties of light was present from at least as early as the ninth century. As knowledge about the nature of light and of the chemistry of glass increased, so the tools of glass improved. The most dramatic impact of this occurred at the end of the sixteenth century.

It is still a mystery how people happened on the idea that by placing two suitably shaped pieces of glass near to each other it would be possible to see faraway things, or very tiny objects. Both the telescope and the microscope seem to have been developed in the Netherlands around the start of the seventeenth century and were obviously related to the making of spectacle lenses.

Without the telescope Galileo could not have developed and proved his fundamental theories. Without the microscope, the world of bacteria would never have been discovered. The developments had other side-effects – on optics, and on the discovery of the vacuum, which was made possible only with a large glass flask within which a vacuum could be created and observed.

Because glass is an inert substance which is not corroded easily, and it is possible to see through, it became essential to the progress of chemistry using glass retorts, flasks, thermometers and barometers. Nowadays almost all scientific disciplines depend on glass, not to mention almost all transport systems, electricity, watches, televisions and much of what makes our civilisation work. Our lives have been transformed. Look around you and you will see how glass is everywhere.

At a more fundamental level it is arguable that without glass the philosophical and emotional bases of both the Renaissance and modern scientific thought would not have been established. Sight is humankind's strongest sense. By providing new tools with which to see an invisible world of tiny creatures, or to contemplate distant stars invisible to the naked eye, glass not only made possible particular scientific discoveries, but led to a growing confidence in a world of deeper truths to be discovered.

It became clear that, with this key, people could unlock secret treasures of knowledge, see below and above the surface of things, destabilise conventional views. The obvious was no longer necessarily true. The hidden connections and buried forces could be penetrated.

It is also clear that the spread and improvement of glass technologies through Europe from the fourteenth century had profound effects on mathematics and geometry, and hence on perspective and art. So glass is a perfect example of the movement round a triangle. There is some new knowledge, then some new artefacts, and finally the mass dissemination of these artefacts which can lead back into further new knowledge.

Does technology always help?

Good glass-making techniques, including the blowing of glass, were known in China and Japan almost as early as in the West. Yet in those two countries there was little use for the substance. The major drink was hot water or boiled tea. For drinking tea, the excellent pottery and porcelain manufacture provided a perfect set of containers, from the humblest beaker to the most precious tea-bowl. Thus there was little market for glass containers which were much more fragile. In Europe glass was particularly developed in order to satisfy the demand for wine goblets.

Glass-making was developed in the cold northern part of Europe for letting in light but not wind. Some of the earlier glass could be afforded only by rich religious institutions and this was often partly decorative, stained to the amazing colours we can still see in Chartres Cathedral or King's College Chapel in Cambridge. The use of glass for ordinary windows spread rapidly in the sixteenth century, particularly in the wealthier houses of northern countries.

In China and Japan, however, window glass was not developed because it was not desirable. In Japan, the frequent earthquakes would have shattered the glass. The buildings made of bamboo and wood would not have been suited to glass windows. There was the presence of an excellent and much cheaper alternative, mulberry paper, which could be made into movable walls. All these combined to make window glass unattractive. Furthermore, glass-making requires kilns fired to a very high temperature where the glass is kept continuously molten. It is very fuel-intensive so can be made only in areas of thin population and thick forests. China and Japan seldom met these conditions.

Another use of glass is most directly linked to the tools of thought, that is its use for spectacles. It is one of the ironies of life that just as many reach the peak of knowledge, in their mid-forties and -fifties, they find it impossible to continue reading. They have to hold a book at such a distance away from their eyes that they cannot distinguish the characters. This was a serious drawback up to the fifteenth century, especially for bureaucracies and institutions where the most skilled in literacy and accounting could no longer read. It became an even more serious disability after the printing revolution made books for scholarship or private enjoyment widely available.

It was exactly around the time of the printing revolution that the making of spectacles developed rapidly. The increase in knowledge arising from this development was enormous, lengthening the intellectual life of some of the best-trained minds.

What makes people creative?

The rapid development of knowledge and artefacts needs an exact balance between what we can call 'boundedness' and 'leakiness'. At the extreme, if a system has no bounds, then nothing will have time to grow before it is swept away by the next thought or invention. It is like a flat surface, swept by rapid winds or tides, or a bare mountainside with no crevice for plants to grow in, no ledge for the poppy.

Yet at the other extreme, if the ledges turn into impassable barriers, there is the opposite difficulty, of involution or stasis. Change and improvement have many foes and there are always more reasons for not doing things than for doing them. If almost complete control can be maintained within a bounded unit, as happened in China or Japan for long periods, then few new things can happen.

New ideas, coupled with the threat of being outflanked and outmoded, make people inventive. However, ideas must come in at a constant, controlled rate. This happened in Japan over the century from 1868. It is happening in rather different ways in China today. If they pour in too fast, as with market capitalism in Russia at the end of the twentieth century, they can overwhelm a civilisation. From the ninth to the nineteenth century Europe combined bounded political and cultural entities within a highly interconnected landmass. So ideas and artefacts could rapidly drift from place to place.

The interconnections between a number of independent centres of innovation are very important. Because of the difficulties of achieving major breakthroughs, it is unlikely that they will often occur within a bounded unit all by themselves. There is too little data available, very highly trained and able thinkers are few, and people are blinkered. Thus major break-throughs tend to occur when scientists communicate with each other at a distance.

The major scientific discoveries from the twelfth century to the present were the results of wide European contacts. The ease of such networking in Europe was made much greater by a common religion (Christianity), a common language (Latin) and many common traditions. There was a fraternity of scholars and inventors. Good ideas travelled very fast. The impact of printing as a way of moving ideas rapidly across Europe was obviously also crucial.

A major motive in the search for increasingly reliable knowledge is curiosity. The European experience increased the number of puzzles that faced people. Huge amounts of new information poured into Europe from the fifteenth century from long-distance travel, the discovery of America and voyages to India, the Pacific and East Asia. The new knowledge challenged current ideas. For a long time the bracing effects of the mixing of cultural traditions in the relatively small area of the Mediterranean, in particular between Islamic societies and the Christian civilisation which borrowed from it, also clearly stimulated new thought.

The outcome is the world we now live in, where I am writing this letter to you on a device that was unimaginable to me only twenty years ago, the laptop computer.

··· 14 ···

*C*an education destroy knowledge?

Dear Lily,

Many people assume that the purpose of education is to make us think. We live in historically unusual societies where this is indeed often the case. Yet education can just as well be seen as a device to constrain thought. It is often used to direct people to think acceptable ideas, so that the only thoughts that are thinkable are those that one's teachers (and the society as a whole) consider appropriate.

Knowledge has been passed on through most of history by word of mouth. This does not allow much criticism. Nothing is written down, so different versions cannot easily be compared. There is no external 'truth' or 'way' providing an orthodoxy from which there can be deviations. Formally recognised differences came later with the development of writing. Such writing was again usually monopolised by the rulers in order to preserve the status quo. It was not an instrument for questioning the system.

The tendency thereafter was for those who developed writing systems to use them to instil traditional and accepted wisdom. The educators concentrated on the classics, whether religious – Buddhist sutras, Sanskritic texts, the Koran, the Bible, the Torah – or secular, such as the writings of Confucius or Aristotle. The assumption was that the truth had all been revealed long ago. The task of education was to instil this truth in young minds through repetition. There was no questioning, just some explanation, elaboration, teasing out of obscure meanings.

This tendency was reinforced as wealth increased. There were more priests and teachers; the ability to pass the examinations on the texts became ever more important as the key to power and status; the period of education became ever longer. This was true in the past just as it is today: where once a good school grade might have got you a reasonable job, then a good Bachelor of Arts or Science at University, nowadays you need a doctorate as well.

In this expansion and formalisation of education there was little pressure towards independent, questioning thought in the sense of encouraging originality, doubt and difference of opinion. Mental worlds were, if anything, increasingly closed. Truth was asserted and given sanction by being written down. Knowledge of the world was unquestioned and what was read was self-evidently true.

This tendency, as we see it developing in many great traditions of scholarship, ended up after some centuries in an almost total lack of change. There was nothing new to be said or thought. The aim was not to lose any of the accumulated wisdom. The knowledge and thinking of the charismatic founder – Confucius, the Buddha, Jesus, Muhammad – was distributed to his followers who earned a reasonable living by interpreting it and passing it on to their pupils.

The tendency shows itself still in the appeal to authority and the learning of things by heart without really understanding them. Persuading, intriguing, encouraging young minds is very strenuous work; much easier to assert and dominate using authority and telling students merely to copy down the wisdom.

If changes are to be made, they must be so small that they are invisible to the teachers. Tinkering on the edges of knowledge, 'shifting the mental furniture around', is all that is allowed. Since this requires much less mental effort and often brings prizes and even serious wealth, tinkering is often preferable to trying to make advances in deeper understanding even today.

Another widespread tendency is towards a situation where for every really creative thinker, there are dozens of less talented critics. It is often easier to live by destroying other people's ideas than by generating many of one's own. The 'frogs in a well' syndrome, where humans, like frogs, pull down any frog escaping from the well – the misery of all is better than the escape of a few – is widespread. It is combined with the growing ethic of 'limited good', where it comes to be believed that another's success does one down, while another's failure pushes one up. These are insidious pressures working against the increase of knowledge. Many have experienced this in schools when peer pressure will soon create an anti-work, anti-achievement ethic where a 'swot' is picked on.

Why does knowledge dry up?

Knowledge tends to become private. Yet over-privatisation, over-concentration on intellectual property rights, sets individual against individual, organisation against organisation, in a world of secrecy and excessive competition. Good science usually operates best in an open market for ideas and through co-operation.

There are periods when an individual or institution may be forced into secrecy for a while, as in the famous case of Charles Darwin's concealing of his theory of the evolution of species for over twenty years because of fear of upsetting the religious hierarchy. But the ultimate aim is to publish the results and earn praise and gratitude by providing a rung upon which others can climb.

In contrast, in many societies all deep knowledge is by definition *esoteric* (specialist and secret). It is developed by a particular family, sect or organisation and the widespread feeling is that it should never be made generally known. Yet all this is the opposite to modern science in the West where findings are, in theory, published and open so that the hypothesis can be fully tested by colleagues. The scientists and philosophers of Europe lived off their ability to spread their knowledge. The intellectual or priest in many societies lives off his monopoly of secret knowledge.

All this works against the rapid expansion of reliable knowledge. In a world of falsehood and deception, of secrecy and privatisation, where is the 'reliable' to come from? For most people nothing can be relied on, least of all information from non-related strangers. Why should others tell us the 'truth'?

Knowledge is usually costly to acquire. Once gained, like other capital it should pay dividends. Those who have worked themselves up to the top of the knowledge tree are hardly likely to favour radical thinkers who are hacking away at the trunk. Established systems of knowledge are not dislodged by rational argument but because the older generation dies off or their theories just feel stale and out of fashion. In many societies the senior generation ensures that its successors are so indoctrinated that they never threaten the system.

Why do we know more and understand less?

A hunter-gatherer did not need huge libraries, encyclopaedias or computer databases to store accumulated information. He or she could probably remember well enough all the important things that had occurred in the previous week. If someone wanted to catch a new animal or climb a strange tree, most of the general skills learnt as a child would be enough for the task. We are different.

You may think that as a species we have perhaps become more intelligent over the last fifty thousand years, individually more likely to discover new things using more powerful intellectual tools. This is undoubtedly the case at the level of the whole society. But, at the level of single individuals, I do not know of convincing evidence that there has been such obvious progression. Our brains have not grown, nor is there evidence of new mental processes.

In many ways we seem, individually, to know less and less about how the world works and find it more difficult as individuals to make a major discovery. Indeed, it could be argued that there is more ignorance, forgetting and wasted research effort in the world today than there has ever been in history. If this is the case, why is it so? Why do many societies and individuals seem to choose paths that lead their minds to become more closed and how, occasionally, have individuals and civilisations briefly escaped from these paths?

As knowledge increases through the rapid accumulation of a mass of details, it becomes more and more difficult to see the overall pattern. This is why, for example, a number of enormously learned people have produced so little and tend to produce less and less as they grow older.

Each new piece of information, when added to a complex, interacting system, alters all the existing information. Thus to add a new piece becomes more and more difficult. We know this from our practical experience of storing our belongings. With one drawer containing ten things, it is not difficult to decide where to store or to find objects. With ten drawers, each containing twenty objects, it is far more difficult. Indeed the difficulty of the task grows at an increasing rate.

To find an item amongst ten thousand objects is much more than ten times as difficult as finding it amongst one thousand. These laws explain why the 'advancement of learning', the expansion of knowledge, is so very difficult and seems to become *increasingly* so.

In our early days or when we are starting a new discipline, it is easy to be radical, to make large advances; everything is open and fluid, and the returns on a little labour are great. The easiest advances are made first and difficult terrain can be avoided. But after a time the best mental land is occupied and one has to move to marginal areas. Furthermore, each new piece of information has to be fitted into an increasingly complex pre-existing set of information. Even minor changes come up against vast entrenched obstacles. It seems possible only to tinker at the boundaries. And we may know in our hearts that as the philosopher Karl Popper put it, 'Our knowledge can only be finite, while our ignorance must necessarily be infinite.'

Do computers help?

The problems of knowledge storage and retrieval become greater and greater. Each major stage reaches a ceiling of what can be held and achieved efficiently. Oral cultures can hold only a very small amount of reliable information about the world. Writing created the possibility of libraries of information. Printing extended this possibility enormously through multiplication of texts. By the end of the nineteenth century the system of hand-indexing using slips of paper had reached its limits. Only in the 1960s, with the development of computers, were new potentials for storage and retrieval reached.

At the moment, the position is that the increase of computing power (speed, size of storage media, searching methods) is in advance of the increase in information. The laws of information overload and saturation have been temporarily suspended by technological developments based on science.

Yet there is another area where computers do not help much. Radical innovations become more difficult because the time and energy it takes to master all the professional expertise needed to understand and then change a system start to exceed any human being's normal capacity. At the start of a new discipline, an amateur can make huge advances by pursuing what is really a part-time hobby. By the late-nineteenth century, it required highly organised and disciplined teams to carry out major research.

The increasing complexity is one reason we often see that conservatism, routinisation and ritualisation increase. This happens when processes become more complex, yet the understanding of the way in which they work, that is the reliable knowledge content, does not increase proportionately. This is the trap shown for example by the history of the making of Japanese swords. This technique reached a peak by about 1200 and was scarcely improved over the next five hundred years. In a situation such as this, the only way to make sure such complex processes continue to work is *not to change them*.

This 'lock-in' occurs in all forms of knowledge. It occurs in secular processes (making things, education) and also in most religions (ritualisation and formalism) and politics. Thus the knowledge component levels off or even decreases; the almost exclusive task is to remember how to repeat the words and actions that were passed on by the ancestors and seemed to work. This is the opposite of innovation and invention, which deliberately force us to forget, superseding previous knowledge, making it 'out of date' and irrelevant. Very few civilisations have avoided this tendency towards conservatism for more than a few hundred years.

What blocks our thought?

One well-known difficulty in finding new things has been termed by the cognitive psychologist David Perkins the 'oasis trap'. Knowledge becomes centred in an 'oasis' of rich findings and it is just too risky and expensive to leave that still productive and well-watered zone. So people stick to what they know. This is what happened to a certain extent in China and Japan over many centuries. The huge physical distances between centres of knowledge in China, and the fact that even if one made the effort to travel to another it usually turned out to be little different from that one had left, discouraged exploration.

In Europe in the last eight hundred years there have been numerous oases, separate national cultures a few hundred miles apart, yet each with a very different intellectual flora and fauna. This network of 'oases', each independently developing thoughts and then communicating with other oases, is perhaps the ideal one for the development of new ideas.

Another way of putting it is that in order to advance one often has to go backward, go downhill before one can go up. It is not possible to proceed steadily up the slope of increased knowledge for it often becomes necessary to make a costly detour.

To do so requires great faith, self-confidence and ample patronage. These are assets that many Europeans seem to have had at certain points in history. Yet they are pretty unusual in general. Before an entirely new technology, such as a new weapon or ship, can come up and replace an old one, there may be quite a long period when the new is less efficient than the old, even though its potential is far greater. There is a long, loss-making, period when the older views can still outpace the new, untried and inexperienced ones. Who is going to bear the lengthy development costs?

This difficulty also applies to scholarly progress; often the older, more experienced intellectuals can effectively destroy the half-baked, if ultimately more powerful and 'true', new ideas. Very often, the innovators give up, discouraged. Or they are left hanging from some literal or metaphorical cross. As Oscar Wilde noted, 'An idea that is not dangerous is unworthy of being called an idea at all.' Yet, if it is dangerous, we have to be careful. Sometimes the risk is not worth taking.

Power and order

15

ℋ ow well does Democracy work?

Dear Lily,

You will often have been told that you live in a 'democracy' and that this is wonderful, something that should be exported all over the world. But what does 'democracy' mean and how does it work?

There are, in fact, two meanings. One is what I shall call 'Democracy', with a capital 'D'. This is defined by the *Shorter Oxford English Dictionary* as 'government by the people; that form of government in which the sovereign power resides in the people'. It means that one person has one vote, with everyone over a certain age having such a vote. In practice it should mean that there is a choice. One-party Democracy is something of a contradiction in terms.

The second I shall call 'democracy' with a small 'd'. This is defined by the same dictionary as 'a social state in which all have equal rights'. The *Oxford Reference Dictionary* suggests 'an egalitarian and tolerant form of society'. So this 'democracy' implies a feeling of freedom, equality before the law and equality of opportunities.

The system of Democracy, or the sovereignty of the people, is opposed to 'autocracy', rule by one, which has many forms. These include oligarchy (rule by the few), plutocracy (rule by the very rich) and monarchy (rule by a single hereditary ruler or king). 'Democracy' itself can take several forms, including republicanism, as in the United States or France, or limited monarchy, as in Britain.

Was Democracy expected?

Since Democracy is now the aspiration of many and the most popular form of government on earth, you may think that it has a long and successful history. Not at all. One hundred years ago no one lived in a Democracy in the strict sense of the word. In the middle of the twentieth century the few existing Democracies were nearly wiped out by fascism (the ideology of state power) and communism (the ideology of abolition of the state and private property).

Until 1980, Democracy was still a minority form of government. The majority of governments, and the majority of people, lived in autocracies. Only with the fall of the Soviet Union in 1989 did Democracies outnumber autocracies. So why have many countries gravitated towards other forms?

The difficult thing in politics is to tread a middle path. Usually at certain points in the history of civilisations there is too much chaos and factionalism. We find the 'disintegration of the state' over much of Europe after the fall of Rome, in China after the Opium Wars, or in Eastern Europe after the collapse of the Soviet Union. Local chiefs, lords, commissars and war-lords increase in power and bandits roam. The state is dismembered and cannot maintain a monopoly of the use of force. This is deeply unpleasant for most of the inhabitants, trampled over and pulled this way and that.

If wealth and technical efficiency increase and temporary

alliances turn into permanent ones, everything changes. Political power increases at the state level and local resistance is crushed. Often this coincides with the banning of all alternative groupings. So a movement from disintegration to over-integration, or at least *attempted* total control, is the normal pattern.

Very rarely does an alternative emerge. In small city states or in the early history of empires this alternative is often called republicanism. Citizens, that is the free members of a republic, whether in Athens, early Rome, the Florentine Republic of the fifteenth century or the Dutch Republic of the seventeenth century, although usually a minority of the population, share in government. There is no single ruler, no king or dictator.

Yet this is an unstable arrangement, which soon drifts towards some form of monarchy. For instance, it took only a few years for the Commonwealth under Oliver Cromwell in England to drift back to the unpopular idea that Cromwell's successor should be his son. It took little time for Napoleon to set himself up as ruler and establish a new dynasty after the French Revolution had established a republic in France in 1789.

Power is soon concentrated in the hands of a single ruler, his family and close circle. Republics not only are short-lived but are usually found only in small political units. Until the later eighteenth century, there is no case of a large state (the size of France, Spain, Japan or China) being a republic for more than a few years. In the twentieth century new forms of autocracy took power away from traditional rulers (in Russia and China) or the people (Germany, Italy, Spain) and placed it in the hands of the Communist Party or the fascist state. The present swing to Democracy is strange and unprecedented.

Why is Democracy so fashionable?

Some say that Democracy has temporarily triumphed because it is economically successful. Democracy is part of a package which ensures that individuals can pursue their economic goals in safety and indeed are encouraged to do so. So it tends to generate economic and hence military success. Yet there are difficulties in this argument.

It is clear that Democracy does not automatically generate economic growth. It is possible to point to periods in the history of Democratic societies, including the recession in the United States in the 1930s, when there has been economic decline. Secondly, there are forms of autocracy, as in China today with its amazing economic growth, that are temporarily more successful than most Democracies. There are one-party, bureaucratic states such as Singapore or, some would argue, Japan that have had extraordinary growth without democracy in the normal sense of the word. So neither is Democracy a guarantee of growth nor is it the only path.

Others suggest that Democracy is successful because it wins the affections of people who feel empowered by their right to choose their leaders. They treasure the feeling of liberty when they can, through such choice, run their own lives. There is clearly something in this. Yet the speed with which people have abandoned Democracy when it failed economically, as the rise of Hitler and Mussolini shows, makes us pause. The fact that most people in Britain now do not bother to vote in local and European elections, and that the number voting in national elections in the United States is shrinking so dramatically, suggests that the emotional appeal is less strong than might be assumed.

Does Democracy satisfy?

There are good reasons why people fail to vote. In ancient Athens, 'Democracy', while proclaimed, was largely incomplete. Only a very small part of 'the people', that is the free male citizens, had any say in government. Full suffrage in Britain took a long time to achieve. It was not until 1928 that women got the right to vote in parliamentary elections.

There are other dangers. One is known as the 'tyranny of the majority'. According to the logic of Democracy, the government should obey the will of the majority. This majority may well be fickle and have illiberal views. It may be swayed by newspapers or orators to be intolerant, bigoted or even, as in Maoist China or Hitler's Germany, very unpleasant. Minorities can suffer badly from the majority view. This has been found historically by the Jews. In many parts of the world asylum-seekers, homosexuals and gypsies have also suffered from the intolerance of the majority.

An equal danger lies in politicians doing what they feel is best for the country, even if most of the people who elected them did not vote for their specific actions and may not agree with them.

Another difficulty resides in reducing the complexity of life to a single decision between opposing political parties. At national elections the parties put forward their ideas in a manifesto. Many people agree with bits from each of the opposing party programmes. But you can vote only for one side. When they come to power the politicians may refer to their manifesto (which most have not read) and then pursue policies that those who elected them did not anticipate. People consequently feel cheated and there are allegations of 'elective dictatorship'.

Furthermore, the party in power often brings in new ideas, after a year or two, with which people who voted for them totally disagree. They fight a war, or bring in new taxes or criminal legislation that are unacceptable to even their strongest supporters. People can write to their Member of Parliament, but they feel this has little effect. As the British Labour Prime Minister Clement Attlee candidly admitted, 'Democracy means government by discussion but it is only effective if you can stop people talking.'

What is the strength of Democracy?

Many think that the only real virtue of the system is that the politicians are accountable at the end of a limited term in power, through the need for re-election. This tempers the arrogance of power. The fact that there is an almost automatic swing against whoever is in power, since they soon appear to be the source of our present discontent, means that the government is periodically purged. After a while in office, every government appears shabby. This may save a country from the drift to autocracy.

The fact that almost all our leaders, once they are in power, appear to us as fools, pathetically inadequate or seriously deceived, shows that the system is working. On a recent visit to China I met many young people who had recently discovered that their leaders appeared to be old, stupid and corrupt. These young Chinese were cynical, and yet upset by this realisation. I reassured them that it is this very cynicism, rampant over the last three hundred years or more in England, that is one of the glories of Democracy. Those in power should never be trusted fully. We should always remember the novelist Daniel Defoe's short verse: 'Nature has left this tincture in the blood,/That all men would be tyrants if they could.' The British Prime Minister Winston Churchill observed, 'It has been said that Democracy is the worst form of government except all those other forms that have been tried from time to time.' It is often a sham, a mask for power, but it is difficult to think of a better system.

Should our rights and freedoms be enshrined in writing?

People have suggested that we would be better protected against our rulers and the tyranny of the majority through a written constitution. Certainly the American Constitution was a noble document, guaranteeing individual liberties and freedom of conscience. But it has worked because the principles it enshrined were very vague and general truisms, a statement of the obvious ideas transferred from the unwritten British political system. It could be, and has been, interpreted in entirely different ways by different people.

Written constitutions, in themselves, are no guarantee of liberty. The French, Italians and Germans have had many written constitutions over the last two hundred years but these have not protected them against tyranny. Attempts to introduce a European Constitution are causing considerable alarm since there is a feeling that it is too open-ended, too easily amendable, too undermining of subsidiary powers, hazy about the level of responsibilities. The new order will soon be overburdened by trying to specify too much. By its silences and omissions it may destroy rather than increase liberty.

What is liberty?

There are two types of liberty: negative and positive. Negative liberty is the core of the English tradition. There are certain things that others, including the state, cannot do to you. They cannot seize your body or your wealth without due process of law. They cannot take away your freedom of speech, action or right of association with others without legal warrant. A very few negative rules cover most of life. They are encapsulated by the philosopher John Stuart Mill when he wrote, 'The liberty of the individual must be thus far limited; he must not make himself a nuisance to other people.'

Positive liberty on the other hand is the right, and often

the duty, to do certain things. The right to health care, the right to be employed, the right to schooling. This sounds fine, but the problem is that much more has to be itemised. Anything not specified explicitly can be assumed to be absent as a right.

Positive liberty is the essence of the past continental European tradition. It tends to end up in overblown bureaucracy and much extra work for lawyers. With well-meaning attention to minute details it can stifle true democracy and even Democracy.

Many have felt that laws and politicians should not tell you how you *should* behave. That is the province of religion. Fascism and communism are an attempt to bend the will of the people towards what the leaders think is the moral way; they combine the roles of religion and politics. And many feel that the law and politicians should stick to stating what you must *not* do.

Does freedom from interference help?

One advantage of the negative definition of liberty is that it gives greater flexibility in a multicultural world. If we examine games, we find that their openness comes from the fact that rules are negative, not positive. In football there is just a minimal set of negative rules: you must not pick up the ball (unless you are goalkeeper), trip people up, get 'offside' and so on. There are no positive rules telling you that you must be nice to anyone who smiles at you, always show courtesy, always shake hands with your opponents at any opportunity.

One of the greatest achievements of the United States has been the way in which, over the centuries, it has absorbed waves of immigrants. Although we no longer believe that it is a melting-pot, certainly many groups with different origins live moderately amicably together. They can be Americans because to be so does not demand their hearts and souls. There are things you cannot do, to your fellow countrymen at least, as an American – kill people, steal their property, forbid them from saying things. But there are few positive things you *have* to do or believe. Even saluting the flag, and eating apple pie and Thanksgiving turkey are optional.

Likewise in the British Empire there were negative rules of a universal kind. But, with some exceptions such as the banning of widow-burning and head-hunting, individual consciences and variations in belief and culture were not to be interfered with. This was different from the Catholic, continental European, tradition. This may be one of the reasons why many British look with such apprehension at the attempts to introduce positive laws and positive discrimination, positive human rights, a new political and legal order, by way of the European parliament and constitution.

What are the deeper roots of Democracy?

The British unease about the European constitution can be understood only if we look at a thousand years of history. The English view is that modern Democracy was nurtured and grown in England in its early form, and only later exported. They argue that the social and mental underpinning of Democracy, that is democracy in the wider sense of responsibility and power passed down to lower levels, is a very old affair.

These historians examine the workings of the unwritten English constitution. They note the balance and separation of powers, delegation of responsibility, and set of intermediary institutions – that is things like the universities, companies, religious organisations, clubs and associations which lie between the subject and the state. According to the dominant ideas of the last thousand years, the ruler was not absolute, but first amongst equals. There were many loyalties or obligations; only some of them were to the state.

England was in some respects the most integrated and powerful state in history. Taxes were high, there were few over-mighty subjects, there were few banned institutions. Every subject was bound into the political system. Although for a very long time only a few of the richer landholders had a vote, so the majority of the population and particularly women were disenfranchised, many people had a say in part of the running of their own lives.

So there was relatively effective government combined with a good deal of delegated power. It was not full Democracy in the modern sense, but it was a particularly open, liberal and tolerant society, and there was equality before the law – with the partial exception of lords (peers) – making it an unusually egalitarian one, a 'democracy' of a sort.

Is Democracy the solution to the world's woes?

People living in parts of New Guinea noticed that when the white people arrived, they often built airfields. Planes would then arrive to spill out huge quantities of desirable things or 'cargo'. It seemed clear that the airfields were the key. They attracted the planes. So people hopefully built airfields and then waited for the cargo to arrive. They were disappointed.

We have become the same with 'Democracy'. We have observed that democracy is often associated with consumer success and some forms of freedom. Democracies, we feel, deliver the goods. We conclude that if we set out and 'build democracies' around the world, by persuasion, bribes or force, the benefits linked to democracy will automatically follow. If we put out the ballot boxes, the rest will soon occur. We will be equally disappointed. We have forgotten that 'Democracy' is the result of many other things. It is as much the consequence as the cause of things we appreciate. We have become political cargo cultists.

Can Democracy last?

It may well be that economic growth is necessary for the success of Democracy. The Soviet Union collapsed largely because of its poor economic performance. Democracy has won because it delivers wealth. Yet Democracy, as we have seen, does not guarantee growth. Other systems may be more efficient, not just in the short term as in many of the new nations in Asia, but perhaps in the long term as in China.

Nor does Democracy guarantee equality. It may well be that equality before the law and the rule of law are necessary for Democracy. But Democracy and such equality do not guarantee any specific outcome in terms of actual equality. The increasingly pronounced extremes of wealth and poverty in the United States contrast starkly with the extraordinary economic equality in the largely one-party Japan. This suggests that while individuals may be politically 'free' in a place with Democracy, they may be materially unfree – the poor being worse housed, worse educated and less healthy than the rich.

History has not come to an end, as some prematurely alleged. The triumph of Democratic capitalism is not assured for ever. Only vigilance combined with luck will ensure that the least bad of all political systems lasts for another hundred years in those parts of the world that desire it. Humility is the best way to ensure that it spreads to other countries which have as yet not enjoyed its blessings and its frustrations. Active participation by the people, combined with deep scepticism, may keep the system alive.

$\mathscr{W}$here does freedom come from?

Dear Lily,

You may have heard people talking about 'civil society' and wondered what it means. The talk is of exporting this idea to places that formerly lacked it, namely the communist zones of Eastern Europe, the former Soviet Union and China. You will certainly be aware that many people talk of defending the values of 'democracy', 'freedom', an 'open and tolerant society' against those who attack them. Yet in all this discussion there is seldom any explanation or questioning of where these strange commodities, that is freedom and openness, came from.

'Civil society' usually refers to the world of associations and organisations that lie between the state and the individual. In many societies it is the family group and sometimes the religious caste that inhabit this space. Yet in the modern West these are less important.

What is very widespread is a multitude of organisations to which people belong, but which are not run by the state. Schools, universities, trade unions, political clubs, sporting clubs, religious groups, scientific and literary clubs, economic institutions, these and many others enable someone to belong to an organisation. This can provide strength through numbers and the pooling of resources.

In most civilisations in the past, and in fascist and communist nations in the last century, all these institutions were banned, or controlled by the state. Individuals owed their allegiance to the state or party, not to other organisations. Civil society was prohibited. How is it, then, that these associations and groups now flourish in such a lively way in much of the world? And what effect does this have?

Where did an open society come from?

The revival of Roman law, which spread over all of continental Europe between the fourteenth and seventeenth centuries, brought with it a homogenising, flattening tendency. This set almost all of Europe along a new path. Yet during this important period England retained its (Germanic) common-law system.

At this time, a legal accident occurred in England that was to change the world we live in. Lawyers were, as ever, trying to find a way round a tax regime. When a wealthy man died, his landed property, granted to him by the King in accordance with the strict feudal system, was forfeited back to the Crown. In order for his heirs to reclaim it, they had to pay a heavy death duty on their estates. Naturally the rich did not like this. Their legal advisers saw that the problem could be avoided if they made the man at his death no longer the owner of the property. If he did not hold the property at death, the Crown could not seize it and insist on a tax before it passed on to his heirs.

So the lawyers invented the device of the trust. A group of friends of the property-holder were chosen and the estate was legally conveyed to them. They held it 'in trust for the use of another'. It was legally theirs to do what they liked with, but the owner trusted them to pass it on at his death to his heirs and to carry out his wishes in whatever way he had privately told them.

The trust created a strange and anomalous thing. Trustees were appointed to work together to hold and administer property and to take collective decisions. The trust had a name, a separate existence, a body that existed through time. So it was technically a 'corporation', a 'body'. Yet it had not been set up by the state, it had not been 'incorporated' or licensed by the state with a formal document. It had been set up by a group of private citizens, yet it was recognised by national law.

Such entities were threatening to the state if they became powerful, since trustees could make their own rules. Trusts also allowed citizens to work together and create alternative loyalties. Consequently they were banned during the French, Russian and Chinese revolutionary periods, and by Mussolini and Hitler. In England, Henry VIII tried to destroy them but it was too late. Abolished for a few years, trusts were restored by a technical legal trick.

How did we get freedom?

From very early on the trust idea spread beyond the simple avoiding of death duties. The idea provided a device that could be used for any need. In the field of economics, any group who wished to set up a mutually supportive, private, non-state entity could now do so. Whether it was a great trading organisation such as the East India Company, a bank or insurance company such as Lloyds, or even the Stock Exchange, the device of the trust was ready at hand. Much of Britain's success came from this form of organisation. The United States has widely used the same idea as the foundation of the mighty trusts and corporations that now rule the world.

In the religious sphere, the trust sheltered the growing independence of the Protestant Christian sects. Without the ability to set up meeting places and independent organisations provided by the trust, the Quakers, Baptists, Methodists and other religious nonconformists could never have flourished. Much of what we call religious liberty was made possible by this device. Without it, in certain Catholic countries, the Jews, Masons, Lutherans and others were persecuted almost to extinction.

When the state becomes more powerful it does not usually tolerate rivals. The growth of parties and of political clubs and organisations grew out of the trust concept. The early clubs of the Whigs and Tories, the later clubs and associations of working men, the trade-union movement, all were based on the legal device of the trust.

Likewise, the whole system of devolved government, the shires with their magistrates and local power, the parish councils and many other local and regional bodies were given strength by the concept. Local educational and church organisations, grammar schools and vestries, all were trust-based.

Normally rulers come to believe that power is their private property, that they own it. The strange thing in Democracy is that power *is held in trust for the people*. The present rulers are trustees; they have been entrusted with temporary power, which is not theirs but has to be passed on to their successors. When they are felt no longer to be performing adequately, they are replaced by another 'board of trustees', or as they are called, the government. The corruption of power is held in check by the limited period for which it can be held.

In international politics, the trust idea formed the core of an extraordinary empire. All other empires in history have been held, usually through force of conquest, by the imperial country entirely for its own purposes. Rome, Spain and France 'owned' their empires. In the British Empire, however greatly the ideal became tarnished in practice, the concept grew that the imperial territories were held 'in trust' for the people who inhabited them.

In theory, at least, Britain held its vast dominions in trust. When the children or grandchildren of the people from whom the land had been appropriated had grown to 'adulthood', that is to a position where they could assume responsibility, the trust would be ended. Thus the idea was that wealth raised from different parts of the Empire should, as in a trust, be put back into the trust for the future welfare of those on whose behalf it was held. There was, in other words, responsibility as well as power. Even if it is largely a myth, and some would say hypocrisy and humbug, it is a powerful and inhibiting one. Nationalists such as the lawyer Gandhi could use the rhetoric to gain freedom for India.

How did we get social and intellectual freedom?

The trust gave the British two of their most famous institutions. There were the social and philanthropic clubs and associations: the Women's Institute, the Boy Scouts and the Girl Guides, Oxfam, Amnesty, the Samaritans, the Salvation Army, the National Trust, the Royal Society for the Prevention of Cruelty to Animals, the Royal Society for the Protection of Birds, the National Society for the Prevention of Cruelty to Children, the Lions, the Rotarians. There were numerous working-class clubs and organisations, funeral societies, pigeon-fancying leagues, leek-growing fellowships, discussion groups, sports groups. Many of the clubs and institutions that have spread around the world were invented in Britain on the basis of the idea of non-governmental clubs.

Secondly there were the team games – cricket, football, rugby football, hockey – which are now the world's great passion. Many of the team games played in the world today were invented in Britain, and others like baseball and American football developed in the other land of clubs and associations. They all revolved round the club and the clubhouse (as did golf, from Scotland, and tennis, originally from France). Some of the clubs were famous, such as the Marylebone Cricket Club or MCC, or the institution that was described as the most powerful political body in nineteenth-century Britain, the Jockey Club. Many others were local and small. The concept of the club run by trustees formed the shell within which team games could be nurtured and enjoyed.

The universities and learned societies, whether of the élite (the Royal Society, British Academy) or the masses (working men's clubs, local libraries and institutions such as the London Lending Library), were based on the trust idea. Without these, the meetings of engineers, philosophers and others in the coffee clubs, Lunar Society (an eminent eighteenth-century British scientific club) and hundreds of small groupings would not have occurred. These clubs had an incalculable effect on the development of scientific and industrial knowledge.

What happens if we don't trust people?

The trust idea encouraged that rare commodity 'trust' to develop. Without this, the economic, political and social foundations of modern democracies could not exist. The hybrid device of the trust runs counter to most of the powerful tendencies in the development of civilisations. Almost always any advance in wealth or power in a society has, after a short while, been gobbled up by the central power. Knowledge is power, so it must be incorporated into the centre. Social status is power, so it must be harnessed. Economic wealth must be absorbed. Religious loyalty must be channelled towards the state in alliance with the clergy. The state demands all of this. If the state is threatened, or pretends to be threatened, its demands are almost impossible to reject.

Other threatening institutions are systematically extinguished or enfeebled, until in the later periods of every empire, whether that of Rome, China, the Habsburgs, the Ottomans or France, the peripheral powers are weak. There develops a central power which aspires to be all-powerful and which is supported by an ever growing bureaucracy and standing army. When the absolutisms of the twentieth century emerged, with their superior forms of surveillance and advanced technologies of control, even the family group was shattered. Nothing stands between the individual and Joseph Stalin, Chairman Mao or Pol Pot.

The state is like a machine for cutting grass, a lawnmower with its blade fixed at the maximum setting so it is very close to the earth. It cuts off and absorbs into itself anything that sticks up more than a tiny way. If the universities, the monasteries, the cities, the traders and merchants, the industrial producers or anyone else starts to accumulate visible wealth and power, especially if they start to proclaim their own rules and independent government, the state officials savagely prune or eliminate them. Only two types of organisation can survive such a system which confiscates any conspicuous wealth and destroys all alternative power structures.

One is the secret, banned, organisation whose members hide from the state. The mafia, yakuza, triads and even, in a somewhat different way, the Masons, are forced into a negative existence as a black or inverted civil society. These are outlawed groups which provide services to the individual, often with the partial complicity of some state officials.

The other survivor is the thick, flat, entangled, low-level cover of strong family ties. Through most of history, all that seems able to give ordinary people some protection, to provide an area of safety against the predations of the state, are the natural bonds of birth, or the constructed bonds of kinship through such institutions as blood brotherhood or godparenthood. Only in the family can we trust. A world of suspicion and tight family groups usually emerges, as we find from Italy to China or South America.

How are trust and democracy linked?

Through an accident, civil society, that is the thick layer of organisations that lies between the state and the individual subject or citizen, continued and flourished, and the civil liberties and rights of free thought and free association became increasingly valued.

Such a flourishing of civil society and alternative centres of power had, of course, happened before in history, as in Athens in its great period, or for a time in the Italian city states. Yet in most cases the experiment had been small and short-lived. Only when the trust coincided with two other developments (which it also helped to bring into being) could a new type of civilisation be established.

One of these was a new way of obtaining reliable knowledge about the natural world (the scientific revolution). The other was a new way of harnessing that knowledge to generate new power and wealth for humans (the industrial revolution). When these two were joined with the trust, there developed a powerful form of political and social system, which we often term 'the open society'.

Yet it is well to remember that the creation of an open society was an accident, an unintended consequence of many other forces. It was not the result of superior virtues or intelligence on the part of people living in one part of the world. We should also remember that it is constantly under pressure from forces from both the left and right.

The danger of the lawnmower blades' being set too low and stifling all independent power (communism) is matched by an equal danger from rampant capitalism. In several parts of the world at present the blades are set so high that vast wealth is accumulated in private hands and the whole nation suffers as a result of overgrown corporations and obscenely inflated private fortunes.

So there is nothing to suggest that a vibrant civil society

will continue indefinitely. It does not take a great deal to erode it, or even to snuff it out entirely. Throughout history we have seen strong tendencies towards centralisation and the erosion of lower-level liberties. Some see them today behind the activities of the advocates of increasing European centralisation and integration.

Even more ironically, those who are most vociferous in their condemnation of assaults on the open society by terrorists and others often slip into an attack on the very civil institutions, such as the media or the due legal process, that they claim to be defending. They can act unwittingly as the very agents of the enemies of the open society.

17

*W*hat is bureaucracy for?

Dear Lily,

As soon as societies developed complex organisations – the state, churches, cities – they needed organisers and managers. Almost all activities, in fact, need some rules and adminis-tration. No games could be played, no arts performed, no knowledge transmitted, no products made if there were not rules and umpires, referees and teachers to administer them. Schools, hospitals, courts of law, libraries, universities, indus-trial firms, parliament, all need rules and all need bureaucracy. Unadulterated foodstuffs, uniform measures and standards, agreed rules about behaviour, all need supervision.

So bureaucracy is one of the great tools of civilisation. Nowadays most organisations need an accountant, a lawyer, a secretary and an administrator. Our lives would collapse into disorder without bureaucracy.

As a form of government it has many things to commend it, especially when compared with its competitors. The aim of the bureaucrat is to apply uniform rules to uniform cases, to work by a recognised code. Favouritism, corruption, the emotional tugs of power, patronage, family ties should be rejected. Impersonal rules should be imposed. All of this is very commendable. In this letter, however, I shall concentrate on the negative side of bureaucracy, for this is less often noticed.

How do people keep order?

Under traditional authority, society is held together by rulers whom we obey because they represent the past, the ancestral and customary wisdom. Obedience is unquestioning, passed on from generation to generation by succession to offices of power vested with authority. A king, a chief, a priest, all have this type of authority.

From time to time such traditional authority is challenged and sometimes overthrown in a moment of creative chaos by the personal insights and dynamism of a single individual. Why such moments of 'charismatic' (literally meaning a laying on of hands) authority occur, whether through the life of the Buddha, Jesus Christ, Genghis Khan, Oliver Cromwell, Napoleon or Chairman Mao, is a large question.

What is certain is that the periods inaugurated by a charismatic leader tend to last only a short time. Soon the founder dies. Yet he or his followers may set up institutions which live by the rules or precedents that he outlined, whether he was St Benedict or Karl Marx. This leads to the third type of authority, the setting of impartial rules and standards, operated by trained officials in a 'bureaucracy' (literally power in a place where paper is stored).

All of history can be read as a tension between these types of authority. In fact they usually coexist rather than one replacing another. The prophet relies on bureaucratic structures; the Civil Service relies on the charisma of politicians.

Why do organisations grow?

The benefits of bureaucracy make it attractive to many. Increased efficiency can lead to better medical care, better traffic control, a better economy, and all sorts of benefits that make life run smoothly. Bureaucrats can stand out against the partisan influence of connections and kinship and the corruptions of threat and bribery. Bureaucracy is a powerful bulwark against revolution, subversion and overenthusiasm. It can protect scarce resources, allocate wealth more fairly and protect the weak from the strong. As the poet Alexander Pope put it, 'For forms of government let fools contest;/Whate'er is best administered is best'.

So there is very often a growing desire to control through administrative action, to use bureaucracies as an arm of government. The state holds the people together primarily through administrative centralisation. As it seeks to extend its power, so it increases its chief tool of power, bureaucracy. There is a powerful pressure towards multiplying the number and control of bureaucrats.

A second much more recent trend in modern states is the desire to encourage equality of access and execution of rules. This usually opens with a campaign against inequality, privilege and special favours, with a desire to level and redistribute what there is.

In order for this to happen, everything must be flattened, be put on the same level. Communist societies try to abolish classes and the state ends up with all-powerful administrative classes and a nightmare of incompatible rules which few believe in. It is no accident that the Soviet Union was ruled by something called the Politburo (the political bureau).

For much of the past, bureaucracies were used to maintain inequality, to extract wealth from the mass of the population and distribute it to the privileged. Since the American and French revolutions of the late-eighteenth century, the desire to enforce equality through bureaucratic pressures has been related to the desire to enforce equality and individualism. It is proclaimed that individuals have inherent rights, and if these are infringed then there must be action to protect them.

That is fine up to a point. The problem is that it is much easier to define and protect individual rights than to define and defend the wider community or social rights. It is much easier (and more profitable) for a bureaucrat or lawyer to deal with single individuals than with communities.

Are organisations a disease?

One reason bureaucracies grow is the desire to increase power and pay. As each procedure in an organisation is made into a job, it creates 'ecological niches' or nesting places, as it were, for officials, who live off the institution. Since there is little power, pay or prestige if one has few or no subordinates, to increase their power and importance, each bureaucrat tries to increase the number of their assistants. The number of 'officials' very quickly expands to consume the resources available.

As soon as a germ (administrator) moves into a new body (hospital, school, university, law court) it breeds, dividing and subdividing tasks, creating needs that only new administrators can fulfil. It develops or applies a special status-enhancing language ('goals', 'bench-marks', 'mission statements'). This compensates for the fact that it is in the nature of such professional administrators that they have no particular skill or knowledge of the area in which they work.

They are not trained to give lectures, to perform surgical operations or to teach children. They probably know little of the content. Yet they do know how to work in local politics, how to deal with outside bureaucratic agencies. They are trained to help to bring in money, to minimise risk, to homogenise and generalise rules and to avoid some of the 'corruption' of individual action and subjective judgements.

Examples of bureaucratic systems becoming ever larger and more powerful are widespread. For example, a constant flow of requests for information or the bringing in of new rules has quite overwhelmed the central administration in many universities, hospitals and police forces in Britain. So the administrators try to handle this by creating new posts and also passing on parts of the load down the system. Lower down, the burden rises and new administrative posts are set up, then soon overwhelmed, which again passes further work on down.

The great analyst of bureaucracies C. Northcote Parkinson gives a good example of what happens. In 1914 the British Navy had 62 capital ships in commission, run by 2,000 Admiralty officials. By 1928 there were 20 capital ships, run by 3,569 Admiralty officials. There was, as was noted, 'a magnificent navy on land', since the number of ships had decreased by 67 per cent while that of the bureaucrats had increased by 78 per cent.

To believe that the spread of more administrators will either diminish workloads or even lead to more efficient administration (measured by input/output of time and energy) is as naïve as to assume that computers will one day bring less work for humans or create the paperless office.

What is bureaucracy?

Bureaucracy is an extremely efficient and effective system because it rests on a rational ordering of time and space. It is based on the idea of a bureau or writing desk with drawers in it. Everything must fit somewhere. The fact that many things are untidy, or fit between categories, cannot be allowed for.

Ideally, everything should be placed on an equal level on the desk. Like cases, like solutions; a level playing field, universal tariffs. Do not allow discretion or personal circumstances to cloud judgement. Everything should be comparable. Since *qualities* cannot be compared, as in apples and oranges, they must be reduced to something similar, for example weight or volume.

It is also necessary to generate some principle of filing the information that is collected so that it can be reused. Usually a hierarchical storage system is created, based on stating very general principles and then working to split these, layer after layer, until every conceivable type of case has its own pigeon-hole.

The bureaucracy disapproves of all rule-breaking, which it tends to label 'corruption'. It thrives on the multiplication of rules, attempting to make provision for every kind of situation, and trying to prevent individuals in the group from exercising too much personal discretion.

Another tendency is towards centralisation of power. If possible, decisions are moved upwards in the system; too much delegated power is to be avoided as it might lead to a lack of uniformity, 'unprincipled exceptionalism'. If it can be shown that different parts of the same institution act differently, this is equivalent to corruption. Usually in a bureaucracy not only is there a hierarchical arrangement of the drawers so that rules are of a rigid kind, but the organisation of roles is hierarchical. This means that every decision of any importance has to be ratified by someone higher up the chain.

Why measure everything?

It has often been noted that assessing is a very strong feature of bureaucracies. They always wish to place things on lists in their attempt to turn uniquely varied qualities into measurable quantities. This is very obvious in all walks of life. In schools there are increasing numbers of tests which are marketed as good for the child, parent and school. Assessments are made available in order to mark progress towards targets and to make some kind of comparison between the intrinsically incomparable. In hospitals, universities and elsewhere it is the same.

One particularly intriguing and rapid growth in one branch of this desire to assess is the wish to try to protect against the future. There is now a huge business in 'risk assessment'. There are many organisations and individuals who spend their lives trying to quantify and specify and hence, in theory, diminish risks. Since life is full of risk, when consulted they usually suggest extreme caution.

Another technique of modern bureaucracies uses the metaphor of the path or track, namely the 'audit trail'. The old saying that justice must not only be done, but be seen to be done, now applies to all administration. It is not enough to teach or examine well, but every stage must be put on paper so that if there is an inquiry or 'audit', the 'paper trail' is clear, unambiguous and correct. The principle of finance, that everything must be accounted for, that life is to be reduced to a double-entry page, that there must be written receipts for everything, is now applied more generally.

There are now teaching audits, research audits, hospital, legal and many other kinds of audit. 'If it moves, salute it; if it doesn't move, whitewash it' used to be an army saying. The equivalent now is 'If it is unpredictable at all, risk-assess it; if it leads to an outcome, make an audit trail'.

Is bureaucracy a danger?

A certain amount of bureaucracy, accountability and organisation is vital for the world we live in. The benefits of bureaucracy do not need to be promoted. Yet the hidden costs of overdoing the regulation are very considerable. As the rules multiply, it becomes so difficult to do anything that one has to cheat or break the rules in order to survive. Indeed, since the rules often conflict with each other and whatever one does breaks some rule, it becomes a question of choosing between illegalities.

I still remember how surprised I was when a building regulations inspector came to check the house we live in. We had put in a new staircase without a handrail. He said it was unsafe and must have a handrail. When we put that in, he said that it was now too narrow for safety. Short of pulling down much of a seventeenth-century structure, we were bound to break the law one way or another.

The system becomes ever more complicated, with more and more rules. Rather than leading to openness and transparency (which was the original intention), this leads to a situation where only a highly trained specialist (professional bureaucrat) knows how it works. There is as a result more space for hidden corruption.

There is also a loss of personal incentives. Humans like freedom and responsibility in their lives. They like to be given basic guidance and then encouraged to get on with things; to be ingenious and creative in their solutions. As bureaucracy increases, people are ever more rule-bound, forced to work 'by the book'. This means that jobs become dead; creative and ingenious solutions are often frowned upon.

The hierarchical nature of bureaucracy leads to duplication, the erosion of trust and individual creativity and the emergence of a 'surveillance society'. It ends up in the typical Japanese office with its endless stamps and fear of being 'the nail that sticks up' which will quickly be hammered down.

One unexpected effect of over-bureaucratisation is the spread of cynicism. For much of English history rules were few but were observed and respected. The proliferation of rules, as in the Soviet Union, means that they are seen as obstacles, nuisances, pressures which work against the individual, barriers to get round and break if possible.

Cunning, cheating, deviance and learning the real rules behind the rules are what it is all about, a phenomenon found in all over-centralised bureaucracies. This breeds cynicism since the less successful, the small-rule-breakers, assume that the successful have got to where they are by cheating, bribery, corruption and breaking rules.

Another harmful effect of overactive bureaucracies is that they divert talent. In almost all organisations, the higher someone's pay and the higher their status, the less practical work and the more administration they do. A head teacher who was perhaps an excellent communicator does not teach any more. An excellent surgeon ends up doing paperwork as head of a hospital. A brilliant academic is finally the administrative head of a university. None of them any longer does the thing he or she most enjoys or is good at. They spend their time as fund-raisers, personnel officers, chairs of committees. It is a widespread tendency: if you can do anything really well, stop doing it and become an administrator.

The aim of the bureaucrat is to prevent 'corruption', which is defined as the use of human contacts, networks, allowing in warmth, affection and emotion. Ironically the proliferation of rules often means that the only way to cut through them is precisely through a form of networking, or as it is known in Nepal *afno manche*, literally 'own people' – knowing someone and using ties of patronage.

A further effect is waste of time and effort, much of it never accounted for despite the fact that bureaucracy is supposed to be based on accountability. In case an institution might need to justify an action, huge amounts of time are spent on concocting audit trails, lengthy agendas, minutes, papers to cover every aspect of everything. The time and energy spent doing all this when set against the cost of any likely harmful outcome is probably out of all proportion. Yet it is held to be irresponsible not to do it. If there is trouble, the lawyers will go for the weakest point, so the bureaucracies have to lumber themselves with huge protective defences over their whole body.

Can we avoid being drowned in paper?

When people looked at bureaucracy over Europe during the period 1200–1800, they pointed to one path that had avoided this almost universal tendency. This was to be found in England. Linked to the growth of powerful middling groups, the absence of the threat of war, the nature of the common law, the proliferation of wealth and the growth of a powerful set of intermediary groupings, the state of bureaucracy in England from the twelfth to the nineteenth centuries represented a strange paradox.

England maintained a curious tension between the most centralised feudal landholding and judicial system in history (with all land ultimately held by and all justice flowing from the Crown) and the most decentralised administrative system, where the legislature and executive were practically separate. Local government was extremely strong and independent down through the county to the parish level. The size of the central bureaucracy in the capital, as well as that of the standing army and the police, was small when compared with almost every other middling-sized state in Europe.

This unusual tradition, which many observers thought was one of Britain's greatest strengths, has almost vanished. Since the 1980s bureaucracy has spread with the so-called 'management revolution'. Every attempt to get rid of the tentacles seems only to increase the problem.

So what can be done? The main thing is to be aware of the reasons for the spread of this replicating growth. The second is to be aware of some of its effects. The third is, if it cannot be altered, to learn how to survive within the increasingly bureaucratic system. These are arts that those living in Eastern Europe or in Italy have perfected.

One obvious way to survive bureaucracy is to join it. This will be a real temptation for you when you are looking for a job. Many people have joined professions and have by their very success been promoted into management positions. Or they have been forced to seek promotion to an administrative post to pay for the mortgage, health insurance, pensions or children's education.

If you are faced with intrusive bureaucracy you will be forced to learn various ways to outwit the system and to get round some of the more unacceptable tests and indices. While these techniques are important, the most important thing is to keep cheerful and positive.

The most insidious feature of bureaucracy is that, like all power, it tends to affect even those who start off as sceptical. People come to believe in the assessments, audits and mechanisms. They tend to take them very seriously and try to fit themselves into the evolving system. Once this concession has been made, there is little chance of escape.

Keeping a sense of humour that mocks some of the more extreme forms of bureaucratic behaviour helps. We need to remember the jokes. Most bureaucracies have an element of the criticism made of the British Civil Service, which provides 'a difficulty for every solution'. A committee can often be 'a group that takes minutes and wastes hours'.

Yet being forced into such joking, and the feelings of wasted talent and time, are a considerable price to pay for supposed gains in efficiency. As in many of the great bureaucracies such as classical Iran or imperial China, cynicism is corrosive of integrity, personal and civic, and of morale, personal and public.

This is the dilemma. We need an uncorrupted civil service and bureaucracy to make life in modern complex societies tolerable. A good bureaucracy can provide a strong counterforce to the power-seeking of politicians. It can run a great university, hospital, business organisation or television company with fairness and efficiency.

For many centuries Britain had an unusually small, yet efficient, bureaucratic system. Many commented on the contrast between the centralised and over-bureaucratic situation on the Continent and the relatively tiny and uncorrupt system on this island and in the United States. All this is under threat, but the older traditions are worth fighting for.

Bureaucracies have a tendency to expand and become over-intrusive. When they combine with the worst aspect of 'management culture', they can become an overwhelmingly complex, time-wasting machine. They limit the freedom and creativity of individuals. Getting the balance right is very difficult indeed.

$\mathscr{H}$ow do we get justice?

Dear Lily,

In most societies the last thing a person wants to do is to go anywhere near a court of law. A lot of money is wasted and you may lose. So if you want to sort out a quarrel you get your brothers to smash up the other person's house or seize their property. Or, in a Nepalese village, you ask some senior villagers to come and settle the quarrel in a relaxed way, sitting on the veranda amongst the grain baskets and chickens.

Are English and American courts odd?

Law is a strange process which in many ways goes against the grain of ordinary life. A court is basically a place where people behave in an odd way. They bring their disputes to a complete stranger who, after listening and asking questions, says one is in the right and the other in the wrong.

If going to court is a strange thing to do, going to an English or American court is an extreme form of this peculiarity. You are asked to 'tell the truth, the whole truth and nothing but the truth'. In most societies there is no belief that there is an abstract thing called 'truth'. There are believed to be many conflicting types of truth – factual, social, religious, mythical. Each is 'true' in a different way. Furthermore, no one but a lunatic or a traitor would tell the court something that would hurt their family or friends. People are expected to lie, or at least to tell partial truths.

When you are judged in an English court it is by a curious standard. The ultimate test in the mind of the jury or judge, both of whether your story is true and of whether you have done something wrong, is to ask themselves, 'Was this the behaviour of a reasonable man?' 'Man' here is shorthand for everyone – men, women, upper-class, lower-class. It is assumed that all individuals should and indeed do adhere to the same idea of reasonableness and that all behaviour can therefore be judged by the same standards.

Almost everywhere else, men and women, rich and poor, old and young are assumed to be 'reasonable' in very different ways. Furthermore, reasonable behaviour entirely depends on the social relationship involved. It is reasonable for a man to strike his wife or his son, highly unreasonable for a woman or son to strike back. It is reasonable for an uncle to find a job in his office for his nephew, but not reasonable to find jobs for unrelated people. It is reasonable to pay a bribe to a customs officer or policeman, but not to someone who has no power.

Much of law is concerned with deciding about the behaviour of people who are by birth or achieved position unequal. In Anglo-American law, it is about deciding between people who are considered to be on a level, not intrinsically unequal, even if they appear strikingly different in their education, sex, wealth or race.

It is assumed in modern law that individuals have rights. Men, women, children, disabled people, even the unborn foetus or animals, all have intrinsic 'rights'. Very few societies in the world share this view. It is usually thought that an individual exists only as part of a group; he or she has rights in relation to others, which are inseparable from responsibilities. There are no *innate* rights which come with birth.

The idea that, in the words of the American Declaration of Independence, 'life, liberty and the pursuit of happiness' are intrinsic and inextinguishable human rights would be regarded by a large part of the world, even today, and certainly over most of history, as an outrageous claim. When the idea was imported into India in the nineteenth century by the British it caused immense confusion and disapproval. A member of a lower caste, a woman, a child, had never been conceived of as having the same rights as a high-caste person, a man, an adult.

This assumption of individual human rights is a very old feature of English law. It has now spread over the world and become a central doctrine of a new form of mission activity. It has many merits. When taken to extremes, without attention to the counterbalancing rights of communities and groups, or the responsibilities that go with the rights, it is as dangerous as rightlessness.

How does law rule over us?

We often hear about the 'rule of law', but what does this mean? One idea is that people are prepared to settle disputes through legal process, rather than by force. A second is that all actions and all power are ultimately under the law. Above the rulers there is something higher; they also are under the law.

Usually legal systems develop in a different way. At first the rulers may say, 'We make the laws and we keep the laws.' But after a time they forget the second half of this. They are above the law. So the law does not rule them; they rule the law. You can see this in Stalin's Russia, Chairman Mao's China, or

France in the later seventeenth century. There is one law for the powerful and rich and another law for the people.

Only in England (Scotland has a different system) for a long period of about seven hundred years have we believed that ultimately the law is supreme and even the King and his ministers have to abide by it. Everybody is under the same rule. Unlike chess, where certain pieces have privileges, the English law gives few privileges, at least in theory.

The 'rule of law' depends on uniform application of laws and a common procedure. It means that the legal process should be separated off from the political, that the judges and the courts should be independent. All of this is difficult to sustain. Powerful forces, economic and political, are constantly hoping to bias law in their direction.

How do courts work?

The great problem is to persuade people to accept what you are doing in the legal process. Law is a dramatic and often elaborate affair. People dress up in archaic costumes, the judge sits high up above the court, long-sounding words are used in a strangely formal way. There are often dramatic public punishments, as in the so-called 'theatre of Tyburn' where criminals were taken through the streets and executed before the crowds in eighteenth-century England.

The legal process takes people out of their ordinary lives where they have become entangled in conflicts. It puts them in an arena that is out of normal time and space. The procedure in the court then rearranges their lives. You have to exert a lot of pressure in order to persuade people to follow a decision that they may think is against their interest.

So the law is like a game of tennis. People go to a 'court'. They play a combative game, either on their own behalf or through their representatives, serving, returning, trying to outwit their opponents. The judge is the umpire. After the case has been heard, their world is changed. One side has won, the other lost.

What are juries?

In almost all serious legal cases you have a confrontation between the state and the citizen or subject. The state has almost all the power and the single individual is inherently very weak. So if the state says, 'You are suspected of an offence,' how can you defend yourself?

When you have a jury system, where it is the duty of your equals (or peers) to decide your guilt or innocence, everything is changed. The jury are not themselves on trial but observers and arbiters. It is one thing to grind down a single individual who is already accused of an offence. It is entirely different to be able to persuade twelve, free, moderately affluent and reasonably educated individuals who have been told on oath to judge as fairly as possible without fear or favour.

So the jury acts as a filter of state power, a protection for the single citizen or subject. It is a key institution in any democracy. Most countries in Western Europe had juries of a sort a thousand years ago. Yet almost all had given up the jury system by the eighteenth century. England has maintained a jury system up to the present. There are now increasing calls by politicians for its abolition in a wide range of cases.

Should we torture people?

The absence of the use of torture in criminal trials throughout most of English history is a notable feature of England's legal system. Very early on, the English courts set their face against torture. People believed that if you tortured someone you would not get a true confession. The tortured person would lie in order to make the torture stop. There was also perhaps a certain appreciation of the force in the philosopher Montaigne's remark that 'After all, it is setting a very high price on one's conjectures to burn a man alive for them.'

In English law you do not need the confession of the accused. You prove them guilty or not on the basis of evidence. It has never mattered what the individual thinks after he has been proven guilty. If the jury thinks that you are guilty, you are guilty. You can go to prison or the gallows tree protesting your innocence. That is your right.

This tradition of avoiding the short cut of torture is also under threat. Some of those engaged in the 'war against terrorism' in Britain and America, where torture is currently banned, are now arguing that it should be allowed, or at least the evidence from those tortured by less scrupulous regimes in other countries should be accepted.

How unusual is England?

The essence of English law is the protection of the individual and his or her rights: to a certain amount of liberty, freedom of speech, control of his or her body and personal space and to everything he or she owns. Ownership includes visible things, like bits of land and houses, but also invisible things, such as intellectual property rights and certain things such as the right to a title or office.

In most societies, law is concerned mainly with interpersonal matters of status and physical injuries. England, in contrast, has been obsessed with property, with civil law, that is cases between individuals who use the courts to sort out disputes about who has rights in what.

Nowadays the principles of an old English system have spread through the former British Empire and the United States. They are so widespread that they have become the normal way of proceeding. Many of the fundamental ideas, for instance the absence of judicial torture, the separation of politics from law and the rules of evidence, have become enshrined in the European constitution and elsewhere. This makes it easy to forget that if we had looked around the world in about 1750 we would have been astonished at the English exception.

Does the English system have advantages?

The sophisticated development of property law and safe-guarding of economic interests have helped to make England and America wealthy. People can afford to trust each other, and if that trust breaks down they can use the legal system. The early development of industrial capitalism could not have occurred without the extraordinary development of English law.

The other main advantage of this kind of legal system is that, on the whole, the majority of people feel safe under it. Without a legal warrant from a Justice of the Peace, the police cannot raid a person's house or business. Most people most of the time – except asylum-seekers and members of some racial minorities – can rest secure that they will not be subjected to arbitrary punishment or imprisonment.

If you are arrested you have the right to call a lawyer and the right to know what you are being charged with, and the right to be freed if no charge is brought within a certain number of hours (habeas corpus).

Under the rule of law, an individual is relatively free from censorship of thought and action. Criticism of the authorities, free speech (within reason) and reasoned opposition to the present system are all tolerated.

Some of these advantages of the rule of law are being whittled away. State officials argue that suspected terrorists and asylum-seekers should not be given legal protection, but should be subject to imprisonment without charge or trial for long periods. There are those who now fear that once certain categories of people are denied basic legal protection, it will not be too long before we all find ourselves in the nightmare world of Stalin or Chairman Mao.

Are there disadvantages?

People complain about the slowness, cost, complexity and at times inefficiency of the English system. There is something in the satirist Jonathan Swift's observation that 'Laws are like cobwebs, which may catch small flies, but let wasps and hornets break through.' It is sometimes impossible to convict someone who is clearly guilty. The inquisitorial system, where the judge can call for more investigation, might well avoid some of these difficulties.

Yet the main disadvantage of the English system is that it can generate an antagonistic attitude. Much of the English practice of politics and social life (including sports) is confrontational. The English legal system is odd because it believes, or pretends to believe, that disputes are resolvable into one person's winning (being right) and the other's losing (being wrong). If this is accepted, then the best way to sort out difficulties is to get those in the dispute to carry out as fierce an argument as possible in front of a referee.

In divorces, for instance, a confrontational legal system can lead to much bitterness. The people who profit most from this are the lawyers, who sometimes have a vested interest in dragging the case out. There is much in life where right is evenly divided and where mediation or arbitration, poorly developed in the English legal system, is a much better approach to settlement.

In a Nepalese village all quarrels are settled outside the court, and in Japan nearly everything is done through mediation or arbitration. The aim of the Anglo-American system is to cut ties, to have a winner and a loser. The aim of many dispute-settlement systems has been reconciliation. Relationships are complex and multi-stranded. People will have to go on living close to each other and interacting in various ways. It is best that their quarrel is smoothed over, rather than settled dramatically in favour of one or the other.

Self and others

19

*W*hy is there inequality?

Dear Lily,

Throughout your life you will encounter the relics of a world where you were treated as second-rate just because you were female. People will not always listen to what you say, they will not always pay you properly, and you may be subjected to indignities that a man would not have to face.

Yet you will also be aware that, compared with most women in the past and present, you are fortunate. Many millions have been assumed to be inferior by birth, to be the mere possession of their family. They have been forced to work and to have children, to wear restricting clothes, to have their bodies mutilated. So you may well wonder why gender inequality is so widespread.

Are men and women the same?

There are arguments that men and women are the same. This causes problems, because they patently are not the same physically and probably differ in other ways as well. On the other hand, if they are accepted as different, then there is always the temptation to build this natural difference into inequality.

In Christianity, with Adam created first and Eve made out of his rib and leading him into temptation, and in some Islamic civilisations, there is a long tradition of the danger associated with women. So religion often tends to suggest the inferiority of women. In much of the eastern half of the Asian continent women have always been seen as inferior. In traditional Hindu civilisation in India, women should be subservient to their husbands and their brothers.

No one has really explained this. Some relate it to the superior ability of men in war and hunting, where strength and aggression are more valuable. But what of the reputed Amazons? Furthermore, in most of these civilisations in the past, a well-armed woman could have defeated a man.

Others say it reflects the relative role of men and women in economic production. They suggest that in societies where women are the main producers of the crops through their work with simple hoes (as in much of Africa), they are often powerful and independent. In societies where men are needed to guard the flocks of animals, or to work with heavy tools such as ploughs, as in India and China, men have the higher status.

There is something in this, but we need to remember that women too can plough – as they traditionally did in northern Spain and Portugal. Also, in Japan and much of China, where the intensive rice cultivation was done with hoes, women were just as important as men in the work. Yet this did not improve their status.

From our own experience we know that the crucial producers, for instance those who worked in the factories and mines in nineteenth-century Britain, were still treated as inferior and expendable. So the roots of the inequality seem to be more than just political or economic.

Again, people have said that the attributed inferiority reflects the way we classify the world. We tend to oppose the cultural world of human artefacts or objects, which are often thought of as male, to the natural world of wild forces. With their bodies supposedly subject to the moon (as in the monthly cycle of menstruation), and their more emotional nature, women are linked to the natural world. Yet all of this seems rather arbitrary and hardly grounds for gross discrimination.

What does seem clear is that women have had their highest status in certain religious traditions that emphasise their direct link to spiritual power, particularly Protestant Christianity and Buddhism. They also seem to have higher status in late industrial societies such as the one now dominant in Western Europe and America.

Women's status is also often high in societies where men are away working, perhaps as shepherds or migrant labourers – as in the Nepalese village where I work, many of whose men went into the army and now go off to work abroad. Recently I visited the so-called 'kingdom of women' in Yunnan, south-western China. There the men traditionally went off for six months of the year to carry goods along the south-west Silk Road to India. The women were left to run the households and the farms and were the central power in the society.

What makes people unequal?

The very simplest societies, those that hunted, gathered and practised agriculture over the planet for a hundred thousand years, were often egalitarian. There were sometimes 'Big Men' and some were richer than others. There were even sometimes captured slaves. Yet there were no permanent divisions into castes and classes.

It was with the emergence of 'civilisation' that real differences in lifestyle and expectations arose. The universal human desire to be 'king of the castle', to dominate in play, to receive the deferential respect of others, to let others work for us, could now be consolidated through the use of new technologies. Those in charge could use superior weapons to enforce their dominance. These included horses, armour, writing, money, law, bureaucracy and even religion.

Because we live in an unusual civilisation which is officially constantly striving towards equality, at least of opportunity, it is easy to forget that throughout almost all of history people have striven in the opposite direction. The general tendency has been for the differences between strata to increase. The basic premise has been that people are born unequal.

On the other hand, the American Declaration of Independence of 1776 stated, 'We hold these truths to be self-evident, that all men are created equal, that they are endowed by their Creator with certain unalienable rights, that among these are life, liberty, and the pursuit of happiness.' Such an assertion would have struck almost everyone who ever lived as complete nonsense. It has been very generally assumed that some humans are by nature better, more intelligent, more gifted than others. Furthermore, no one has unalienable rights to anything.

What kinds of inequality are there?

Inequality expresses itself in different ways. One is 'caste', a term that comes from the Portuguese word meaning 'unmixed/ pure breed'. It is a system that is found in classic form in Hindu India. A person is born into a certain group. Each group has its function: priests, warriors, merchants, farmers. Its meaning lies *in relation* to other groups. This is a hierarchical system of differences which means that one is allowed to have sex with, marry, eat with and even touch the body of only someone within one's group. To do these things outside leads to impurity, spiritual danger and pollution.

A second system is 'class'. This is based on success in life. It is not principally given by blood or birth. It is mainly an economic rather than a religious matter. Some people are wealthier, some poorer; some own the means of producing wealth, others work for them. Often there are three classes, each of which is subdivided. The English are perhaps the most class-divided and class-conscious society in history.

My grandmother was not unusual in thinking of her world as like a large chest of drawers. A few people were in the top drawer; many were in the middle drawers, which were divided into upper, middle and lower (she felt she was in the upper one of these). The drawer at the bottom contained the vast majority of the world, who could be spotted at some distance by their clothes, accents, tastes and hobbies.

The third form of classification is race. This combines inequalities of wealth with ideas of ritual pollution and dirt. A person is not allowed to marry, have sex with, touch or eat with people with skin of another colour, or eyes of a different shape. The extreme case of this was often combined with slavery.

What is the American way?

Outside these is the peculiar system we now try to practise, which we might call the American way. It assumes that everyone is born equal and should have equal opportunities. Yet curiously, with equal chances and equal abilities, some end up very rich, and most end up poor. So there is a paradox.

America, based on the premise of absolute equality, has one of the most extremely unequal divisions of wealth in the world. Japan, based on the premise of inequality, is one of the most egalitarian societies of all.

An added difficulty is that where the society proclaims that it provides equality of opportunity, there is no one else to blame if we end up near the bottom of the pile. In caste systems we may have a lowly position, but that is not our fault. It is written on our brow at the moment of birth.

The strain comes to bear most heavily in our educational systems. If there is no natural inequality, yet people have to be assigned to differently valued and paid jobs, then something other than blood must separate them. So we use education. While we proclaim that everyone is equally gifted, some end up with firsts at a good university, while others leave school with poor grades at sixteen. The latter may bear the double burden of a life with not only far fewer material comforts but also the knowledge that they have 'failed', that they are considered lazy or stupid by the wider society.

Does inequality usually increase?

The normal tendency is towards the reinforcement of both caste and class and the effective enslavement of much of the population. We can see this process at work over much of Europe in the past.

After the fall of the Western Roman Empire some sixteen hundred years ago, much of Europe started with light populations of 'barbarian' peoples mixed in with the remains of Roman civilisation. Slavery had been abandoned and serfdom had not yet started; people were largely free to follow a military leader, work for a patron, or set up on their own. There was little instituted inequality or hierarchy. There were no inherited statuses, little division of labour and task, no huge disparities in wealth and life chances.

If we then look at Western Europe a thousand years later, we see that something extraordinary had happened. As wealth and population grew and more sophisticated technologies were developed, they created great inequalities. The rich and powerful had become superior. Through education and cultural ornamentation they had turned wealth into superior status.

For not only had inequality increased, but much of Europe had become very like a caste society. There were blood differences, that is differences based on birth and enshrined in legal rights. There were the nobility and the ignoble or commoners. There were the free-born and the bound and illiterate peasantry. There were huge gaps between these birth-given orders so that, as in the caste system of India, marriage between the castes was forbidden. Nobles could not marry commoners; a peasant could not marry a bourgeois.

What had happened was that the strong human drive to assert superiority over others, when coupled with new opportunities and tools, had created first inequalities and then hierarchy. The earlier assumption that all men were born equal in the sight of God had given way to the basic premise that some men were naturally superior to others. It was against this that the French revolutionaries in 1789 set themselves, with their cry of 'Liberty! Equality! Fraternity!'

The tendency to drift towards inequality as a civilisation settles down after a period of turbulence can be documented from many other civilisations and periods of history. We see it in various phases of Chinese civilisation, or in the increasing rigidities and divisions of Japan in the seventeenth century.

What was the English path?

There was one notable exception to this almost universal tendency towards inequality and then hierarchy. Although the English to a certain extent moved towards a sort of class system, they did not move towards caste. The basic premise of birth equality had been maintained. There was no legal difference between a gentleman or an aristocrat and a commoner or a farmer. Their children could marry each other; people could move from one status to another through marriage or money in a few years. By the eighteenth century a 'modern' social structure had emerged, in opposition to the increasingly hierarchical path that had been followed by almost all previous agrarian civilisations.

One way in which past writers drew attention to this was in the curious differences in the words given to groups. In France there were definite status groups, named after a mixture of where they lived and what people did. There were the blood-born and superior warriors, the *nobilité*, the religious literate group or *clergé*, the town-dwelling merchants and craftsmen or *bourgeoisie*, and the country-dwelling workers or *paysans*. They were part of the great Indo-European *varna* system which stretches as far as Hindu India.

In England, however, there were strange different labels. In the seventeenth century, for example, no one used any of the above terms or their equivalents. Instead they talked of lords, gentlemen, yeomen, merchants, artificers, husbandmen, of labourers, servants, cottagers, paupers and vagrants. None of these fitted with French categories.

There was nothing like the yeoman in France. The English yeoman was a middling man, who usually lived in the country, but was educated, independent, a voter and a juryman, held substantial property, perhaps did some farming but also might do other things – making, buying, selling. To be a yeoman really meant to be a free and relatively prosperous man. As I sit writing this letter in a seventeenth-century yeoman's house I have a strong feeling of what sort of person he was. There are famous descriptions of him, with silver buttons on his coat, eating good food, sending children to the local grammar school, standing up to the knights of the shire; the 'backbone of England'.

It is a category or class not defined by any particular occupation and which in England existed only in the eyes of others. It had no fixed badges or legal status. People just felt they were, and were regarded by others as, yeomen. Every English village had them, and they were numerous. There has been nothing equivalent elsewhere in the world, though there were hints of something like it in parts of ancient Japan. The kulaks of Russia and the rich peasants of Spain or Italy were different in many respects. If a modern audience wants to appreciate the archetype of the yeoman living in the shires of England, they have only to turn to Tolkien's portrayal of the hobbits living in the shires of Middle Earth. Bilbo, Frodo and their friends are yeomen.

How have some societies avoided caste?

What almost always happens is that as wealth increases, the gaps between groups widen. At first everything is jumbled up and people struggle in a competitive and fairly equal world. The downfall of an empire like that of Rome or the Sung dynasty in China, or a period of upheaval such as the medieval wars of Japan, creates a chaos of confused, overlapping groupings where people fight to survive. As the situation clears and wealth accumulates, the social structure solidifies and small cracks become large fissures which are impossible to leap across. People increasingly live within enclosures; high fences surround them and protect them from other groups.

If a society is imagined as something vertical, then the ladder usually has few rungs and they are far apart and growing ever wider. It is impossible to climb up and difficult to drop down. There are four rungs, as we have seen: the warrior-rulers, literate clergy, traders and manufacturers, and country workers. There may also be outcaste groups who fit nowhere, for example Jews and gypsies. This is the normal tendency towards greater rigidity. Yet it is not the path that led to modern Western civilisation.

For what was odd about the English path was that it did not look like this. There were no 'enclosures', or if there were, the fences round them were so flimsy and constantly broken through that they were almost meaningless. Some elocution lessons could turn a common flower-girl into an upper-class lady, as in Bernard Shaw's play *Pygmalion*. Those within each ramshackle enclosure were no doubt constantly trying to prop up the fences, but then someone would let in another rich trader's daughter or expel a useless son.

In fact there were numerous parallel ladders, each with many, closely spaced rungs. The Church of England is a good example. This was a ladder on its own, mirroring the whole social structure, from the impoverished, poorly educated, hopeless curate in some remote living to the Bishop of Durham or Archbishop of Canterbury, equal to any lord in wealth and status. A very talented, ruthless or cunning individual might climb this slippery ladder.

A parallel ladder could be found in trade and business. From a humble small shopkeeper in a rural village up to the heads of great trading companies, from Dick Whittington when he first arrived in London, with just a bundle on his back and his cat, to his position as a great city gentleman and Lord Mayor, there were hundreds of rungs on this particular ladder. The same is true for the legal, academic, farming, military and office-holding ladders.

Furthermore, one could move up one ladder and then hop across to another, or move one's children up from rung to rung through education. There were countless cases of people who had made a career in one field, say farming or manufacturing, who then moved their children on to another ladder, say the Church or law. There were no true hereditary professions.

This system of ladders means that people are always able to climb up and fall down. Most of us would secretly agree with a man who observed, 'What makes equality such a difficult business is that we only want it with our superiors.' So we concentrate on climbing, as does everyone else, and the system ends up as it is.

20

*W*hat makes us individuals?

Dear Lily,

You are an individual. You act on your own; you have your own rights and obligations. You can practise any religion you choose, vote for whatever political party you like, do whatever job you are qualified for, marry whom you want. You can keep (after tax) any money you earn. Although there are now many people in the industrial and capitalist parts of the world who are in your position, it is still decidedly unusual.

Most people on the planet cannot do these things. They belong to larger groups – the family, caste or village community – who regulate what they think and what they do. This was even more so in the past. Two hundred years ago there was nowhere on earth where you could have been an individual in the way I have described above. So how has individualism, a location of economic, religious, political and social power in the hands of each person, emerged so suddenly and so dramatically?

This is a large topic and a full account would take us into the rise of religious freedom, political democracy, modern industrial organisation and many other areas. Here I will limit myself to the social and economic side. In particular, I will write about the way in which the individual has become separated out from the wider family group.

This separation of the social world of the family from the economic world of the production of wealth is one of the great changes in history and is described as the 'rise of capitalism'. It is particularly relevant to you, since England has often been described as the first capitalist society. In your own country there emerged a new system of individualistic economic and social relationships which now dominates much of the world. How did this happen?

What happened in England?

In the period AD 700–1200 much of Western Europe was uniform. A traveller through northern France, northern Germany, the Low Countries and England would have felt no real sense of contrasting civilisations. There was a relatively light population, ruled by feudal lords and kings, practising a form of Christianity. The people were partially unified by a Latin language and governed by barbarian legal codes mixed with bits of Roman law.

The social system was based on the rather individualistic family systems of the Germanic tribes which gave people much the same roles as the family system today. People were struggling to preserve the vestiges of Roman civilisation and build up a new world. Language apart, English visitors to Spain or Italy would have felt at home.

The society that grew up in Western Europe after the fall of the Roman Empire was feudal, not a family-based one. Its primary bonds were contractual, ones of allegiance and power based on choice, rather than on blood. Between the fifth and twelfth centuries, the collapse of a status-based civilisation gave rise to feudalism.

Yet, from this common base, a curious divergence occurred over the centuries. An almost universal tendency asserted itself. As wealth accumulated, the feudal bonds were loosened and then snapped, and what we can roughly call a peasant civilisation reasserted itself. The details of the process are complex and were uneven over Europe. They included the increasing power of kings, the re-establishment of a centralising form of Roman law, and the growing distinction between a literate class of clergy and nobility and an illiterate peasantry, who were discouraged from learning to read.

Above all it involved the emergence of a form of ownership and production in which the family line again became dominant. The land was given into the private ownership of families. It was owned by them as a group. Every child had birth-given rights in the family property. The unit that produced and consumed wealth became the family. There were real peasants, who stood in opposition to other orders, that is the town-dwellers or bourgeoisie, the nobility and the clergy.

This was reflected in the terminology. In Italy a group known as *contadini*, in Germany *bauern*, in France *paysans*, emerged. Yet there was no such group in England and no native term to describe such a category. There were country men and women, but this only described where they lived. Instead there were many words – husbandman, artificer, yeoman, labourer – to specify status. None of them fitted with the meaning of the word 'peasant'.

Why are there so many peasants?

England was clearly the exception. So why is there such a strong tendency for civilisations to move towards a peasant path? The simplest answer seems to be that it is in the interest of both the rulers and the ruled. To this we may add that the family property solution is in many ways a considerable improvement on what usually preceded it. It works better than communal agriculture or even slavery.

A family-based peasantry is created when the agricultural population are given inheritance rights so that the family as a unit owns the land. Previously families had usually enjoyed very insecure or shared rights, either as members of a larger village community which redistributed use rights from time to time, or holding an insecure tenure granted by large land-holders. Both of these other systems have grave disadvantages for the family. They leave it vulnerable to the tendency for any hard-working person to find that he or she is supporting lazier fellow villagers, or at the mercy of the landlord's whim.

So when the rural dwellers are offered complete ownership of their fields, usually in return for a reasonable tax based on what they can produce, they are hardly likely to refuse. They now own the property and can pass it on safely to their children, who are, in fact, co-owners from birth. They are happy and their children are happy.

The system is often productive and there is likely to be a noticeable improvement in yields. Family members have direct incentives to improve their production which will now benefit them themselves and their close relatives. They can invest in the knowledge that they and their heirs will benefit in the longer run. Effort and intelligent planning are rewarded by increased prosperity for their loved ones, rather than to the nebulous 'community' or a distant landlord.

Meanwhile the ruler is also happy. The production will rise so the taxes will rise. Furthermore, governance will be easier since a mass of peasant families with a deep attachment to the soil can be relatively easily controlled. The family is used as the foundation on which the system works, with the head of the family taking responsibility for the behaviour of his family members.

As in the Confucian or Roman law system, a form of patriarchal power (the power of the senior male) is encouraged. The head of the family rules the younger brothers, the women and the children. Furthermore, in the perennial contest between ruler and over-mighty subjects, a strong peasantry can act as a buffer against the local gentry or lords.

What happens when peasants emerge?

However, there are certain hazards along this usual path. One is that as time passes and the population tends to increase, the position of the peasants deteriorates. The family holding is split between ever increasing numbers of descendants. No one has to leave the holding, but, in the absence of improvements in yield through new technologies, there is less and less per member of the family. The peasants' position deteriorate into that of subsistence farmers where people retreat from the use of money and markets. This is what happened in Ireland in the hundred years before the great famine of the mid-nineteenth century, or in France in the centuries before the Revolution in 1789.

Likewise the rulers tend to make the situation worse. As their power and means of control increase, they are tempted (or with the threat of war forced) to extract more and more from a trapped rural population. So taxes and rents increase. After some centuries what started as an extraction of 10 per cent or so of the crops may increase to up to half the yield of the family farm. The family is trapped in the system.

Another consequence of moving down the peasant path is that alternative paths, whether towards crafts, trade or urban growth, become less attractive. The response to the shrinking of resources, as children divide and subdivide plots and the lords and rulers press their increasing demands, is not to flee or set up new types of activity. These require capital, which would have to be withdrawn from the farm, and are risky. The way out is thought to be to work ever harder and to cut all costs, for example that of keeping animals.

So the peasant path is very attractive to both the rural dwellers and their rulers when it starts. Yet it often becomes more and more bumpy and unsatisfactory over time. It leads, in the end, to a position from which there is little chance of escape. There are no paths down which the densely packed peasantry can now move away from rural misery.

How did the English take another path?

A way out is to move to an even more extreme form of privatisation of property, not down to the level of the family as a group, but to an individual within a family. England moved to such a system of single-heir, individually-held property.

In the English case there was no family-owned land, nor was there community-held land. Over the centuries an unusual system developed whereby there was a combination of two major landholding methods. Between the twelfth and sixteenth centuries, much of the land was held by individuals, not families. It was held on a kind of lease granted by a manorial lord, but in this system there was considerable security. The land could be inherited by whoever one chose as one's heirs, or sold to another, as long as the lord was paid a fee and the transaction was recorded in the manor court.

Alongside this there was freehold property, belonging to the King, but held directly by an individual and to all intents and purposes privately owned. So there was no family property: children had no automatic rights in a holding by their birth into the family unit; the individuals who held the land could dispose of it as they wished within the constraints of the customs of the manor or the laws of England.

In this system the centre was powerful enough to hold each individual in its grip without having to resort to giving families absolute rights. Yet it was also found to be effective to give considerable security to individuals. The absence of the usual threats and pressures of invasion from landed neighbours – because England was an island – was a key factor.

What happened to our sense of Community?

Most of us believe that in the past there were true communities within which people lived. The community came first, the individual second. There were villages or other physical places where a person was born, married and died. It was a community of residence. Since their forefathers had lived there for generations, many of the villagers were related by kinship and marriage. It was a community of blood. There were village organisations, a council, a headman, village customs and laws and a village sentiment. 'We' are of this community; 'you' are an outsider from elsewhere. In extreme cases, as in some Chinese villages, everyone even had the same surname; everyone you met was called Chen or Yan or whatever.

I saw many of these features of what we might call natural or real Community with a capital 'C' when I first visited a Nepalese village in 1968. Many people were surrounded by relatives, and some of the families stretched back for some generations. Even the women, who often married out, retained strong links with their *maita* or birth village. Many people lived out almost all of their life in the village into which they had been born.

Many believe that almost everyone lived in such natural communities until the nineteenth century. Then a revolutionary change occurred, from Community to Association. 'Association' describes our modern world where people are constantly on the move, born in one place, educated in another, married in another, moving several more times before dying. We tend to live with very few kin nearby, and most of our interactions are relatively short-term ones with neighbours or workmates.

Increasingly in large cities or rural commuter villages we do not live in bounded communities. Many people do not feel much about people in their street or neighbourhood. The growth of cities and new patterns of work have created, we believe, the lonely crowd of rootless, drifting, modern individuals.

There is something in this powerful myth of a former close-knit world. When I arrived in a fen village near Cambridge thirty years ago, most people seemed to know each other and there was a sense of the village as an entity. Some of the families were old, and the farming couple who lived next door had been born and were to die in the village. In the course of the next thirty years the village has become a commuter suburb of Cambridge; the blacksmith has gone, and the real shop, two pubs and the village school have all vanished. It is no longer even a ghost of a Community except in its cricket and football teams.

I seem to have witnessed the shift from Community to Association and, indeed, as one of the first outside academics in the village, to have contributed to it. Yet as I feel this nostalgia I have to remind myself that my historical studies of English villages over the last seven hundred years suggest that there have never been real Communities in the 'place, blood and sentiment' sense. Considerable mobility, the fragmented family system and developed economic exchanges have meant that unlike in China, India and much of mainland Europe, it is difficult to find 'natural' communities in England at any point in its history.

So the rootlessness we see today is a very old phenomenon. It is a peculiar feature of England that people have never been absorbed into a very powerful 'Community' which gives security while making it impossible to be a free individual. We live instead in temporary, constructed and partial 'communities' – groups of friends, co-workers, neighbours, club members.

What are the consequences for your life?

So you can begin to understand why, though you live in a country village, grow vegetables and flowers and enjoy the trees and rivers of East Anglia, you are not a peasant and you do not live in a natural village Community. Unlike almost everyone in the world up to about a hundred years ago, you do not belong to a largely illiterate, household-based set of people who pay up to half their income to support a tiny élite who are totally different from you and live in cities and castles. You were not born in the street you live in now, nor will you, in all probability, stay there for more than a few years.

You are not in the absolute control of the dominant male (father, husband, brother) in the household, nor, if you marry, will you ever be under the practical control of the leading female (mother-in-law). You can own property in your own right and sell and give it away as you like. But you cannot automatically expect to inherit from your parents. You will leave home and set up on your own. You are able to make your own way, not tied down within a family or community with all the advantages – and disadvantages – that that brings. Indeed, in all true senses of the words, you, dear Lily, are a free spirit.

$\mathscr{W}$hy do many people work so hard?

Dear Lily,

People usually prefer leisure to labour. Even if they say they like work, it is often preferable to watch others doing it, or to contemplate doing it sometime in the future. Jerome K. Jerome joked, 'I like work; it fascinates me. I can sit and look at it for hours.' So most people have to be compelled to work, especially if, as is usually the case, it is boring and physical. How are people forced to work?

One method is the system of 'free' market relations, labour for wages, which is the one you are familiar with. A second form is serfdom. Serfs have to do certain labour services for their lord and pay animals as a form of rent. They cannot sell or alienate their holdings without their lord's agreement in the manorial court. They are under pressure to have their grain ground in the manorial mill. They have to consult with their neighbours about what crops they will grow. They cannot enclose their strips of land without permission. Often they have to pay a tax if they marry off their children. Sometimes they are not allowed to move from their holding without the lord's consent.

On the other hand they are not slaves. They should not be physically abused by their lord. They cannot be bought and sold. They can own personal property. In other words they are not things, but active and right-bearing human beings, though tied down to a particular place and occupation. Such serfdom existed in England until the fifteenth century when its last remnants mysteriously vanished. In Eastern Europe, it remained the major form of labour condition until the nineteenth century.

Then there is a widespread form of organisation that often overlaps with, but is different from, serfdom. This is family-based or household production. Its central feature is that the compulsion to work is exerted neither through the market (wages) mechanism, nor through direct lordly power (serfdom). It comes at one remove from the lord through the compulsion of the family. There is often an enormous pressure towards hard work, but this comes to bear on the individual through loyalty to the family line. There is also a desperate need to extract a living and pay rents to the lord. This is the characteristic form in much of Africa, India, China and South America, as well as many Mediterranean countries.

A final form is slavery, which is characteristic of ancient civilisations. Here people are bought and sold as goods; they are the property of others and have no rights. The technologies of metals, writing, weaving and ploughing led for centuries to the use of slaves. Rome was the last great civilisation in the West to be based on slavery, the end of an era lasting over three thousand years. There were periods of revival, such as that in the southern states of America, but the system has been dying out. Although there are still many slaves in parts of North Africa, South and Central America and elsewhere, slavery is not the world's way of working any longer.

Both slavery and the family farming system make people unwilling to use animals or machines. It is almost always 'cheaper' to work all hours than to keep capital invested in animals, mills and other machinery. These systems, which covered much of East Asia and India, and to a certain extent Mediterranean Europe, tend to drive out labour-saving tools. Slavery and family labour make human labour a priority. Only a free-market system, and sometimes serfdom, makes it highly desirable to replace humans by machines.

How did we get to our world?

If you had looked at the world in around 1750 you would have seen that much of it seemed to have reached a plateau where it could not get any richer. Indeed, much of it was already getting poorer. With the technologies then known it was impossible to improve the general position of mankind. Nor could the earth feed many more than the five hundred million then living on the planet.

There were, however, two exceptions. One was North America, which was experiencing the fastest economic growth in the world. Its population was tiny and the resources vast. This looked as if it would be a temporary phenomenon once again, for the country would quite soon use up its immense resources of soil and timber. There would be a burst of growth as there had been in China, India and the Mediterranean, and in a century or two America would arrive at the same plateau.

The other exception was England. It had started at a low level, a trading nation sucking in materials from elsewhere. The country had an odd social structure: there was no large poverty-stricken rural group, but rather a large and prosperous, increasingly urban and urbanised culture. It had a highly efficient farming system. For centuries it had grown gradually richer and it was continuing to do so. By the 1750s it was, per head and in terms of energy available per person, the wealthiest and technologically most sophisticated country on earth.

Yet in 1750 it seemed inevitable that even England, in due course, would hit the invisible buffers. The conversion of energy from the sun using plants and animals will yield only a certain amount for humans. Another century of growth, at the most, and then England, like America, would end on a high-level but flat path, another civilisation that could not move in a new direction.

England's special state was plainly visible. People noticed the improving technologies of production, and the interest in wealth creation and scientific discovery. They even noted the increasing use of fossil fuels and the growth of wealth flowing in from the British Empire. Yet no one at that stage could see the impending revolutionary change. For the English had harnessed the power of steam.

Who could have foreseen that the long path of replacing human labour by animals, wind, water and increasingly coal, and doing this through sophisticated machines (especially mills), would suddenly transform the world? Who could have known that what was at first merely a change in scale, a movement along a pre-existing path, almost a natural evolution, would suddenly alter everything and become a revolution?

What did the steam engine do?

The steam engine was only a small adjustment to a device that had been known to the Romans and the Chinese for thousands of years. Hitherto it had had no significance whatsoever. Now the fact that humans could convert coal into energy by way of fire and steam was to alter life on earth.

The human species stopped having to live off supplies of energy from the sun, a current account whereby the sun's energy was converted to human use through living creatures. Instead, it began to draw on an immense deposit account, the energy locked up in fossil fuels. Of course, living off stored energy was not entirely new. Humans had often done this by using the stocks of fish, timber and rich land on new frontiers. Yet in the past they had quickly burned up much of this surface energy.

What the steam engine did was to sit at the top of a funnel which went down into the vast reserves of highly concentrated sunlight that had fallen on the earth over millions of years. The stored energy in the fallen timber had become coal. Later the process was repeated with oil. In each case, the thin trickle of energy available to each person from the sun became a gushing torrent. A world not only of vast energy resources but also of many other side-products in alloys, chemicals and plastics opened up.

We could not have predicted any of this in the middle of the eighteenth century. Even as late as the middle of the nineteenth century many intelligent people could still not appreciate what had happened and its implications. The economic laws that had limited humankind for thousands of years had been temporarily suspended.

This new technology could be exported. But it was not an easy or obvious change: even after the first model of how the industrial system based on steam had been revealed, it took almost eighty years for this success to be repeated anywhere else, in Germany, Japan and North America. The huge momentum of China and India was leading them in other directions, and it was over a hundred and fifty years after the start of the British industrial revolution that a similar change began to happen in those great civilisations. For the move towards industrialisation is not easy, even when there are successful models to follow and much of the technology can be bought off the shelf.

What are the possible paths through time?

It is clear that these various pressures constitute a series of paths. A society or civilisation starts off with new potentials. It has fresh, unused soil and forests, a good stock of animals and knowledge of the technologies of the wheel, fire and simple mills to use water power. Its social structure is fairly firm and just.

Yet, over time, the normal tendency is not towards bettering the lot of the majority or finding new ways to get nature to yield up its goods. The flocks and herds do not increase, the coal seams are hardly exploited, the winds and waters are not increasingly harnessed, the agricultural tools are not decisively improved. A shortage of working capital leads people to borrow against their future harvests at a very high rate of interest. The power of lenders increases and the ordinary villagers become debt-ridden and increasingly impoverished.

We might have expected human labour to be supplemented and hence human material life to be improved. Yet the desire of the powerful to become more so, a growing population's pressing on resources and the fear of shortages constrain people and force them in a direction that is, in the long run, harmful to them and their descendants. This leads away from the one possibility of an escape from agrarian labour.

Unless we understand these powerful paths which lie behind the long-term development of civilisations and become self-reinforcing, we cannot begin to see what has happened in the world. We have to understand that the great civilisations of India, China, Japan and much of continental Europe were heading towards, or had already reached, a high-level path that could not lead towards industrialisation. They were, if anything, moving away from an industrial solution.

Why do humans often give up using animals?

Domesticated animals are the earliest and most effective 'machines' available to humans. They take the strain off the human back and arms. Used with other techniques animals can raise human living standards very considerably, both as supplementary foodstuffs (protein in meat and milk) and as machines to carry burdens, ploughs, lift water, grind grain. Since they are so obviously of great benefit, we might expect to find that over the centuries humans would increase the number and quality of the animals they kept. Surprisingly, this has not usually been the case.

In Japan, domesticated animals were quite widely used in the period up to about 1600. There were large numbers of horses and oxen. After that, as the population grew, the animals were gradually replaced by human labour. By the later nineteenth century there were practically no large domestic animals in the intensive rice-growing areas of central Japan. All the land was being used to grow crops, so there was nowhere for the animals to be kept. In any case, human labour was cheaper.

I saw this same process happening over a very short period of just a couple of generations in a Nepalese village. In the middle of the twentieth century there were large numbers of buffaloes, cows, sheep, goats, oxen and other livestock providing milk, meat and manure and working as plough animals. By the end of the century three-quarters of the animals had disappeared. People could no longer 'afford' to keep them. It was cheaper to hire a man to carry goods up to the village – a five-hour walk up a steep mountain – than to keep or hire a mule.

It was not only in Asia that this was happening. It is possible to see the same pattern over many parts of Western Europe. For instance in France, the animal energy available per head in terms of oxen, horses, sheep and goats was higher in the thirteenth than in the eighteenth century. It seems a law of nature that animals are replaced by humans and that people have to turn from a protein-rich to a carbohydrate diet.

Animals are in many ways a luxury. Only the relatively well-off can afford them. Poverty edges them out. A son will replace a donkey or ox, carrying goods on his back, or dig with a hoe or spade rather than plough with an animal. Domesticated animals have no collective bargaining power.

Why does 'more' often lead to 'less'?

Animals are just one example. The use of wind, water, wheels and gunpowder, rather than increasing as civilisations grew in population and sophistication, tended to decline. Almost everywhere human labour replaced every other form of power. A form of virtual, and sometimes actual, slavery was the answer.

Sometimes this concentration on human labour was increased by the ecological conditions in a civilisation, and particularly by the nature of the staple crop. Some crops, such as wheat, encourage the use of animals in ploughing and of mills in grinding. Others, like rice, encourage the use of humans in planting, weeding, cutting, threshing and husking.

Rice also has the special ability to increase the population size, since the usual law by which, after a certain point, extra work brings less and less reward, is slow to act. Extra children improve the output of rice for a considerable time. Furthermore, much of the fertilising of rice plants is done by natural processes in the water so that less animal manure is needed. The decline of domesticated animals has a less harmful effect than it does with wheat, maize and barley. Growing wet rice encourages hard work rather than the move towards non-human power, that is to say industrialisation.

Rice is such a fruitful grain that it tempts people down a dangerous path, away from progress. Temptation also comes from other plants such as bamboo, which is so wonderfully versatile that it inhibits the use of other woods and metals. Likewise the paper mulberry tree saved much of Asia from having to develop the much more difficult rag-based paper of the West. Yet it was the effort of pounding the rags that helped the development of machinery and water power. So there was a vast difference between a bamboo and paper civilisation, such as China and Japan, and a wood and stone civilisation such as Western Europe.

In Asia, nature provided the raw tools which merely had to be shaped. In the West, nature was stingier and more effort had to be put into making the substitutes in glass and iron and stone. Yet the extra effort and increased knowledge paid off in the longer term.

For most of history, the Asian solution was far more effective in bringing a reasonable standard of living to many millions of people. In the end, however, it was the path through coal, iron and steam that led to our modern world of industry.

That many of us no longer have to labour for long hours in the fields is a merciful release and a giant accident. The changes that occurred on one small island in the eighteenth century constituted the second great productive revolution in human history, equal in impact to the domestication of animals and plants. It is very recent, and it still alleviates the stress of hard physical work only for fewer than half of those who live on this planet.

22

*W*hat made our digital world?

Dear Lily,

You have been watching television since you were a few days old. You started surfing the internet as soon as it became available. You now have your own website and digital camera and can phone almost anyone you like from anywhere. Perhaps you do not need to be reminded of how your life is awash with the effects of information technology and how different all this is from your ancestors' lives. Yet you may not know much about how this extraordinary world came about and how recent it all is.

What is information technology?

For almost all of human history the major way in which humans could communicate was by using their voices or their bodies. This was the age of oral and performance arts.

Then, more than five thousand years ago in the Middle East, people started to develop a simple form of handwriting. So the age of signs and symbols, which had earlier been present in another form in rock painting, developed. This age lasted until two hundred years ago. The only way to capture and pass on information, apart from via the senses, the voice and the body, was by transforming it through the brain in painting, writing or mathematical notation. Most of our great art, literature and science comes from this process. The period is subdivided into two by the development of the movable-metal-type printing press in about AD 1450.

The third age was that of mechanical reproduction. With the invention of photography in the 1830s, it became possible to use machines to gather and pass on information. This age of recorded information has continued up to the present. It can again be subdivided into two phases: the era of the development of photographic and film-making machines, until about 1950, and the electronic or digital era of television and the computer since then.

These three ages of oral, representational and recorded communication, subsplit into oral, writing, printing, photographic and electronic technologies, built on each other. One mode does not wipe out the previous methods, but cumulatively adds to it. So you still use all of the technologies – talking, dancing, painting, writing, printing, photography, television and computers. Each has special strengths and certain weaknesses. Much of the art of modern life consists in deciding which is appropriate in order to learn about the world and to share your ideas with others. The layers of coexisting technology are one of the reasons our world is awash with information.

What is the difference between speech and writing?

Writing is, in many ways, much more powerful than speaking. It eliminates the need for both the speaker and listener to be in the same place at the same time. The reader can now read when she likes, at a distance, and can take up or put down the writing, reread and concentrate and compare versions, make amendments.

The power of writing made world religions possible. Once there was literacy, religious truths could be written down so that we have what are known as the 'religions of the book', that is Hinduism, Buddhism, Taoism, Judaism, Christianity and Islam. There is now a written and definitive version of the standard truths. There is a universal and uniform message from God or the gods. There is a literate priesthood to interpret these truths. There are increasingly firm boundaries between Good and Evil. Religion as we know it is a by-product of writing.

Likewise the economy is based on writing. Accounting, money, credit, taxation, rents, private property, exchange, all of these are virtually impossible to develop without some way of storing and transmitting information outside the individual human mind. The huge trading networks and complex bureaucracies of early civilisations could not have developed without writing. Similarly the presence of writing inaugurated the state. Leaders could now control space and time in a new way and turn tribesmen into subjects. State officials and state organisation all require writing.

The development of law as a separate sphere was made possible by writing. There were legal codes and written precedents; judges and lawyers emerged to interpret and adjudicate. People could leave property through written wills; contracts could be made and witnessed, and written evidence presented in court. Indeed a new concept of an external 'truth', existing outside the biased opinions of individuals and universally applicable, arose. This was the basis not only of law, but also of science.

All of these developments became even more powerful when the Greeks perfected alphabetic, non-pictographic, writing in about 900 BC. Writing no longer took the form of little pictures of reality (pictographs), but became an incredibly powerful symbolic, that is arbitrary but meaningful, tool. With writing, humans could pursue truth and transmit their emotions in an efficient and cumulative way.

What is the Gutenberg Galaxy?

When Johannes Gutenberg invented the modern (movable metal letters) printing press in Germany in the 1450s, it almost immediately changed the Western world. Printing was, in a memorable phrase, the 'gunpowder of the mind'. It caused a vast change in religion, politics, arts and sciences. Here was a way of preserving, exchanging and accumulating information which was as large a leap for humans as today's computer and internet revolution.

Gutenberg and then others very rapidly developed a device for the mass production of identical artefacts. This early mechanical production was applied to the multiplication of ideas. Within a hundred years, printing techniques were vastly improved, and over the three hundred years from 1550 profound changes occurred, leading to the production of colour plates, mass publishing of cheap books, steam presses. Today, in Britain alone, over one hundred thousand new books are published every year.

The appearance of the printing press coincided with and heightened the political and religious divisions in Europe. It is doubtful whether the Protestant Reformation would have occurred without the distribution of anti-Papal texts and Bibles in local languages. Now people could interpret God's message for themselves, reading it in German, French or English, rather than in Latin.

Without the focus on local languages in which the new books were printed, there would not have been the growth of nationalism. Some people started to think of themselves as 'Germans', 'Spaniards', 'Italians' and so on.

At a deeper level there are numerous hypotheses as to the effects of the 'Gutenberg Galaxy' on how humans think. Printing almost certainly changed theories of perspective, of the linearity of truth (in the West we read across or down the page and assume that truth is so read), of time. It undoubtedly altered the way reality is perceived, strengthening the concept of the individual, of the external 'text' which contained truth, of the change and progress and improvement of ideas, of an expanding universe of knowledge.

The arrival of printing in Europe suddenly gave a particular impetus to what we call the Renaissance. Many have suggested that without the multiplication of texts made possible by printing, it would have been much more difficult for the sixteenth- and seventeenth-century scientific revolution to have happened. So it would seem that a relatively simple change in technology was behind much of the political, religious and intellectual ferment in the West since the fifteenth century.

Does printing change everything?

Yet what is surprising is that this is not a feature of printing in itself. The results were not inevitable. Like all technologies, which are extensions of the human body, printing was just another tool. It could be used to enable, promote and maintain revolutionary changes, or it could be used to conserve the *status quo* and prevent change. It did not necessarily lead to fresh ideas. We can see this clearly if we look at the other end of the landmass of which Western Europe is one small tip, at the great and much more ancient civilisations of China and Japan.

In China the press with movable print was invented at least three centuries earlier than in Europe. Books using movable type or woodblock plates, mainly religious texts, multiplied and were printed in enormous numbers. Yet after the first invention there was little advance. There were few major innovations in the next five hundred years. Although the printing and publishing of books grew hugely in Japan and there was more widespread use of books than in any part of Europe, the technology of printing did not change much.

The revolutionary effects attributed to printing in the West, that is political revolution (nationalism), religious revolution (Protestantism) and psychological and intellectual revolution (individualism, ideas of progress, open thought, science), were absent. There was rapid growth in printed matter, but little else.

The Chinese and Japanese cases remind us that none of the effects we see in the West was a necessary result of printing in itself. Printing became the agent of changes which were equally the result of other pressures.

How different are paintings and photographs?

A new era of communication began in the 1830s when it became possible to use a machine to capture a slice of the natural world. The ancient device of the camera obscura, which let light into a dark box through a pin-hole thereby producing an inverted image, was modified. United with chemistry, it produced photographic plates. From this evolved modern photography and, from the 1890s, moving pictures or cinema.

Photographs gave an instantaneous cross-section of reality in ways that not even the greatest artists could achieve. They were multiplied into many copies through books and photo-journalism. Photographs gave permanence to the ephemeral and allowed humans to dissect the almost invisible, revolutionising our knowledge of micro-organisms and disease. The camera shrank and expanded the world, bringing far-off lands close, and allowing humans to capture distant space so that when combined with the telescope it helped us map the universe.

The world began to be seen through glass. Improving lenses made reality sharper and brighter than it had ever been. We became saturated in images which fed our desires and created new ones through advertising. We became tourists of reality, consumers of fantasies.

When these still images were strung together into moving sequences, the power of reproductive technology was further increased, and from the 1930s the addition of sound and colour led to the modern cinema. Films changed our concepts of time and space, became an art form alongside novels, creating powerful fantasies and myths. The effects were increased immensely with the development of television from the experiments of the 1930s.

What is the digital age?

Television is fundamentally different from film, both because it enters our living rooms and because the way the signal works provides a particularly involving experience for human beings. It gives us an instantaneous and highly emotional picture of other lives. It has broken down the boundaries between public and private life, undermined (while at the same time paradoxically highlighting) divisions and inequalities.

As the writer on media Joshua Meyorwitz has put it, 'Television has helped change the deferential Negro into the proud Black, merged the Miss and Mrs into a Ms, transformed the child into a "human being" with natural rights ... It has led to a decline in the image and prestige of political leaders, it has demystified adults for children and demystified men and women for each other.'

Television has turned our diverse and spacious world into a global village, helped destroy communism by showing the advantages of consumer capitalism, and altered the way we see the natural world. Even in the most appalling slums, television brings a little glamour and hope. Yet its effects can also be overstated. While television is switched on for many hours in many homes throughout the world, most people hardly watch it. They just have it on as a background to their lives, like a talkative old grandfather muttering in the corner chair.

When did we start to hurtle through space?

This has been the story of only one strand of communication technologies. You will know that there are many others. One set relates to travel. There have really been two great changes here.

For many thousands of years it was impossible for humans to travel at more than about twenty-five miles an hour (on horseback). Then in the 1830s the first steam trains suddenly rushed people into an era where they were soon travelling at two or three times that speed. The railway system altered life in numerous ways, changing the nature of cities, the patterns of leisure, the concepts of landscape and space, and opening up continents such as North and South America, India and China.

The second great change was the car and plane revolution of the early-twentieth century. With steam-driven ships and now jet-propelled planes, people can move huge volumes of goods (including themselves) at incredible speeds. The love affair with the car, once described as 'the mechanical bride' (or bridegroom), began. The effects are so much with us that we tend to forget them.

I always find it a great shock to reach the limits of the wheel at the top of a valley in Nepal. There I realise I have moved back to a world where everyone has to walk or ride on animals. The recompense is clean air and a sense of time slowing down. The disadvantage is aching arms and legs and a gruelling life for many poor people.

Is e-mail addictive?

Another great change has been in one-to-one electronic communication. Until the middle of the nineteenth century the fastest a message could travel was again limited to the speed of an animal or bird (pigeon post), or, over short distances, a drumbeat. Then, when the telegraph was invented and cables laid across land and ocean, and with the spread of the telephone, the speed increased to thousands of miles per second, the speed of long distance phone calls.

This great leap was made even more powerful at the end of the twentieth century by the unplugging of the phone. Now we are all potentially connected to almost everybody all the time. Physical and social space have become disconnected. We form virtual communities and may be 'closer' to someone in India or China than to the person standing next to us.

These telegraph and telephone connections have been revolutionised by digital connections through e-mail. I remember my resistance to e-mail in the middle of the 1990s when it first appeared. For several years I found it an irritating and threatening new technology. Once I had succumbed, like many people I became an addict.

When it works, it builds on the best features of letter-writing: having the time to deliberate, to change what we want to say; the fact that we do not have to catch the other person's attention directly. Yet it is better than a letter. It is cheaper, much more immediate, gets there very much faster, and you can send pictures and attach documents easily. You will forget that a world existed before e-mail and you will certainly leave far less trace of your life and ideas than we, the last letter-writing generation, have done.

If technologies of information in the past have often had such profound, but unexpected, effects, it is not difficult to imagine how the powerful modern media must be changing our world today. It would clearly be impossible to run a modern economy or society without them. Publishing, newspapers, banks, the Stock Exchange, airports, hospitals, universities would all collapse if the electronic media were switched off. Down to the details of many people's lives – trying to meet friends on a busy platform or ordering shopping on-line – our lives are media-entwined. High-density internet links (broadband) are transforming India and China, as earlier media transformed the West.

And this is just a start. You are standing on the edge of even more amazing advances which it is impossible to predict. I remember being told in the 1970s that one day all the books in the largest library in the world would fit into something the size of a sugar-lump. I was not told that this sugar-lump might then be connected to other lumps of data and all available on a wrist-watch communicator. Nor would I have believed any of this at a time when the largest computer in Britain could not hold what will now fit on to a compact disc. Yet we are now close to that sugar-lump.

How can we survive in the digital age?

Do not forget that swallowing the largest library in the world can cause indigestion. With thousands of websites, television channels, computer games, text messages and phone calls awaiting and assailing us, it is easy to become drowned, to become media addicts in a world of virtual reality. Are there any things I have learnt to help me survive?

One is to try to stick to one medium at a time. There is a temptation to try to absorb too much in too many ways, to enjoy music on our CD Walkman or iPod while at the same time e-mailing someone on our laptop and being interrupted by constant bleeps from our mobile phone and in the corner the TV trying to attract our attention. Add a meal we are trying to eat and some young children demanding our attention and the result is exhaustion.

To a considerable extent we have a very narrow receiving mechanism, and if we try to absorb too many things at once they often conflict. Just the action of talking absorbs much of our random access memory (RAM) as it were, and to try to talk about complex subjects and drive well at the same time – as your granny often reminds me – is pushing my abilities to their limits. This is one of the reasons why people still go to cinemas for good films; it is a total experience and all mobile phones are switched off. Many forms of communication are only really enjoyed one at a time.

A second thing is to try to understand a little not only about how one reads or passively receives a medium but about how it is constructed. The best way to understand the way we are tricked and seduced by television or photography is to learn how to make films (filming, editing) and how to photograph and modify photographs (in the old days developing, now using a computer program). Thousands of lessons at school are devoted to the craft of writing and reading, but we are left largely to ourselves in the craft of how to construct and decode the much more powerful visual media which now dominate our lives.

In some ways this self-education has become much easier. The tendency over past centuries was for individuals to become more and more the passive recipients of media. In early societies, most people would be involved in the creation as well as the appreciation of song, dance, formal speech. But writing, printing and then television tipped the balance towards technologies that create an imbalance between transmitter and receiver.

One major factor was the capital cost of the technical equipment, which reinforced things like producer's monopoly, political control and censorship. In essence it is far cheaper to buy a book or television film than to produce one. A television series I was involved in cost about £200,000 per episode. Few of us have that kind of money to spend.

Yet in the late-twentieth century the first great technological innovation that restores a little of the balance occurred, namely the internet revolution. Although there is now the problem of gaining attention when so much is available on the world-wide web, the new medium does suddenly allow each of us to be a publisher, to make as well as to receive.

We can design a website, put photographs and films on it, become a little broadcasting (or narrow-casting) station. Even if only a few people log on to the website, it is out there and in making it we learn some of the tricks that are constantly used to beguile us. Have a look at my amateur efforts on www.alanmacfarlane.com and you will see what I mean.

On the other hand, there is a downside to this. Like all technologies the internet can be used in other ways. It potentially increases the control of authority over its subordinates, a country's foreign office over its ambassadors, generals over subalterns, directors over far-flung agents. Initiative can be stifled and central power extended.

A final very personal bit of advice. Much stress from media comes from people's staring at screens for hours. After a while we stop enjoying the experience, our minds dull, the problems seemingly insoluble. As the old saying has it, 'Variety is the spice of life.' Never do anything that requires the combined deep concentration of the eye and mind for more than an hour before having a break. After half a day stop entirely and do something entirely different. It is not only your eyes that will benefit. With media, as with so many things in life, less is more.

Life and death

$\mathcal{W}$hat are the limits to growth?

Dear Lily,

If a woman marries at about sixteen, survives until about forty and has regular sexual intercourse, she will, on average, have at least a dozen live births. Even if half of the children die soon after birth, each married couple will leave six descendants. You can see that if this happened for many generations the population would grow very fast indeed.

Human beings, like many animals, have the reproductive capacity to increase their populations in a way that leads to what is often called exponential or non-linear growth. That is to say, it follows a sequence: 1, 2, 4, 8, 16, 32 and so on. The curve of growth becomes steeper and steeper. We can see this happening today. While it took over 100,000 years for human populations to reach six billion, it will only take one further generation to reach nine billion.

What are the laws of population?

Populations in history were periodically decimated by three types of disaster: war, famine and disease. People kill each other and destroy their means of livelihood. Famines and food shortages lead to deaths or to a decline in births; diseases kill.

There has been an alternating pattern in history. Some large accident or invention occurs – a new source of food is discovered (rice, potatoes, maize, herrings) or new ways to grow and harvest plants are developed. There will be a boost to the food supply. Health will improve, people can afford to marry younger, and their infants will survive. There will be a spurt in the population growth. For a time there will be a golden age.

Then, at a certain point, the population will build up to such a level that it will usually trigger what we would now call negative forces. People will jostle up against each other and there will probably be violence and war. They will over-exploit the seas and lands, and a slight shift in weather patterns will lead to famine.

As populations build up they will also face another basic problem. There is a biological law that micro-organisms multiply and vary much more rapidly than long-living species such as humans. Their natural ability to do this means that as human societies succeed in building up their populations, the micro-organisms that predate on them build up and vary even faster.

Their human hosts crowd together and create a rich material culture of other animals, clothing, food, drink and masses of excrement. In these conditions, the normal tendency is for the vectors which carry the bacteria and other organisms (flies, lice, fleas) to multiply. The viruses, which survive only with high population densities, also thrive.

Hence there has been a strong tendency through human history for most diseases to increase in variety and incidence. Humans are the prey and as they increase in numbers, so do the organisms that live in and off them. This is a law that is likely to halt the development of all human civilisations. It did so to an extent in the past with bubonic plague, malaria and dysentery; it may be doing so today with AIDS or something worse.

Often these catastrophes feed off and exacerbate each other. Ravaging armies cause famine and spread disease. The population then collapses with huge suffering. The cycle will then repeat itself. This explains why despite the natural potential for growth, the number of people has grown quite slowly over long periods. It is a dreadful cycle, from misery to misery, with brief periods of happiness between. Given the growth in absolute numbers, each time there is a disaster, suffering is greater, a million people dying in a war or famine rather than a thousand.

Why does more work often lead to lesser results?

We are constrained not only by our biology, but also by a basic economic law which is fundamental to the analysis of why the growth of population does not lead to ever increasing economic growth. The law states that in most situations there is an ideal level of work that can be put into a task. After a certain point, however hard one works, the returns begin to diminish. Five people working on a stretch of land may produce five tons of grain. Fifty people working on the same area will not produce fifty tons, but a great deal less. An essay that is quite good and has taken three days to write will probably not be twice as good if you work on it for another three days.

This law of diminishing returns is one of the keys to the negative effects of continued population growth. Through good fortune or invention humans open up a new resource. The first gains are immense. The fish are plentiful, the burnt-down forest produces excellent crops. Soon, however, the returns on further input of labour begin to dwindle. The cleared forest gives less and less, the marginal lands on the hillsides are less fruitful than the valley bottoms. This means that after a certain point a growing population fails to provide extra benefits. Each new mouth, after a certain number, is a net loss. We live in a finite world with diminishing resources.

Are there limits to energy for humans?

The amount of energy available to humans on earth up to about 1750 was very limited. For almost all of human history the major energy source has been the sun, transformed through plants and animals by photosynthesis into something humans can use for food or heating. Yet plants and animals can appropriate only a tiny part of the energy that flows down to the earth as sunlight. The development of agricultural systems increased the efficiency of this absorption, but still very firm limits were set on the quality and quantity of human life.

Almost all resources on earth, even air and water, are finite and tend to degrade with use. At first, with few people, there was plenty. Millions of years of sunlight had been banked in the soils, forests and oceans on the planet. But many of these resources are non-renewable so that with use they decline in quantity and quality.

Deserts expand, the mountains lose their tree cover, the seas become barren, forests are felled. Humans as they become more successful exploit nature and often wreak havoc on their environment. Within a few generations the resources are used up. The movement of humans from island to island in the Pacific, exhausting each in turn, is but one example. Another is the huge ecological stress in China, North Africa, the Middle East and the Amazon basin. Again and again the returns from nature have started to decline through over-exploitation. Now even air and water are under threat.

One partial response to these ecological and economic

patterns is to improve the technology and thereby tap a new source, or increase the efficiency of energy transformation. Yet this is also a trap. New crops or improvements in old ones (potatoes, rice, wheat, vines) often lead to an increase in yields. Yet the new resource often leads to a dead end.

Thus potatoes trapped the Irish into a situation where they became so dependent that when the blight arrived and aid was refused there was mass starvation. Rice is such a good food that it encourages the growth of dense populations. The dispensing with non-human labour – a movement away from any chance of industrial development – is a likely consequence.

Too much can often result in too little. Resources run out. The problems of initial overabundance, of too rich resources, are as much a trap as underabundance. They often lure populations down a route that, when it reaches its limit, is impossible to escape from and leaves people particularly exposed, as we may find with our current dependence on oil.

What hope is there?

You can see in what a fragile and contradictory world we live. We compete with other species and often we have been too successful and eliminated them entirely. Yet there are others, especially microbes, that are more effective than us. We are largely composed of bacteria and surrounded by quickly evolving viruses. Although we now have a growing understanding of these through the developments in genetics, this is not a final triumph. One day micro-organisms will eliminate, or greatly diminish, the human species, just as we have eliminated or diminished others.

Another constraint is energy. The first law of thermodynamics is reassuring since it reminds us that total energy is constant and irreducible. Yet the second law describes the actual world in which we live where energy dissipates, becoming less concentrated and hence less useful. We temporarily overcame some of the constraints on the amount of energy available when as a result of the industrial revolution we started to use stored carbon energy. The development of high-temperature superconductivity, of nanotechnologies, of more effective use of solar energy, may again delay the final outcome. Yet such tactics cannot postpone it for ever.

Or perhaps we will have too much energy and so we will pollute our world beyond recovery. All human activities, that is the manipulation of atoms and the use of energy, cause 'externalities'. Everything we do tends to leave a deposit, even if it is only temporary (like sound pollution) and relatively harmless.

We can see this in garbage, in water and land pollution, and through the use of insecticides and fertilisers, genetic engineering and the production of greenhouse gases. We all know that the more energy we use and the more of us there are who are living at a high standard of material consumption, the more these problems will grow. One way or another, either a shortage of the energy we can tap, or the damage caused by the release of that energy, is very likely to trap us.

So we shall find ourselves caught in the law of diminishing returns. We will try, being a creative and energetic species, to overcome these problems. We will dig away furiously in order to try to escape from the traps we find ourselves in. It is impossible to predict whether these attempts will lead us to new frontiers in the stars or into rapid extinction.

24

Why do so many people starve?

Dear Lily,

In almost every civilisation, sooner or later large numbers of people starve. I am not talking about malnutrition or seasonal shortages, which are almost universal in agricultural societies. Famine is different in degree and kind, a particularly awful kind of catastrophe.

Famine refers to a state where people actually die of hunger or hunger-aggravated diseases. 'They that die by famine die by inches.' People's emaciated bodies suck up the reserves of fat – a horrific way to die. There have been great famines in India, China, Russia and Europe, and now the land of frequent famine is Africa.

What causes famine?

The case of Africa reminds us of some of the most frequently cited arguments to explain famine. These are variations in weather (usually too much or too little rain), war and political dislocation, pests, low prices for crops, corruption and poor communications. There are also, as in many countries in the past, local tolls which prevent the movement of food except at very high costs. Yet while all of these may be important, we have to look a little deeper to understand the almost universal tendency towards famine in agricultural civilisations.

In the majority of societies famine is related to overpopulation. The size of the population increases as a result of a temporary improvement in resources. For a while there is relative plenty. Then demand begins to exceed supply and people are even more vulnerable to food shortages.

Changing from several types of crop to just one can be disastrous. The wide variety of crops and livestock which provide a buffer for people in difficult years is replaced by just one. Everyone grows potatoes, or rice, or wheat, or cotton, or coffee, and little else. When that crop is threatened there is nothing much to fall back on.

Another cause of famine is the widespread tendency for the strong to prey on the weak, to extract from them as much of what they produce as possible, so that most people live with their noses just above the water of disaster. In bad years they drown.

This is a world-wide situation: the pressures of lenders to extract from borrowers are international. The rich countries of the world have lent large sums of money to the poor, and now much of the prosperity of these poorer countries is being sucked out of them in interest payments. The activities of the International Monetary Fund and the World Bank are often criticised for supporting this unfairness. They are accused of putting enormous pressure on developing-world countries to drop their customary agricultural methods and to specialise in crops that then cannot compete against the subsidised crops produced in richer parts of the world.

Often the family in its desperation preys on itself, its members driven to ever harder and lower-paid work, replacing animals and other labour-saving devices by their own labour. As these processes work through time, almost everywhere in the world we see vast areas of poverty. If there is a small variation in politics or weather, disastrous famine often ensues.

What should we do if famine threatens?

An obvious thought is that 'the government should do something about it'. Yet many argue that the amount of damage caused by government interference outweighs the positive effects. They suggest that the so-called 'laws of the market' be allowed to operate. If there is a scarcity, the shortage will raise the price of that commodity: for example, if wheat is scarce, more will then be produced because it is worth producing, and in due course the shortage will automatically be corrected.

On the other hand, government efforts to force farmers to sell their produce cheaply can have a disastrous effect. The grain-producers and merchants hoard their grain for later sales. They also tend to produce less of a commodity from which they gained little or no profit. So, they argue, government interference causes famines rather than mitigating or preventing them.

This theory was reasonable in the context of the commercialised agricultural systems that existed in eighteenth-century England, Holland and North America. Unfortunately it does not work everywhere. When it was applied in Ireland in the 1840s or Bengal (India) in the 1940s it led to disaster.

There are several flaws in the theory when it is applied beyond highly developed commercial economies. One lies in the nature of how food is produced. It may often be the case that over a few years market prices will encourage more production of a particular crop. Yet for those who are starving to death it is not possible to wait for a few years until more grain is planted and harvested.

The theory also assumes the kind of geography, ecology and good water communications found in Western Europe. When there was a threat of famine here in the past one region could supply another since the areas with acute shortages were quite local. This does not apply to the huge stretches of monoculture found in land-locked areas of India, China or central Europe. Wheat or rice or maize is almost all that is grown for hundreds or thousands of miles. There is no way it can be replaced from a nearby area if the harvest fails. So people will starve to death.

In Bengal in the 1940s and Ethiopia in the 1980s, there were foodstuffs available, either in stores or at the end of railway lines. Yet there was no market mechanism available to 'draw' them to the starving. In such situations, ordinary people lack the economic power (money) to pay for the food. They may clamour outside the warehouse, but no one is going to give valuable grain away for free. So they starve. The laws of supply and demand do not work because although there is huge 'demand' in one sense (starving families dying in agony) there is no *effective* demand because the starving families have nothing to bargain with.

'Work for food' programmes, the artificial creation of some bargaining power for very poor people, is one solution in a situation where most people have never really entered fully into a market system. Only by making them commercial consumers, giving them 'coupons' so to speak to start them off, can they be given the chance to rise above an impoverishment where they have nothing that the food-producers want, not even their bodily labour.

These two major arguments as to what should be done to prevent or alleviate famines refer to different cases. One analysis works reasonably in the historical English context, where the population was well above subsistence level, where the market forces operated reasonably, where shortages were relatively local and ways of carrying bulk goods like grain were well developed. The other analysis applies to situations where there is food available but the poor starve because they do not have the means to pay for it.

Neither of these theories, however, is applicable to most famines in history, where there is an absolute shortage of food over a larger area. There is no food, even if there were money to buy it. The available technology and crop patterns do not produce enough to feed the population in a difficult year.

Here the only escape is through much longer-term planning and the creation of a proper system of diverse agriculture, proper communications and decent storage and of a society where people live well above subsistence levels. Yet how can this possibly be achieved?

When did the first escape from famine occur?

On the eve of the industrial revolution, just two hundred years ago, most people in Europe, Asia and Africa lived close to famine. Yet in England, a different situation had emerged. While even close neighbours, Scotland, Ireland, France, were still famine-prone, England had somehow escaped from the normal tendency. How had this happened?

The extraordinary fact, which everyone began to notice from about the fifteenth century, was how affluent the rural dwellers of England were. Highland Scots and French, Italian and Spanish peasants were often poorly dressed, fed and housed and very often overworked and ill. Yet many of their English counterparts wore reasonable clothes and good leather shoes, ate a good deal more protein, drank beer and ale, lived in reasonable houses and worked moderate hours.

Ordinary housing can be taken as just one example. England is the only country in the world where the houses of ordinary villagers of the fourteenth to seventeenth centuries have survived in large numbers. As I sit writing this in a village farmer's house which has changed little for over three hundred years, I can see that the old houses still provide a comfortable and spacious environment for affluent country men, even in a relatively poor area of the Cambridge fens.

The relative affluence of the English can be seen from their eating habits. They have been able to let their wildlife teem around them. They cherish songbirds, leave much of the flora and fauna on their beaches untouched, do not like the idea of eating their horses or things like snails and frogs.

I still remember my amazement when I went to a beach in France and found many people combing it for tiny creatures and seaweed of a kind that were left untouched on the beaches of my childhood in England. I also remember my feeling of sadness as I walked through the silent woods of France and Italy, where no bird sang or animal moved.

Of course there were exceptions to this picture. There were some who starved on the streets in England. Yet by the eighteenth century, while almost all the country people of Europe and Asia had reached a level only just above subsistence, many of the English were modestly affluent. Famine was a thing of the past, as it has recently become in much of China and India.

Are famines inevitable?

How the divergence between a few fortunate societies and others occurred cannot be explained from within the framework of a discussion of famine. The immediate cause of famine is food shortage, but food shortage is just a symptom of other things. The conditions that lead to the shortage are cumulative, just as the escape from famine is the result of cumulative changes. We can see this in the second half of the twentieth century.

Africa did not, on the whole, suffer from famines in the 1960s, while India and Bangladesh did. Now, despite terrible droughts or flooding, India and Bangladesh seem largely to have escaped from famine, while parts of Africa have almost perennial famine. Perhaps the climate has changed, but ultimately the reasons for these shifts are only partially related to that. Famines are ultimately man-made, even if they may be precipitated by nature.

Nor are famines directly and inevitably the result of absolute numbers of people. When China or India had half or a quarter of their present population they had serious famines. There are now many more people and yet no famine. It was sparsely-inhabited Highland Scotland, not relatively densely crowded England, that had famines in the eighteenth century.

Ultimately the presence or absence of famine is about human relations. Great inequalities breed famine. If, as in England, property is secure, people will benefit from their own work and from their own creative improvements. A large middling group will expand and absorb more and more people. Then a world where famine is only a distant memory can begin to emerge.

In the case of Africa today such a virtuous circle could be created, but only after a careful analysis of all the potential traps these countries face: disease, poor soil, inadequate communications, political instability, the conditions attached to aid programmes, the policies of the international agencies. The difficulty is that all the traps have to be avoided simultaneously. It is not enough just to improve agriculture, or education, or to provide political stability or to minimise malaria and AIDS.

The whole package or system has to be altered; open politics, security of property, these and many other assurances are needed. This is not easy when much of the wealth and attention of the world is devoted to attacking hidden threats of supposed terrorism or absorbed in making weapons for the lucrative arms trade.

25

*W*hy are we diseased?

Dear Lily,

The world, including the human body, is full of tiny organisms. When there are either too many or too few of them they can be harmful to humans. These include those without life such as viruses and prions, as well as the vast array of bacteria and similar living micro-organisms.

Some diseases are with us all the time; others suddenly sweep across the population. Endemic diseases, such as malaria, dysentery, leprosy and the common cold, are present all the time. Epidemic diseases, such as influenza, measles, cholera and plague, burst out suddenly for a few months or years, then usually subside when their hosts have been destroyed.

There are four main ways in which major diseases spread. There are bacterial diseases which are carried into the body through the mouth, in contaminated food and drink. The various forms of dysentery, typhoid and cholera are examples. If we are to understand how these types of disease change over time, we need to look at human eating, drinking and cooking patterns and the ways in which human and other excrement is dealt with. A change such as eating a new foodstuff or installing a new sewage system can alter the pattern of these diseases.

Then there are the vector-borne diseases which are 'injected' into parts of the human body by creatures like fleas, lice, mosquitoes, flies and other insects and snails. Major diseases of this kind are plague, typhus and malaria. These are affected by housing, clothing, footwear and bodily hygiene.

There are also diseases that spread through bodily contact. These include leprosy, venereal diseases and various skin and eye diseases. A new one is AIDS.

Finally there are air-borne diseases, viruses that travel short distances when people cough or sneeze or just breathe, such as smallpox, measles, tuberculosis and influenza. These are very difficult to protect against, as are a number of other diseases whose causes are little understood, such as various forms of cancer.

Why do diseases become more deadly?

Early successes in increasing human resources in the past led to denser populations in large cities and a more congested countryside. This situation would provide sufficient population density for viral infections such as influenza, smallpox or measles to be sustained and spread. It would also lead to increased dirt and pollution of water supplies which would raise the levels of diseases such as cholera, typhoid and dysentery.

When war or famine occurred, the final death toll would be accounted for largely by the deaths from diseases afflicting a weakened population. As the population built up, cities and towns would become slaughterhouses, gobbling up immigrants who died of the diseases of crowding.

Until very recently this seemed an inevitable tendency. Human populations could reach only a certain density before automatically creating a situation where numbers were cut back again by one disease or another. The rise and fall of ancient civilisations, as well as the collapse or stationary state of many European and Asiatic societies at various times in the last thousand years, can be accounted for by the ravages of disease. No escape from this pattern seemed possible.

Did we have to wait for modern medicine?

Many aspects of the history of the rise and fall of diseases up to the present are still a mystery, but one or two things are plain. There seems to have been a dramatic improvement in health in England from about the middle of the eighteenth century. One feature of this was the disappearance of recurring bouts of plague.

By 1750 it seemed clear that in both England and Western Europe as a whole plague had disappeared, bringing an end to constant anxiety about this horrific disease. Yet no one really knows why, after 1665, plague suddenly vanished within about ten years.

The fact that bubonic plague vanished within a few years over all of Western Europe suggests that the disappearance cannot have been caused primarily by a change in the type of rat (from black to brown) which in any case occurred fifty years later. Nor is it possible that all over Europe there was a dramatic change within a few years in the nature of the fleas or the bacillus, in housing conditions, standards of living, clothing or climate or in any of the other factors usually cited.

Some of these may have contributed. Yet the only plausible pan-European explanation is that the periodic entry of plague through shipping from Turkey was prevented by the quarantining of ships when they arrived in Western European ports.

Another significant change in England was the rapid decline of malaria. It was noted that in 1700 about one in twenty of the London population died of malaria. By 1800 malaria was unknown as a cause of death in the city. The previously heavily malarial regions of East Anglia and the Kentish and Sussex marshes were no longer centres of danger.

Again we do not really know why this happened. The explanation that it was due to improved drainage, better houses, or changes in animal husbandry is not convincing. All that is certain is that while southern Europe and particularly Italy were becoming more malarial, England in the eighteenth century became almost free of this disease.

A third change concerned smallpox. Smallpox did not disappear, and there is much argument about whether early vaccination had any positive effect. But this disease certainly began to infect and kill different people. By the 1750s smallpox affected mainly children and in many cases did not kill them.

Why did fewer babies die?

Dysentery, along with malaria, is the greatest killer in history. One of the main ways harmful micro-organisms enter the human body is through the mouth, particularly in the two to four pints of liquid that every human has to absorb daily in order to stay alive. A couple of pints of liquid could contain enough dysentery bacteria to kill the inhabitants of a small city. Almost all liquids that humans drank in the past, particularly milk and water, were contaminated.

People with dysentery evacuate the micro-organisms in their faeces; these micro-organisms then pass on to hands and clothing and, in particular, enter the water supply. Others become infected. At least half the infant deaths in most societies in the past were caused by infant diarrhoea which dehydrates the body.

As a population grows denser it will pollute the water supplies with human excrement. London, a city that grew hugely in the eighteenth century, was a classic example, and dysentery rates should have been soaring as the population increased. Yet from about the 1740s there was a reversal of this trend. Mortality from dysentery had risen until nearly the middle of the century and then, suddenly, it started to fall. This meant that the largest city on earth enjoyed relatively low rates of infant and adult dysentery. This was one of the greatest reversals in human history. How had it been achieved?

Again we do not know for certain. All we do know is that all the conventional explanations – that it was due to improvements in medical knowledge, in hospitals and in the treatment of disease, or to changes in the nature of bacteria, in the food supply, in public sanitation and hygiene and in housing – are unsatisfactory. Many of these did not occur at all. Those that did were not significant enough to explain the change.

What did people drink?

What we need to do in solving the problem of this escape from the dysentery trap is to ask what the English were drinking from the 1740s. If they had been drinking water, then a rise in dysentery (in the absence of water purification and proper sanitation) would have been the result. In fact the majority of people did not drink water. In England the usual drink had become tea.

Tea became the staple drink of the English in the middle of the eighteenth century. The boiling of the water to make tea killed many of the dangerous amoebae and bacteria. Furthermore, the tea contained a substance called tannin (phenolics) which is one of the most powerful antibacterial agents known to man. Typhoid, cholera and dysentery bacilli when placed in even a cold cup of tea will be destroyed within a few hours. By drinking tea people wash out their mouths and stomachs, ingesting a liquid that is not only sterile (because of the boiling) but also a powerful antiseptic.

The Japanese, and before them for some centuries the Chinese, had benefited from this, and now the British too began to enjoy the healthful effects of tea. It was largely an accidental benefit, for tea was drunk mainly for its taste and invigorating effects. Yet the accident led to the escape from one of the apparently unavoidable death traps. Even infants, drinking the phenolic-infused milk of their mothers, benefited from the practice.

What other reasons are there for the decline of disease?

England did not suffer from any successful large-scale foreign invasions for almost a thousand years. It did not endure totally devastating civil wars. Famine and food shortage were less severe than in most agricultural societies. The standard of living for the majority of the population was well above subsistence level. This meant that many people in England in the past, at least compared with rural workers in many civilisations were relatively well fed, clothed and housed and did not overstrain their bodies in manual labour.

Thus, through a set of interconnected, and often accidental, features, the normal tendency to more sickness as population grows was temporarily avoided. This was not through a triumph of medical science or the accident of bacteriological or climatic change. It seems largely to have been a side-effect of social, economic and political institutions which had created an unusually stable, modestly affluent and well regulated population.

The English could still be subject to new diseases, for example cholera and influenza, just as we are subject to AIDS today. Yet England was starting to escape from an almost universal path. This path had always in the past meant that the efficiencies created by a larger number of people living close together in cities and small towns led to a health disaster.

The modern rise in population transformed a sickly, war-ridden, famine-prone world of half a billion into our present one. In theory, it is possible for twelve times that number to live in relative peace and plenty (though perhaps only half of the world's population actually do so). This was unimaginable in 1750. Yet it has happened. The first phase of this had occurred in England by 1800. The second would follow from the later nineteenth century when a truer understanding of micro-organisms was reached and effective treatments for many of the major killers developed.

Yet the story is far from over. The spread of many new diseases (AIDS, SARS, MRSA), the return of old ones (malaria, tuber-culosis) and the growing resistance to antibiotics reveal the continuing struggle between species. Humans are predators on many other species. They are also an easy prey for microbes.

There is still enormous suffering from disease. Better food, better water supplies and better sewage systems – which could be installed throughout the world for a tenth of the cost of current production of weapons of war – would halve the rates of many types of illness. An observer from another planet might be puzzled. As a species we prefer to put our resources into threatening and killing each other rather than devote our attention to alleviating the pain that blights millions of people in their disease-soaked lives.

26

*W*hy have children?

Dear Lily,

In an insecure political environment, the family group is often the only protection. The more children a person has, the better. In an insecure social environment, the only people we can trust and be relaxed and honest with are close relatives. So the more relatives one has, the merrier. Having many children adds to a woman's standing in the community and increases the prestige of the group in general. It helps to overcome feelings of loneliness and isolation.

In most civilisations, much of economic production depends on human muscle power, so the more workers the better. Crises are frequent; sickness, accident and loss of home or livestock are always feared and in such predicaments only family can be depended on. A person spreads the insurance against risks by investing in people. This is far safer than hoarding money which can be stolen.

Family members are particularly essential as an insurance for old age where there are no pensions and few social services or hospitals. In such circumstances, without sons and brothers a man (or woman) is at high risk. All this encourages large families. The joys and pleasures of children is another attraction. There is also the biological drive and the pleasure of sexual intercourse.

The desire to have as many children as possible is both reflected and reinforced by the family and religious system. In most societies a great emphasis is put on the family line. The ancestors are important and still interested in their descendants. They require people to keep their shrines attended and a child (often a son) to carry through an effective funeral ritual.

Even God or the gods are concerned that a person has offspring. The fertility of animals, crops, humans and spirits all becomes intertwined. Continuation of the society and continuation of the family and the individual are all linked in popular thought. The Chinese used to have a saying, 'The lack of filial piety to one's ancestors and family is seen in three ways; the first and most serious is having no child.'

Is it difficult to have many children?

Many infants die at birth, others in childhood, women in childbearing, men in work and war. In order to ensure even a couple of living male descendants, given such risks and the unpredictability of the gender of infants, a family will need to use every device available to maximise fertility.

Girls will be married off at, or before, sexual maturity. Those families that do not have the right number of heirs will adopt them from other kin. This is a world of enormous pressure on the individual and family to produce as many children as they can.

For thousands of years this pressure has been felt in the majority of human societies. It tends to produce large numbers of births balanced by high numbers of deaths. In good years births dominate, then a crisis occurs and the gains are wiped out by war, famine or disease. Despite this crisis, the family and the society, having built up a surplus, survives.

The fact that a number of these crises are partly precipitated by the preceding high fertility is not appreciated, or, if it is, seems unavoidable. Heirs are generated in excess to protect against crises which are partly caused by the overproduction of heirs.

This is a situation we find almost everywhere in the past. It is a pattern of high birth and death rates which has profound implications. Any resource improvement, a new crop or technology, will almost inevitably soon be swallowed up by rapid population growth. A more precarious situation is the outcome. Yet, given the interlocking set of pressures, it is difficult to see how individuals or families can behave otherwise. Political alliances, social status and co-operation, economic production and religious merit, all are dependent on having large families.

Indeed, over time, the situation becomes more difficult. Any success in overcoming an obstacle will lead to greater population. This then feeds back into increased political risks, higher mortality from the diseases of crowding, and a larger number of priests and elders to tell people that their spiritual salvation requires that they have many descendants. In particular, as more human labour becomes available, it characteristically becomes cheaper, driving out alternatives such as animals. Diet deteriorates as meat and milk are replaced by cereals, and the strain on the human body increases. More children to labour in the fields are needed.

Why have fewer children?

The puzzle is why people sometimes want fewer children. Some argue that there is a three-stage sequence. In the first period, high numbers of births and deaths more or less balance each other. In the second period, the number of deaths falls dramatically. After a period of very rapid population growth there is a drop in the number of births. Deaths and births balance each other at a new, lower, level.

Reasons for the move to the final stage are crude but plausible. The number of deaths is reduced by external factors – a vaccination campaign or clean drinking-water system in a developing-world country, for example. After a few years of experiencing children surviving in larger numbers, people begin to realise that they do not need so many in order to ensure heirs. So they limit their fertility.

Are there cases that do not fit?

In the seventeenth and eighteenth centuries, in a few parts of Europe such as Norway, Switzerland and England people were not reproducing at the 'natural' level. Some were not having children at all; most women were marrying some eight to ten years after they had reached childbearing age. All this in a period when there had been no obvious medical or sanitary revolution.

There is no real evidence that England ever had a high birth and death rate. Instead it seems that the number of children was controlled by conventions that encouraged late and selective marriage. There is no evidence that, apart from the higher aristocracy, women married in their teens. On the other hand there is evidence throughout the ages of quite large numbers (perhaps up to a quarter) of women never marrying at all.

In England there was no possibility of legal adoption until the later nineteenth century. There is no need for descendants to ensure a prosperous afterlife and no worship of ancestors. There is no inspection of the bride to see if her childbearing potential is unsullied. There is no special interest in having large families. Women's status has never been dependent on how many children (particularly sons) she has. Men's power and authority have not depended on kin. Children were historically of only minor importance, in crises or old age. Children were ultimately, as one person put it, 'pretty things to play with', an antecedent of modern consumer durables or pets.

What part did marriage play?

Whereas marriage and having the maximum number of children are 'natural' in most societies, in England they have been turned into matters of choice and conscious weighing of advantages. There are arguments for and against getting married and we find them throughout English literature from the earliest fragments of poetry. These arguments are given particular expression in the system of romantic love which I described in another letter.

This peculiar and long-term English pattern which ties marriage to love and makes children an option, a cost as well as a benefit, is not easy to explain. The key lies in the way in which biology is linked to other forms of continuation of the society, that is to say the reproduction of power (politics), wealth (economics) and spiritual status (religion). If all of these are closely linked together, then in order to reproduce them, the production of human beings will be emphasised. If there is little or no connection, an individual can decide whether he or she wants the pleasures of children.

Almost everywhere, the family is the foundation upon which society is built. Whether in India, China or elsewhere, much of the political, social, economic and ritual world is based on family ties. What is odd in the English case is the separation of these different spheres. The political and legal system, developed from Anglo-Saxon England onwards and maintained to this day, has not rested on the family but rather on abstract relations between those living within a state, subjects of the Crown. The political and legal security of the English has been mainly guaranteed by contractual links and not by birth and blood.

There have been few economic pressures to breed. As today, historically there was a downward flow of wealth through the generations. Children cost money and time to raise, train and marry off. Children are always costly, of course, but in England unlike almost everywhere else they could not then be depended on to return the expenditure. They, in turn, could not automatically expect to receive anything from their parents. At any point a parent could decide to leave his or her property to a chosen heir and, if necessary, exclude one or all of the children.

Nor was economic production based on family labour. There might be, as there are today, family firms. Yet the normal work-force consisted of a group of fellow villagers, manorial tenants, apprentices or servants, hired workers. The work-force was recruited on the basis of market forces, not family ties. There was no institution similar to that in China, India and many parts of Mediterranean Europe whereby parents and their married children, or one married child, jointly owned and produced as a family enterprise. Nor did brothers and their wives co-own and co-produce.

Once a person had left home or married he was economically, as well as politically, independent. Thus there is no evidence from Anglo-Saxon times onwards of those extended families that appeared over much of Europe in the later Middle Ages and which are the dominant form in Eastern Europe, China and India.

Finally, spiritual reproduction was not linked to the family. There might be family prayers or even, among the wealthy, a family chapel. Yet for the vast majority, and particularly after the Reformation of the sixteenth century, religion was largely a private matter. Christianity in general set its face against any acknowledgement of a link to dead ancestors. Then as now, even for the rich, the memorial services and feasts held by descendants were not expected to bring blessings or avert wrath, but merely to be a thanksgiving and remembrance.

Heaven is not barred to those who do not have a son to light the funeral pyre (or instruct the crematorium attendant how to dispatch the dead). Parents are as little concerned with their children's religious beliefs as they are with their political and economic opinions. The sins of the father are only indirectly visited on their children through loss of income or bad upbringing. The sins of the children are not visited on their parents.

This has always been unlike the situation in most societies. For instance, in ancient China nine generations of a family were to be executed for a serious crime committed by one member, often involving hundreds of individuals from the great-grandfather's generation down to the great-grandchildren of an accused individual.

With chastity so cherished by Christians, it seems clear that God has little interest in whether a person has children. Indeed sexual intercourse and childbearing are widely considered a second-best, a fall from grace, a sometimes necessary but unfortunate effect of our fallen nature. If possible, abstain from sex and marriage; if not, then marry and have children; this is the message of Christianity.

How did choice become possible?

So the political, social, religious and economic worlds were split apart and dealt with by different institutions. The market as a separate institution with its own rules was already beginning to be developed in England over a thousand years ago. Political life and legal matters were also partially segregated, as were religious and ritual activities. Each had its rules largely independent of the family. The family gave comfort, companionship, meaning, love and child-rearing support, as it does today. Yet it was not the building-block out of which society was constructed.

Where society continues free of other pressures, people can respond in an unusual way to changing circumstances. If there are strong demands for human labour and reasonably-paid jobs are plentiful, people are optimistic and there may be a rise in fertility, as there was in the later eighteenth century in England. People feel that they can 'afford' to get married and have a child. In many ways childbearing is like house-buying and the demand for mortgages: when the economy is booming and confidence is high, a house and children seem inviting.

On the other hand, when the economy is flat or in decline, or people start to want goods rather than children, then the number of babies per family starts to drop. Consumerism may lead couples to prefer cars or holidays to children. Women may decide not to get married at all or to postpone marriage and childbearing until some later date.

This is a very different attitude from that in the majority of societies where having children is encouraged for everybody. Yet it is an attitude that is sweeping across the world as part of the package of individualism, consumerism and capitalism. Many people now feel that they can 'afford' only one or two children.

Body and mind

27

What makes us feel good?

Dear Lily,

Amidst all the numerous pressures, frustrations and injustices which I have described in these letters, humans still survive and sometimes glory in their world. They create masterpieces and feel intensely. I will tell you now in a different kind of letter of a few of the things I have discovered about the pleasures of our senses.

Our senses stir us to our greatest efforts and our greatest achievements. Yet they also entrap and ensnare us, lulling us, diverting us, overpowering us, compelling us away from freedom and creativity. Even the tools we create to heighten our enjoyment of them – styles in art, music, cooking and many arts and crafts – can soon become cramping and inhibiting, creating ruts out of which it is almost impossible to escape.

Why does smell enchant us?

As I write this in late May our garden is filled with the scent of flowering honeysuckle, and the first yellow roses are out as the lilac dies away. The Japanese tea-house in which I write has the memories of rich incense that we have burnt and the aroma of green tea. This evening the smell of onions and tandoori chicken will fill our house.

Smells give us a vast amount of pleasure, even if we are not as sharp-sensed as a dog or a tiger. Developing the pleasures of smell, suddenly being wafted back to other places, times and people, all these enrich experience. They carry us in an instant across space and time. The smell of a particular herb takes me in a fraction of a second to the Philosopher's Walk in Kyoto, Japan, or to a hot terrace in the Nepal Himalayas.

The sense of smell has been developed more intensively in some cultures than in others. An extreme case are the Japanese. In the eleventh-century novel about Prince Genji there are frequent scent-guessing competitions. The Prince himself can be smelt well before he enters a room because of his particular exquisite mix of scents. The military rulers of Japan tradition-ally stored their wealth in precious incense sticks, rather than in gold. Apart from gold, the most precious gifts that the three wise men could offer to the infant Jesus were frankincense and myrrh.

Yet we are hardly conscious of how smell affects us. Body smells of loved ones, the fragrance of newly-cut grass, the aroma of wood-smoke evocative of summer barbecues or winter bonfires, all these are parts of a rich tapestry of almost invisible pleasures. Likewise we are warned of danger by smells that disgust us, like those of rotten meat or faeces. Every age, every culture, every group selects from a repertoire to highlight certain smells. Even the gods can be enticed by the smell of blood or burning flesh, of precious incense or sweet flowers.

Every society and civilisation has its own smells, and one of the delights of travelling in India or China or South America is the new palette of smells that absorbs us. If you smell euca-lyptus leaves or a salty breeze, you will be taken back to your childhood in Australia. Each reader will be able to reflect on the smells that instantly take him or her backwards: perhaps herbs, flowers, cooking or just the air, full of dust, or earth smells or the fumes of buses and cars.

How has taste changed our world?

From infancy we are very aware of nice and nasty tastes and a great deal in between. Smell enhances taste, but perhaps less obvious is the connection between taste and sight. This became apparent to me when a Japanese friend tried to explain the comparative virtues of Japanese and Indian cooking.

He said, 'We Japanese eat food with our eyes.' The more elegant meals are beautifully presented, exquisite colours and arrangements on the plate or table. 'Turn off the lights,' he said, 'and eat it in the dark, and much of the food is so delicate that it hardly tastes of anything.' The presentation works by tricking our brain through associations. It is poetry on a plate.

On the other hand, to his way of thinking, an Indian curry was rather boring to look at. It consisted of a pile of white rice, with various brown sauces. Nothing to please the eye. Yet turn off the lights and eat it with one's taste buds and nose, as it were, and it was really delicious.

Certainly the joys of taste are ones that can hardly be over-emphasised. Great civilisations have revelled in food and cooking. It is very easy to argue that the heart of Chinese culture is food, its preparation and eating. Or again, much of American culture is now carried around the world in its food and drinks, the hamburger and cola culture. Italy is for many a series of delicious pastas, the eastern Mediterranean one of various cooked meats and kebabs.

Other civilisations are known for their drink. A notable contrast between the two great religions of Europe is between the Catholic wine-drinkers of the south and the Protestant beer-drinkers of the north. It is not difficult to argue that beer and the pub have long been one of the central identity-markers of English culture, just as whisky is for the Scots, or *sake* for the Japanese.

The connection between Catholic cultures and wine reminds us that not only are food and drink among our greatest pleasures, but we project these pleasures on to the gods. In almost all religions the chief offering is a sacred drink – wine, millet beer, rice wine – or foodstuffs, such as bread or sacrificial meat. Like humans, the gods delight in incorporating the material world through their mouths. Only a part of the pleasure we get from eating and drinking comes from filling our stomachs. Much of it is an expression of other things, including creativity, delight and fellowship.

How did a 'nice cup of tea' make all the difference?

I did not fully appreciate the significance of consumption and the importance of what we eat and drink until, with my mother, I wrote a book on just one small part of the vast sphere of foods and drinks, namely the history and influence of tea-drinking. As I worked on this, I began to realise to what an extraordinary extent we are what we consume and our lives are shaped by our scarcely examined sense of taste.

In Japan, the introduction of tea-drinking some six hundred years ago altered almost every aspect of life. It had a very deep influence on aesthetics, in particular pottery, but also architecture, painting and poetry. It influenced politics as the tea ceremony became a place where warring factions could meet. It fundamentally altered religion, for tea and Buddhism were inextricably mixed together. One cup of tea was worth an hour of Zen meditation.

Tea altered economics. The cultivating and exporting of tea was vital to the growth of the Japanese economy. The extra energy provided by the caffeine in tea enabled the Japanese to work incredibly long hours. It deeply affected health, for the boiling of the water, and the chemicals in tea that destroyed bacteria, almost eliminated water-borne disease. In sum, the 'Way of Tea', as it was called, and the 'Japanese Way' became almost identical. Tea was Japan, and Japan was Tea.

Meanwhile, at the other end of the Asian continent, when tea began to be imported in quantity into Britain in the early-eighteenth century it also affected everything. It altered relations between men and women, parents and children, shopkeepers and customers. It changed the nature and timing of meals. It altered architecture, furniture, pottery, shipping, navigation. It helped make the industrial revolution possible through improving health, and added to people's ability to survive fatigue and poor food. It provided the secret weapon to sustain the creation of the largest empire the world has ever seen. Without tea our modern world would be very different from what it is today.

This is just one substance. I might have rehearsed the history of sugar, potatoes, tobacco, beer, rice, herrings or any of many other foods or drinks. Each would show how far the culture of human beings is almost invisibly, but very powerfully, shaped by our sense of taste. The desire for pleasant sensations is, of course, manipulated through advertising and 'market forces'.

How does touching affect us?

When you were little, you had a passion for 'cuddly toys' and spent hours stroking the cats, teddy bears and other little creatures which accumulated in a pile on your bedroom floor. You loved stroking things, moss in the lawn, hazel catkins, sand and smooth stones.

The textures of the world are infinite. The pleasure of running water through the fingers, the different feels of wool, silk, cotton or velvet against the skin, there are so many ways in which half-consciously we enjoy bodily contact with our environment. The poet Rupert Brooke's lines about what he loved struck a chord with me many years ago:

> *Then, the cool kindliness of sheets, that soon*
> *Smooth away trouble; and the rough male kiss*
> *Of blankets; grainy wood; live hair that is*
> *Shining and free; blue-massing clouds; the keen*
> *Unpassioned beauty of a great machine;*
> *The benison of hot water; furs to touch …*

There can be no doubt that we are animals who enjoy touching and feeling. The hugs, kisses, brushing and encounters with many surfaces through our lives give us immense pleasure, not least in our sexual life. These pleasures are again very variable across time and culture.

What opens magic casements?

Humans are almost defined by their ability to articulate and interpret sound, particularly through language. Remove our vocal chords and we would never have flourished at all. The variations and importance of languages through history is immense. Two of the forms in which sound has given me particular pleasure are poetry and music.

It is difficult to overestimate the degree to which the rhythms and rhymes of poetry and popular songs infiltrate our lives. I find that lines of poetry haunt me through every waking hour.

'To cease upon the midnight with no pain'; 'Drips wet sunlight on the powder of mine eye'; 'Had I the heavens' embroidered cloths'; 'Surprised by joy, impatient as the wind'; 'The glory, jest, and riddle of the world!'; 'With beaded bubbles winking at the brim'; 'Shall I compare thee to a summer's day?'; 'As numberless as leaves in Valambrosa'; 'When the hounds of spring are on winter's traces'; 'O the mind, mind has mountains; cliffs of fall, frightful, sheer, no-man-fathomed'; 'A green thought in a green shade'; 'And drunk the milk of Paradise'; 'The savage wars of peace'; and a thousand other fragments (some of them no doubt slightly misremembered) echo through my life and give richness and consolation.

Without their cadences, and of course the accompanying worlds of plays, novels and other literature whose sounds echo in our minds even if we do not say them aloud, our life as humans would be immensely poorer.

What passions cannot music raise and quell?

The world of sounds where words are subordinate to the sound itself, which we can roughly term 'music', is as rich as that of intellectual sounds. This may be the music of nature – birdsong, water falling, a fire crackling, the wind of autumn sighing through the trees, waves breaking on rocks. Yet the special human pleasure is composed music. Here, of course, there is an almost infinite variety, from 'pop' in all its variants, through 'jazz' to classical, east and west, north and south.

Music is indeed a very deep form of communication, entering us in a way that we cannot put into words. The melodies and harmonies affect us at the level of our animal being. Music moves us to feel the most powerful of emotions – hate, fear, jubilation, love and calm. We are both liberated and trapped by its entangling enticements.

Since it is so powerful, we believe we can trap and entangle others, in particular the gods. For, as with taste and smell, it appears that the gods share our enthusiasm for music. Not only, we are told, are there heavenly choirs, but the angels play trumpets and harps to please God.

In particular, spiritual powers can be called by a distinctive sound: the deep note of a Tibetan horn in a Buddhist ritual, the bleat of a conch shell in a shamanic rite. Breaking continuous time with an abrupt sound is particularly effective in summoning the gods. Whether it is the clapping to attract the Shinto gods, the cymbals and drums used in many death rituals, or the ringing of bells large and small in Christian churches, the cacophony of gongs, bells, drums and cymbals is central to much religious ritual.

What are the pleasures of the eye?

Humans are basically visual animals. Something like three-quarters of what we absorb in the way of information about nature and other human beings comes into our brains via our eyes. It comes in as a mass of meaningless fragments of light, and then we start to interpret it. Although we do not have as powerful an eye as a hawk or a fly, we far outstrip either because of the size of the brain which makes sense of what the optics give us. We have the eyes of a predator, looking forwards. We notice very minute variations that stimulate our curiosity.

What to say of the pleasures of the eye? There is so much that I shall arbitrarily confine myself to just one form, painting. The pleasures of painting have grown on me over the ages, but they are obviously ones that have given you enormous happiness. I have watched and filmed you drawing and painting from a time before you could speak.

How do we learn to see the world so clearly?

Although I have become increasingly interested in looking at paintings, I did not think that I would ever come to write or think explicitly about the history and meaning of art. So it was a surprise to find myself proposing a new theory to answer

part of the largest question in the history of artistic representation: how, after many centuries of symbolic, non-realist, art,
did some painters with their brilliance, realism and accurate
perspective become intense mirrors of their worlds? What
caused the Renaissance in Western Europe and why did it
happen only in that one small, relatively backward part of the
Asian landmass?

My attempt to answer some of these huge puzzles led me
to read the major historians and critics of art. I began to understand a little of how, as children, we start by seeing the world
quite clearly. Then, as we grow older, we are systematically
taught to distort and bend the world, both as we perceive it
and as we represent it, to fit into the current fashions.

Yet, for a magical moment, roughly between 1380 and 1450,
the whole visualisation of nature changed in one area of the
world and the earth became bathed in a glorious light making
everything look even richer than what we normally see with the
naked eye. How did this technology of enchantment become so
rich, and the world consequently become enchanted in a new
way?

My suggestion is that it happened primarily because of
the rapid development of the one substance on earth that has
directly affected what we can see, namely glass. As Leonardo
da Vinci wrote, 'The mirror is the master of painters,' and the
glass mirror started to alter Western vision dramatically in the
century up to the time he painted. Not only did it allow proper
self-portraits, but it changed the angle of vision on the world,
disturbing our conventional views and allowing the painter
to check what he saw against another exact image. It doubled
reality.

Coloured glass in churches 'stains the white radiance of
eternity', and panes of glass frame the world and make possible
new ways of perceiving the world. Glass prisms and lenses were
used in experiments to determine precise laws of perspective

and allowed the artist-mathematicians to understand how light and the eye work. All these developments suddenly shocked one part of the world into a new way of seeing.

That shock and surprise occurred only in Western Europe. It occurred only in areas where fine glass had developed and it did so at precisely the moment when glass manufacturing became far more sophisticated.

What is the garden of earthly delights?

The garden is one source of delight that brings together all the senses. It combines smell, touch, sound, taste and sight in a powerful and evocative way. My large rambling English garden full of roses, honeysuckle, fruits and trees is an illustration of this and it seems to me deeply natural. Yet I also know how very odd both its form and my intense feelings for it are.

People in many cultures appreciate gardens, but they are often rather formal affairs, and shortage of space or wealth makes it impossible for many to have a reasonable-sized garden. The semi-wild garden is somewhat unusual. The English share the essential spiritual view of the irregular and 'natural' garden with the Japanese. Yet there is a marked contrast between the often miniaturised rock and pine gardens of Japan, the exquisite complexities of Chinese gardens, the formality of great French or Italian gardens and the tumbling pastoral woodland I have created. It is part of a wider difference in attitudes towards nature which has long intrigued me since I roamed the hills and woods of northern England as a boy.

I think the key to my English garden lies in the controlled confusion. Some have suggested that the British love of artificial wildness was originally the result of the alienation caused by the industrial revolution of the eighteenth and nineteenth centuries. In their proximity to the machines and daily horror of urban squalor the British were cut off from nature. Yet they simultaneously regarded it with all the more emotion. They broke the link with the natural world, but at the same time tried to create a deeper link. In order to gain peace and serenity, they began to worship nature. They artificially constructed nature, yet pretended that it was natural.

Personally I think that the mixture of manipulation and sentimentality, of calculative exploitation and uncalculating spontaneity, is much older than the eighteenth century. I believe that there is an unbroken tradition in the attitude to nature from the Anglo-Saxon period, through Chaucer and Shakespeare, up to Alexander Pope, the Romantics and the Pre-Raphaelites. Now we see the obsession with gardens in flower shows, in garden centres and on the television.

This ambivalent attitude, the creation of an artificial feeling of the countryside – the garden cities, the parks and widespread tending of small plots – arises out of the tension of an unusual social structure. The English have invested their landscape with a strong commercial mentality and morality from the Middle Ages onwards. Nature has not been really wild or untamed for a thousand years. Yet to preserve oases of tranquillity and non-calculative, non-competitive, not over-rational space in the midst of all the daily bustle, the garden and the park were preserved as spaces for feeling and spontaneity. There the human senses of smell, touch, hearing, tasting and above all seeing could be liberated and the body refreshed.

Certainly this is how I feel about my garden. After an exhausting day at committee meetings or teaching, of struggling through traffic or buying the week's food, like many others I find the natural world a deep solace, a 'haven in a heartless world'. Many find this restorative power in walking, mountaineering, deep-sea diving, sitting on a riverbank fishing. I find it in my garden, supplemented by walks up the reedy fen rivers or in the foothills of the Himalayas. Gardens and walking release the mind, allow us to become animals again for a brief moment in our over-cerebral existence.

Why do children delight?

Participating in the lives of children also mixes our senses and helps us shed the brittle shell of adult rationality for a while. Our own children are often a great source of joy, but also of ambivalence, strain, guilt, tiredness and confusion. They are too near us for unalloyed pleasure. My pleasure in children has reached its peak through the privilege of distance and closeness combined. I first learnt this pleasure amongst children in Nepal, and it has been repeated at an even more intense level in the pleasure of watching you, Lily, grow up.

It is difficult to say what is the ultimate source of this joy. Some of the ingredients are clear enough. You are certainly very beautiful and sometimes when the sunlight weaves into your hair or you look up with a startled smile, I suddenly see again the worlds of Cleopatra or Héloïse. Certainly you are very clever and as I listen to you, discuss with you, or watch you solve problems or learn to paint or read, I am awestruck at the complexity and brilliance of the human mind. Certainly you are full of humour and rumbustious fun and inventiveness, and when you and Rosa used to pretend to fight and tumble I was reminded of so many childhood games and pretended terrors.

So, as we explore together the virtual world that hovers on the edge of this material life, the many imaginative territories you inhabit bring back another reality. I catch glimpses of my own childhood wanderings on Pook Hill, to Toad Hall, Narnia, the land of hobbits, through Mowgli's jungle. All these are deep pleasures which combine all my senses and momentarily transport me into another dimension of living.

So if I were to bring it all together I would say that amidst all the misery, fear, injustice and pain which I am explaining to you, I hope you will not forget moments when all this fades away into periods of innocent joy. It is when we bring all our powerful senses together, perhaps in a moment in the garden of earthly delights, perhaps when we encounter again the first Eve, that we triumph over despair.

So a moment when Lily danced to Handel, or when she sat in a pool of buttercups, or gravely took part in her first tea ceremony, these are the moments I treasure. They are, with similar moments with other friends and loved ones, what makes being human bearable. They are also what makes me want to write these letters to you, Lily, for helping to remind me of all this.

28

*W*hat is sex and is it good for you?

Dear Lily,

I was not sure whether to write to you about sex. You are my granddaughter and I felt a bit uncomfortable at first. Yet I think I should try, since it is clearly something you will wonder about a great deal, especially at this time in your life. We have discussed almost everything over the years so I feel we can look at this personal issue without embarrassment.

If it does make you feel worried at all, imagine that you are just one of the eighty or so first-year undergraduates at Cambridge to whom I used to try to provide a simple survey of the huge varieties of sexual behaviour and attitudes among human beings. I tried to treat it in a matter-of-fact way. I did this to put their own lives into context and to relieve them of some of the kind of guilt that certainly I felt as a growing boy.

What can I say about the patterns of sexual relations?

In the era before effective contraception, a sexual relationship outside marriage was not only widely regarded as sinful, but dangerous as well. The woman, in particular, took a huge risk. Having an illegitimate child often led to disgrace, even imprisonment in a mental asylum, or a life of prostitution and perhaps infection with a venereal disease.

I was brought up on the edge of that period, and the idea of having sexual relations before I married was still considered sinful and dangerous. You will know how things have changed and how the age at which these things happen has dropped alongside the fall in the age of sexual maturity. There is little that I can say here that you cannot learn from good books and frank talks with friends, teachers, your parents and others. Perhaps the most important thing is that if you make decisions you then regret, you should as quickly as possible admit them to more experienced people and work out a good remedy.

Another thing to say is that sexual relationships have long been regarded as the very height of human experience. Sexual symbolism is widespread in the Bible, as in the Song of Solomon, and in the writings of great religious mystics. By bringing together our senses of touch, smell, sight and sound, and uniting them in a moment of mounting pleasure, we seem for a moment to reach a reality and happiness that transcends this mortal life. To miss this dimension is very sad.

Yet most of those who have thought deeply about the matter have also stressed that for sex really to satisfy it should be part of a wider relationship. It is not just an end in itself, but also part of a communication with another. If it occurs within a context of trust, commitment, and long-term and deep friendship, it will attain heights that fragmented and momentary bursts of pleasure cannot.

Another comparative point is to remind you of what a peculiar civilisation you come from. In the majority of societies, sexual relations have been embedded in social relationships. It is socially wise or stupid to be engaged in them at certain times or places or with certain people. The gods are sometimes involved if a taboo is broken, but generally sex is not really much to do with religion.

We can see this in, for example, Japan. Sexual relations there are mainly seen as a form of bodily function, alongside eating, drinking, working, defecating. They are pleasurable in themselves and there is no reason to be ashamed about them. The body itself has not been historically a sexually charged object.

In much of the West, however, there has been an association between sex and religion. God is concerned with the 'cleanliness' not only of our bodies but also of our minds. To read the tortured autobiographies and novels in the Western tradition, with their constant deep sense of guilt and conflict, is to be in a different world from that of the literature and art of much of India, China and Japan which openly celebrate sexuality and its pleasures.

It is a matter of balance. You will be aware of the way in which those who are trying to sell you drinks, cars, clothes or cosmetics are constantly trying to use the power of sex to sway your mind. You will notice how television and other media are obsessed with the subject. Much of your conversation is about it. You may be disgusted or intrigued by all this. You will certainly need to be wary of this constant pressure and try to stand back from the insistence to treat your body as primarily a sexual object.

On the other hand, you should also be aware of the still remaining traces of a guilt-ridden Christian civilisation, with its anti-female bias, its concealments of the 'shameful' side-effects of sexuality, its trading on guilt and embarrassment. If you accept that we are sexual beings, that the survival of the species depends heavily on making sexual intercourse a delightful sensation, that we can sometimes express our most intense love through such behaviour, then you will not loathe your body.

All of this is made more difficult for you by various things.

Though there is overlap, men and women are different and their desires and pleasures in sex are not the same. Be frank with your partners and do not through embarrassment cover up hidden conflicts of aim or achievement. Furthermore, as Bob Dylan put it, 'the times they are a-changin''. The liberation of sexuality in Western societies is one of the greatest social changes I have witnessed in my lifetime. At my all-boys boarding school we were not allowed even to talk to girls. Now what was my boarding house is a girls' house in that same school!

Relaxation of standards, better contraception, all this has brought new pleasures and reduced anxiety about the consequences of sex. Yet it has also put new strains upon you, made it more difficult to say no, threatened you with new dangers (sexually transmitted diseases, including AIDS). There is both a gain of experience and a loss of innocence.

Are homosexual and lesbian relations natural or cultural?

Almost all of us are physically attracted at some stage in our lives to someone of the same sex, and almost all schoolchildren go through a stage of feeling love for a person of their own sex. The attitudes towards this and the statistics are often not in line. Twentieth-century estimates suggested that more than four in ten men in the West have had same-sex relations leading to orgasm and that more than one in twenty adult males are exclusively homosexual. Amongst women, about one in five females in the United States have had physical relations with other females, and half have had 'intense emotional relations'.

In some cultures in the past, for instance in Ancient Greece, the love between men and boys was thought to be deeper than that between men and women. We find it referred to in the Bible and in great love poetry.

Yet in other societies, including England for long periods, same-sex relationships were looked on as perverted and deeply sinful. They were regarded as unnatural, shameful and subversive. The case of the writer Oscar Wilde, imprisoned for his relations with other men, is just one example. In many parts of the world, for instance China, it is still not easy to talk about same-sex relations. Yet some people, whether by nature or by upbringing or a combination of the two, clearly end up more attracted to members of their own than the opposite sex.

Recently, the question of marriage between same-sex partners has been much discussed in Europe and America, and such marriage is now allowed in an increasing number of countries. This is a really dramatic change and it is causing a huge debate, particularly in the United States, since it is claimed to subvert the true nature of marriage.

What is the incest taboo?

You may well have heard of the myth of Oedipus, who unknowingly killed his father and married his mother and was hounded down by the gods. Another Greek legend, of the love of a father for his daughter is the origin of what is known as the Electra complex. The other common form of incest is sexual relations between brothers and sisters, sibling incest as it is known.

Many have thought that the prohibition of such relations and the horror that surrounds the breaking of the taboo are universal. Indeed, some have argued that it is this rule that distinguishes us from animals (who often avoid close kin but do not seem to have a 'taboo') and hence is the start of human culture. And it is indeed true that, because it confuses the patterns of power and the flow of blood in the family, it is almost universally banned.

Yet most myths of origin tell of incest between brother and sister, and this was relatively common within ruling dynasties such as the pharaohs of Egypt. We even read of many cases where ordinary people married their true brothers and sisters and had children together, as in Roman Egypt.

The important thing to realise is that almost everyone during their life will be sexually attracted to someone among their close relatives. The art is to understand this temptation, but at the same time not to give in to it. As many have pointed out, the confusions caused by having sexual relations with a father, mother, sister or brother can cause very deep problems. Yet it is often the horror of others that turns a temporary and often minor deviation into something enormously destructive.

For example, the religious reformer Luther was told that through an accident a young man had unknowingly impregnated his own mother; Luther was then asked whether those involved should be told of what had happened. This was a decision made all the more difficult because the young man had now fallen in love with, and wanted to marry, the woman who was simultaneously his sister and his daughter. Luther advised that they should not be told and should be allowed to marry.

How sacred is marriage?

In the majority of human societies in history men have had several wives or women have had several husbands, or both. In other parts of the world it is the custom to marry only one person at a time, though in practice many people have several marriage partners one after another. In Christianity, in particular, it is thought that, once married, a person should not have sexual relations with anyone but his or her partner. Adultery – a strangely old-fashioned-sounding word nowadays – was traditionally a serious offence.

Again the attitudes and the statistics are in conflict. Twentieth-century investigators thought that about half of married males had intercourse with women other than their wives during their marriages, and recent analyses of the DNA of new-born infants has suggested very high incidences of children not being the real blood children of their supposed father.

It has been usual in almost all societies where there was a rule that sexual relations should be contained within the married pair for there to be a 'double standard'. Men could have other liaisons, but if women did so they were in real trouble. This has been particularly marked in a belt of societies that includes many Catholic and Islamic nations, much of traditional India, China and Korea. A woman caught in adultery was to be driven out, or even stoned to death. A man was treated much more leniently.

What about masturbation?

A number of societies have looked on sex with oneself, mastur-bation, with horror. In the Christian Old Testament, it was called 'the sin of Onan', who 'spilt his seed upon the ground'. In Victorian England it was often thought of as degrading and even medically dangerous – leading to blindness, loss of hair, even madness. This fear continued well into the twentieth century.

This is all rather peculiar. To start with, while those who masturbate may think that they are a lonely, perverted minority, almost everyone does so at some point in their life. A set of famous surveys in America in the twentieth century showed that over nine out of ten males and seven out of ten women masturbated to orgasm at some point. In early adolescence, the average was two and a half times a week among males, and it is very widespread among unmarried women.

Although I have never visited a real or virtual sex-aid shop, I suspect that it would show the vast ingenuity of humans in dealing with a very widespread demand for self-gratification.

With this near universality, it seems strange that it should have been so frowned upon.

Yet the horror is not universal. Anthropologists have found societies, for example in the Himalayas, with a much more relaxed attitude. In some societies boys or girls go out in groups and masturbate as a form of communal activity. In others there is no disapproval of the practice.

In Britain in the past, the pressures leading towards masturbation were very pronounced. People were forced to marry some ten years or so after reaching sexual maturity, and indeed many did not marry at all, yet there was a ban on sexual relations unless one was married. At the same time there was a strong attitude of horror. The result was a deep sense of guilt.

Is sex in the head or in the body?

Almost five hundred years ago the philosopher Montaigne noted how variable human culture is. He described how in one nation 'if a tradesman marries, all the other tradesmen invited to the wedding anticipate him with the bride ... and yet in that place strict fidelity is recommended during marriage'. Elsewhere 'there are public brothels of males, and even marriages between them'. In some countries 'fathers lend their children, and husbands their wives, for the enjoyment of their guests, in return for payment'. There were countries 'where a man may, without scandal, get his mother with child, and fathers consort with their daughters and sons'. Anthropologists have discovered examples of all of these and many other variations which seem bizarre to us. This sets one wondering what, exactly, sex is about.

One of the strangest things about sex is that it seems to be as much a mental as a physical matter. We know that the powerful urge to mate is biological. Yet the object of our attention, what arouses us, seems to be so variable. In our own experience we know that we may be thinking of entirely different things when suddenly the curve of an image, the movement of an eye, the flash of a piece of flesh can quickly arouse us.

It was a similar recognition of the way our minds cannot control our bodies that suggested to the medieval Church authorities that women should cover their hair in church in case members of the congregation – and, so it was alleged, even the angels – found their thoughts turning to lust.

Such a belief can be seen in the covering up of the bodies and faces of women in many parts of the world today. The incredible lengths to which societies have gone to put women in purdah or seclusion in many societies are well known. Sometimes they are walled in – in upper-class Korean families to such an extent that the only chance women had to see outside the walls was to invent swinging and jumping games which gave them a swift glimpse of another reality. Sometimes, as with the millions of Chinese women whose feet were broken in childhood, they are crippled to prevent them from wandering off and becoming the objects of men's lust.

Yet what modesty consists of is enormously variable. One of my favourite stories is of a nineteenth-century American visitor to Japan. When he tried to help two young Japanese ladies over a fence, as he would have done in his country, they fled in embarrassed confusion. But when he came to the next town, he was invited by them with great warmth to go into one of the communal bath-houses where the naked young ladies were bathing totally at ease.

What becomes clear is that while the sexual drive is strong, it is almost entirely subject to the invisible mental categories that tell us what is attractive and what is not interesting. Sex is an appetite very similar to that for food. Some like steak, some like vegetables; I hate prunes and marmalade while you, Lily, like both.

It is the same with sex. Some fall in love with people much

younger than themselves, some with rubber dolls, some with their pets or other animals. The extraordinary images on the internet we hear about have made us aware that even the most lurid fantasies of psychiatrists are dwarfed by the ramblings of human desire.

What attracts us and what is allowed are fairly arbitrary, but there are always rules. This is one reason why the anthropologist Robin Fox declared that 'sex is in the head', and it is why I would like to move on now to the last letter on a specific topic, namely the way in which our minds control us without our being able to do much about it. Let's move from sex to money, time, space and language.

29

*W*hat controls our minds?

Dear Lily,

Many of us believe that we can think what we like, even if we may have to be careful in what we say or write. This is an illusion.

From the moment we are born our minds are being moulded to think in particular ways, to see certain objects, to make certain connections, to establish particular patterns, to value specific things. Other things around us are invisible, unregistered, unvalued. This filter influences the way in which I write and you read these letters. It also shapes the way in which readers in other parts of the world, whose mental spectacles are different from English ones, understand what I am writing.

Time flies like an arrow – or does it?

In most human societies, time has not been seen as a straight line. It has usually been thought of as circular, reflecting our normal experience. In plants and animals there is birth, maturation, ageing, death, perhaps rebirth. So it is with the days and nights and with the seasons of the year. Time does not advance, it is not split into tiny elements, its rhythm is slow and repetitive, it is not independent of us. The very movement of the stars in the sky declares that motion is circular.

And we know from our experience that time feels elastic, sometimes passing too fast or too slowly. The posh name for this is relativity. As Albert Einstein explained, 'When you are courting a nice girl an hour seems like a second. When you sit on a red-hot cinder a second seems like an hour. That's relativity.'

Yet you and I treat time in a more mechanical way, and no one is sure why we now have this peculiar attitude. We not only subdivide it into tiny bits, but look on it as a scarce commodity, draining away, to be saved or spent. It is also thought to be going somewhere, aiming towards some future event, like a river or an arrow, and it ticks away irrespective of how we feel about it.

We are not like the nomadic Arabs who knew that it was autumn when they came upon a valley with a certain kind of mushroom growing in it. We know when it is autumn and go to that valley specifically to collect mushrooms. Except in the jokes about confused tourists who wake up and say to themselves, 'We are in Tokyo, it must be Thursday,' we tend first to think of time, and then arrange our lives around it.

There are several theories to explain our obsession, our battling, with time. There is a religious element. Judaism, Christianity and Islam seem to have an idea of time as a progression or straight line. This is very different from the circular concepts of Hinduism, or the idea of the annihilation of past and future in certain forms of Buddhism. This particular thread was given heavy emphasis when Protestantism emerged in the sixteenth century. From then, God was particularly concerned that we did not waste time or our talents. Accounting for what we do, making every moment count, turning time into profitable activity were strongly encouraged.

Time had been thought of in all previous civilisations as reflecting the circular rhythms of nature. Sundials and gravity clocks using sand or water were the only ones that existed until the tenth century AD. Then something strange happened which set time free. A device was developed (the escapement) that broke the continuous motion of gravity into little equal bits. It rotated back and forth regularly like the tick-tock of a clock. There is disagreement as to whether it was invented in China or the West, but certainly it was in the latter that it was rapidly developed.

It is also argued that the regular, enclosed rhythms of the monastic orders, with their bells and tight time schedules, required such a precise clock to be developed. In other words a new sense of time-accounting was already present before the mechanical clock was invented. Others suggest the opposite. They say that it was the new clocks available from the twelfth century that gave us a more exact sense of time.

Whatever the answers to these questions of cause and origin, it is not difficult to see how much we are obsessed and ruled by time. We learn to internalise it, to fear or fight against it, to think of it as a commodity to consume. Even with the spread of mobile phones, a recent check among my students suggested that the watch is still the most common machine we carry around.

We now imagine microscopic slices of time, microseconds and nanoseconds. Our attention spans have shrunk and our civilisation ticks to the clock and whirs with ever faster travel and computers.

Do we look to the past or the future?

In most traditional societies, people tended to look to the past. They revered their ancestors, tried to retain the traditions, lived in a remembered world. In contrast, increasingly for us the past is a foreign country where strangers lived. Most people, especially in rapidly changing societies like America or China, tend to think much more about the present and particularly the future than about the past. They see little or no connection between themselves and previous generations. The threads are cut; they have nothing in common with the landscape they live in, except as 'heritage'. Science fiction rather than historical fact interests them.

Again it is difficult to know why this great change has taken place. Its roots are partly religious and philosophical. Most religions had their great moment in the past, in the life of Buddha, Muhammad, the prophets or Confucius. Christianity, however, looks forward, to 'the Second Coming'. Like communism, it is a Utopian faith, travelling hopefully towards a world where all sin and misery will be cleansed from earth.

Technology also plays a part. Rapid change cuts us off from the past. The great inventions of printing, the compass and gunpowder meant that the seventeenth-century philosophers felt that they were no longer the same as the ancients. They were no longer living in a circular world, for there was real progress. Now we often feel that those who lived before electricity, cars, photography and modern medicine must have been very different. Technological change is so rapid that a world before the internet, the mobile phone, genetic engineering and the latest generation of weapons seems a different one, with little to teach us.

Societies based on the premise of the hierarchy of caste tend to emphasise links with the past. Previous events explain and justify present inequalities. Noble families treasure their family trees and pay respect to their ancestors. Even ordinary families maintain their position by attention to past origins.

When a new world was created in the United States, based on equality at birth (at least for white people), the interest in the past was cut off in one stroke. We ourselves make our own way in life. What our family was or did in the past is largely irrelevant, or just a leisure interest, as in the great interest in family genealogy. Live for the future, make and remake your world is the view of many.

The majority white population of America only arrived relatively recently. Yet its citizens hope and sometimes believe it has a great future. I remember my surprise on my first visit as I passed through customs and instead of being asked 'How are you?' (or as I would have been in my Nepalese village, 'Have you eaten rice?') I was greeted with a cheerful 'Have a good day'.

Why does money matter?

'Time is money' is an old saying, showing the connection between two of our obsessions. What then is money, this strange thing which, like time, consumes much of our attention and dominates our lives to such an extent?

Money is a trick or a fiction; it is a symbol which has no intrinsic value. Gold, silver, jewels, bits of paper or cowrie shells are in themselves useless and valueless. Value is injected into them by humans. This explains why almost anything can be 'used' as money.

At school money was sometimes marbles, sometimes white mice, sometimes sweets. In many parts of Asia, tea blocks are still used as money. They are in many ways a good form of money since they can at least be boiled up and drunk in an emergency. In others, salt, pepper or spices are used, or precious incense. These items seem to have intrinsic value, not merely something injected into them.

Whatever form it takes, it turns into full-blown money when the object can simultaneously be a store and measure of value and an item of exchange. It is our attitude to it that determines its value. Hence it is not money itself that is said to be the root of all evil, but, according to the Bible, the love of money.

Money stands for a relation of power over others. It is like oil in a machine, for it allows the parts to function without grinding against each other. It is a translation device, a leveller; it makes objects in different spheres exchangeable. It allows us, having created one commodity, then to exchange this for another. It has no morality, no inner essence, but it can enter almost all of our life.

We do try to protect specific areas with invisible signs: 'No money here'. Certain beautiful things are beyond the reach of money. I cannot sell King's College Chapel, or even the hundredth part that I appear to own as a Fellow of the college. I cannot buy or sell true love or friendship. I cannot buy or sell truth or religious salvation, although the Catholic Church did at one time sell indulgences. I cannot buy part of the public park in the centre of Cambridge. I cannot buy a place in a cricket team or an orchestra or a chance to study at King's College.

Yet in much of our life, money holds us to ransom. It slips through our hands in a slithery way. The more we have, the more we seem to need. Few people admit to having too much, and many have less than they need or want. Indeed much of our capitalist world is propelled by an apparently unavoidable shortage of money. This is created by the desire for the substance itself. It seems, as in many fairy stories, to turn into dust when it is touched.

In comparison with most of the planet, in Britain we are 'affluent' or rich. Our world is awash with the things that money can buy. Yet few of us feel satisfied. At the other extreme there are some simple societies where people wander about in forests and savannahs. They appear to have hardly anything at all, yet it is reported that they feel satisfied with their lives.

This paradox arises from the fact that satisfaction comes from the relation between means and ends, income and expenditure. This was immortally put by Mr Micawber in *David Copperfield* by Charles Dickens: 'Annual income twenty pounds, annual expenditure nineteen nineteen six, result happiness. Annual income twenty pounds, annual expenditure twenty pounds ought and six, result misery.'

Some simple hunting and gathering societies have a finite need for food and water, for shelter and clothing, and for leisure and social relationships. There is more than enough of all of these; 'income' exceeds demand. We, on the other hand, often reach for the stars, have an open-ended demand and a deep craving for more and more.

Very soon we forget that what made us happy yesterday would not satisfy us for a moment today. I met a Chinese man in his thirties. He said that as a country boy all he wished for in life was one day to be rich enough to have boiled dumplings every morning like his city cousins. Now his daughter wants a PhD from Peking University. The 'revolution of rising expectations' condemns many of us to eternal dissatisfaction. Buddhism calls understanding this the second 'noble truth'.

Each choice we make is a minor deprivation. At the restaurant of life we can gorge ourselves only on a certain amount. If we choose the curry, there is sadness that the pizza or stew is untasted. The Romans made themselves vomit so that they could enjoy the taste of more food, but in the end even they were satiated and could not eat everything. We always want more. Happiness is seen as lying in some future bonus or better job.

Yet we are constantly brainwashed to think that money really exists, and that the more we have of it, the happier we will be. The whole capitalist consumption machine would crash to the ground if we could not be persuaded to spend, spend, spend. The billboards, television advertisements, lifestyles of media and sporting heroes constantly shout 'Money, money, money' at us.

It is therefore sensible from time to time to stand back. We can try tasting a bit of money in our mouth. It tastes (unless it is tea or pepper) of nothing. Nor does it last. As the Irish philosophically put it, 'A shroud has no pockets.' That wise economist Adam Smith pointed out that if we want to escape from the trap of anxiety and dependency on money, the thing to look at is not how to get more money, but how to spend less.

For though we can never earn enough to satisfy our ever expanding cravings, through frugality we can learn the pleasure of being free from care. We certainly need sufficient money in the present world and, as the comedian Woody Allen observed, 'Money is better than poverty, if only for financial reasons.' We can also perhaps start to enjoy one of life's greatest delights, which is seeing how a little of the extra which we have saved can give relief and pleasure to others. For, as the philosopher Francis Bacon wrote, 'Money is like manure, not good unless it be spread.'

How sensible are our categories?

Our culture teaches us to create a grid or map of the world, placing things into boxes. Some things are alike, others are different. Those that straddle the borders are often dangerous or dirty. We believe that these things really are what we believe them to be because of their innate qualities, that apples and plums belong to one class of things, cats and dogs to another.

A delightful undermining of our categories is shown by the arrangement attributed by Dr Franz Kuhn to a Chinese encyclopaedia called the *Heavenly Emporium of Benevolent Knowledge*. This divides animals as follows:

(a) those that belong to the Emperor; (b) embalmed ones;
(c) those that are trained; (d) suckling pigs; (e) mermaids;
(f) fabulous ones; (g) stray dogs; (h) those that are included
in this classification; (i) those that tremble as if they were

*mad; (j) innumerable ones; (k) those drawn with a very fine
camel's-hair brush; (l) et cetera; (m) those that have just
broken the flower vase; (n) those that at a distance resemble
flies.*

The logic behind this is not easy to see – and we may wonder
what would happen if innumerable suckling pigs became
frenzied and broke a flower vase at a great distance!

We might think that this Chinese example is somewhat
fanciful, but the Japanese numbering system is quite similar.
For each class of thing there is a different series of numbers.
The ordinal numbers

*are divided into nearly as many series as there are classes of
objects. There is one class for all animals – except the flying
and swimming species, and insects. Another for birds, in
which, however, hares and rabbits are included! A third for
ships, and junks, and boats; a fourth for liquids drunk with a
glass, as water, wine, tea etc.; a fifth for things having length,
as trees, pens, sticks, masts, beams, radishes, carrots, fingers,
brooms, pipes etc. and so on ad infinitum.*

The author stopped there 'in despair, foreseeing that they
would fill a volume by themselves'.

Yet, arbitrary as these classifications look, your or my classification would probably look just as arbitrary to a visiting
spaceman. For instance, why do we classify the bottom of
things as more stable and truthful than the top, so that what
appears at the bottom of a television screen is more 'believed'
than that at the top?

Our mental worlds are filled with reflections of the present
and past worlds which created them. These reflections in turn
reshape and determine what we can think. They are instilled
in us by our family, school, media, friends. Only a considerable

effort makes it possible to stand back and examine what have been called 'the idols of the mind', the things we fall down and worship without much thought.

How can we talk about our world?

The difficulty of examining our mind's hidden paths is made even greater by the entrapment of language. As Rudyard Kipling rightly observed, 'Words are, of course, the most powerful drug used by mankind.' Their power is not just mental. As the Japanese proverb puts it, 'One kind word can warm three winter months.' Almost everything we do and feel is affected by language.

So although language does not determine our thought, it does set a grid through which we see, feel about and report our world. The comparative linguist Benjamin Whorf wrote that 'We dissect nature along lines laid down by our native language … Language is not simply a reporting device for experience but a defining framework for it.'

For instance, by contrasting English and Hopi, Whorf tried to show that in English, time is divisible into past, present and future, while in Hopi there is just a division between those things that are manifest and those that are still in the process of being manifest – there is no equivalent of past, present and future tenses. This alters our way of perceiving time.

In Japanese there are no tenses, no way of knowing whether something has happened, is happening, or will happen. There is no use of pronouns, so one does not know if I, you, we or they are doing something. There is no positive and negative distinction. So if we invite someone to dinner and they say 'hai' it means yes or no. This is combined with many other, to us odd, features of grammar and syntax and the fact that sets of characters (there are three systems in Japan) can mean entirely different things.

I well remember sitting for fifteen minutes while a Japanese companion went through a menu with the waitress and tried to ascertain what certain dishes on it really were. When the food finally appeared, it bore little resemblance to what we thought we had ordered. It is no wonder that the Japanese have a proverb 'Language is a barrier to communication' and prefer *haragei* or body language to the spoken form.

Each language has its peculiarities. English has very little grammar, but lots of words. Romance languages (the ones that come from Latin, including French, Italian, Spanish) compel us to specify the gender of all nouns. Certain American Indian languages oblige people to indicate whether an object is near or far from the speaker and whether it is visible or invisible. It is not difficult to see why in the Himalayas there are three forms of the verb 'to come', meaning to come up, to come down, or to come on the flat.

It is an endlessly enthralling topic. For example, can we see things for which we have no word? Among the people I work with in Nepal the word *pingya* means both blue and green. Can they see the difference if they cannot speak it?

A clue to the answer is given by the fact that in Russian there are two words for 'blue' which roughly mean light and dark blue. A Russian anthropologist studying us might come to the logical, but incorrect, conclusion that because we do not linguistically differentiate the two blues, the Oxford and Cambridge boat-race teams could not tell each other apart. When I asked my Nepalese friends they said that of course they could see the difference between the green grass and the blue sky.

The nature of the primary colours, and the very idea of what 'colour' is, varies greatly. In China, Japan and Korea there are five primary colours: white, black, green-blue, yellow-red, brown-red. We do not consider white and black to be 'colours' at all, but have a different range of primary colours including yellow.

Thinking is our strongest survival tool, and language and culture the expressions of this. Yet we are constantly trapped into certain habits of the mind. Much of our world goes unnoticed, or noticed too strongly. Yet these blinkers are at least half-explicit and we are taught a little about this at school, especially if we learn other languages. Deeper and less examined are the seductions of our senses, the ways in which we absorb knowledge by apprehending reality through our body.

30

*W*hy are we here?

Dear Lily,

I have written you lots of letters about all sorts of things. In this letter I won't try to summarise or conclude. I will just jot down a few impressions of some of the things that seem to have emerged.

Is our world just an accident?

Most people in the past, and many in the present, believe that the way in which things develop through time is laid down by God or the gods. God is a master craftsman, artist or mechanic, who designs an elaborate system. People argue that all this present complexity cannot be the result of pure accident. There must be a purpose behind it. If you believe this, it will solve many puzzles and make it easier to accept apparent chaos.

Personally I cannot see evidence for a human-like force behind creation, though I do accept that there is an extraordinary degree of orderliness. It seems to me likely that this is the result of basic biological and physical laws, operating over millions of years. These lead to constant small variations. Those that work, that improve the chances for the survival of plants and animals (including human animals), are retained. Add to this the nature of human beings, with their conscious experimentation, their cultural memory and their desire to improve their world (and ability to make a hash of their attempts), and it is possible to account for how our world could have reached this point.

In all of this the many 'accidents', such as the shape of Cleopatra's nose, the wind that destroyed Kubla Khan's fleet off Japan, or the birth of Napoleon, have changed the world. On the other hand there are deep forces and laws, the laws of population, economics and politics which I have told you about, which also operate alongside these one-off accidents. So we can see a mixture of chance, of unintended consequences, and comprehensible and more general laws.

What are the interconnections?

When we are faced with an immensely complex problem, it often helps to break it into manageable sub-problems and to solve these one at a time. So we study different topics at school, economics, biology, history, literature, physics and so on. That is fine and necessary. After we have separated them, however, we also need to bring these bits back together again. To get very far in understanding our world we need to see things in relation to each other.

We cannot understand how our family system works without knowing about how it fits with law, economics, religion and politics. We cannot understand population changes without knowing something about biology, economics, law and religion. And so it goes on. So while we study one particular sub-discipline or subject at a time, we need to be constantly aware of how each one fits into a larger picture.

Why compare?

You will have noted my frequent allusions to different parts of the world, particularly to the Nepalese village where I study and to Japan which I frequently visit. To understand ourselves we need to step back from our narrow everyday world and get a wider perspective. One of the best ways to do this is to compare our world with the many other actual and possible worlds that exist and have existed. We can do this through travel – literal physical travel or the infinite forms of virtual travel available in books, films, television and friendships with people from other cultures.

Our own lives and systems very quickly become so familiar that we do not see them. Only when we look elsewhere and then back at ourselves do we notice the air we breathe and have taken for granted. Much of our world is constructed artificially through history, an invented culture. Yet because it is ours, we tend very quickly to see it as natural, the only sensible way to live.

Are the English (and Americans) blind?

This temptation to think that our world is natural and does not therefore need explaining is particularly strong if, like you and me, one is English. As islanders we have been slightly cut off from foreign influences. We have lived in a corner of a continent and, as has been observed, people who live in corners always think they are special. Instead of this leading to our thinking we are odd, we have tended in our arrogance to think that our way is natural and does not need justification and that everyone else is odd. There is supposedly an English newspaper headline: 'Fog in the Channel: Continent Cut Off'.

The very success of many things English or British in the last two hundred years has increased this arrogance. Through luck, Britain gradually developed the largest empire on earth.

Through this empire it spread many of the basic ideas by which many people now live. Industrial production, the scientific method, democratic politics, the simple family system and love marriages, private property and commercial capitalism, religious tolerance, team games, and much great literature are all parts of the package. This influence was reinforced by the United States, which refined many of these ideas and gave them strong backing.

Much of the world now speaks English, thinks English, plays English, runs its capitalist economics, its individualistic social life, its democratic politics and its legal system along English lines. Of course this is an exaggeration and oversimplification because many changes are made to these things when they move elsewhere. Furthermore, most of what we take to be 'English', as I explained in the second letter, was originally imported.

Yet it is true that if you travel you will find strong reflections of your own and American culture. To a certain extent the modern world has come to us through a narrowed funnel: the past, like sand through an egg-timer, has narrowed down and then spread out through an English passage. This again makes your own country seem rather natural, universal, invisible in many ways. It also tends to make many of us notoriously bad at learning and speaking other languages and hence limits our ability to enjoy interacting with non-English speakers.

Is England odd?

Yet once you step away from these assumptions you will soon be aware that both historically and cross-culturally what seems 'natural' is indeed very odd. England is like Charles Darwin's Galapagos Islands, a place where strange creatures have developed because of their partial isolation.

I don't think I need to remind you of all these oddnesses.

These letters are full of them. From the curious way we bring up our children, fall in love, believe in 'the truth', believe in equality before the law, through to many things I have not had the space to talk about, like our odd sense of humour or our odd food, we are a bundle of peculiarities and contradictions.

Are humans odd?

If the English are pretty odd, they are only an example of the oddness of the species revealed in these letters. The contradictions between reason and emotion and between body and mind and many others mentioned in my first letter have been amply shown. Much of this comes from one central paradox described by the essayist William Hazlitt: 'Man is an intellectual animal, and therefore an everlasting contradiction to himself. His senses centre in himself, his ideas reach to the ends of the universe; so that he is torn in pieces between the two, without a possibility of it ever being otherwise.'

On the one hand humans are companionable and social beings in their family, love, friendship and playful behaviour. Yet they also engage in great violence in war and persecution. They desperately search for faith and knowledge and constructive understanding to build a better world. Yet they also search for power and order and domination. And so it goes on.

This is why it is really impossible to say that humans are basically of this or that nature. The species is a mass of contradictions, very malleable, full of potential for good and evil. Often it makes you despair as you study its antics, but occasionally you draw your breath in wonder at the beauty it creates and the truths it has discovered.

How did we get here?

These letters have tried to tell you how the world you live in has come about. I have suggested it has done so by a mixture of evolution and revolution. In England there has been a long evolution for over a thousand years. Although things have been constantly changing in small ways, and there have been moments of more dramatic change – for instance in the middle of the seventeenth century or during the industrial and urban upheavals after 1780 – there is no moment when everything changed at once.

Revolutions can be defined as times when not only do the players change, but the rules are altered. People decide to stop playing cricket and start to play football. The English have basically always played the same game. The legal, linguistic, family and other systems are recognisably the same from the Anglo-Saxons to the present. Yet the rules have been modified day to day to fit a changing world.

Many societies and civilisations have had a less continuous history. They have tended in one direction, then suddenly switched to another. They play cricket, then football, then hockey. The famous revolutions in history, in particular the French of 1789, the Russian of 1917 and the Chinese of the 1940s, are examples of this happening. Yet even in these there is often much more hidden continuity than people imagine.

Just as we are now constantly told that our world is undergoing revolutionary changes because of globalisation and new technologies, yet we feel that there is also a great deal of continuity, so many French people feel that their Revolution altered only some things and many Chinese argue that Chairman Mao was really just another emperor. The Japanese have been through huge shifts in their history, successively going through a Chinese, a feudal, a neo-Confucian, a European and an American phase. Yet below all these there is a set of deep structures, a customary way of thinking and doing, a grammar of actions which has been curiously continuous.

So England and Japan in particular can best be described by the contradictory phrase 'the changing same'. They are like the famous shoe. The shoe was patched with new leather, given a new heel and a new toe. It was entirely new material, yet was also in shape and function the same old shoe. No wonder the philosopher in the story could not decide whether it was the same or a different shoe.

What constrains us?

I have tried to show you something of the deeper tides below the surface of history. Beneath the daily events there are a number of continuing structures and strong tendencies. To change the metaphor, there are paths along which civilisations move and though there is room for straying, they are under some compulsion to stick to the path.

These tendencies and paths are determined by physical, biological, economic, political and social forces. They constrain our lives in the same way that language constrains, but does not absolutely determine, what we can think and say. The best way to harness their power is to understand what they are. In knowledge is freedom. When the fly realises it is trapped in the fly bottle, it has established some freedom. It may even find the exit from the jar.

These paths vary between civilisations. None is intrinsically morally better. Each has its advantages and its drawbacks. The current dominant one, the individualistic, democratic, capital-istic, industrial and scientific system, has a number of attrac-tions. It leads to a good material life for many. It gives a feeling of equality and control over our life. It can avoid fear and oppression. Many civilisations are impressed by it.

On the other hand it has a lot of drawbacks. It can leave

individuals lonely and confused. It often leads to a feeling of guilt and inadequacy. It puts a great burden on the individual. It promises equality, but can lead to gross inequalities. It can sap all real meaning from life and in particular can turn work into boring drudgery. It creates ecological desolation and areas of the world filled with drugs and pornography. It is no surprise that even in the midst of its affluence and openness many reject what it offers as empty pleasure-seeking.

What is certain is that all creeds that promise an end to suffering and pain on this earth are deluding us. Buddhism perhaps has the best answer, suggesting that we can transcend the suffering. We are animals, competitive animals. We have survived through living off other species and each other.

We can strive to make the world better, less cruel, less confused, less unfair. Yet to turn it back to an imagined paradise is impossible, not least because there never was such a golden age. Attempts to make heaven on earth, however well-meaning, have usually ended up in the horrors that we associate with movements such as communism and fascism. They tend to lead to hell and not to paradise because they are based on a totally unrealistic notion of what we are and how societies work.

In the end, we can only accept our contradictory nature. We can modestly seek to hurt our fellow humans and the other animal and plant species with which we share this small planet as little as possible.

Let's remind ourselves what a puny and trivial species we are in the words of Douglas Adams's *Hitchhiker's Guide to the Galaxy*:

Far out in the uncharted backwaters of the unfashionable end of the Western Spiral arm of the Galaxy lies a small unregarded yellow sun. Orbiting this at a distance of roughly ninety-two million miles is an utterly insignificant little blue green planet whose ape-descended life forms are so amazingly primitive that they still think digital watches are a pretty neat idea.

What else is there to say?

I've tried to explain how I think the world works. I've kept the letters short and left out most of the detail. Fortunately the arrival of the internet means that I can refer you to other things which will add to this account.

On your very own website, www.letters2lily.com, you will find …

Thirty very short letters from you, Lily. These ask the questions that I imagine you would have asked me to get the letters in this book in reply. You can hear me reading out my answers to four of them.

There are also thirty short letters in which I explain how my own life led me to write certain of the letters in this book. I have listed some of the books and other things that I've found particularly helpful in trying to understand the themes covered here; some of these you know, others you might like to look at.

There are some reactions to this book from other readers. There is also a chance to add your own comments or discuss the topics here in an international forum (chat room). Finally, there are the sources for the quotations in the book and thanks to those who have helped me in various ways to write these letters.

More generally on my own website (www.alanmacfarlane. com) you will see a lot about my own experiences and life and the various books and articles on which I've drawn for these short letters. There are lots of films and photographs from all over the world, as well as things such as lectures I've given and television films I've been in. These chart my pursuit of the riddles and questions about which I have written and will add flesh to the bare bones of the letters in this book.

...

The internet helps, yet there is still so much more I'd like to say to you, Lily. I am reluctant to end. The best way I can say goodbye is to pass on a poem which your great-grandmother, my mother Iris, wrote for my sister.

Petition for my daughter

Time be kind. The dangerous world
Presses on the petals furled,
But as bruising years go by
Promise her a sanctuary.

Let her grow with great surprise,
Guard the wonder in her eyes
For a shining sea-washed stone,
For leaves of satin, twigs of bone.

Trust her with your mysteries,
Butterflies and bark of trees.
Woo her with your winds and grasses
Comfort her when summer passes.

Give her body's flower grace
Into Galahad's embrace,
That in peace she may discover
Man as friend and friend as lover.

Time be kind, be gentle. Teach her
There are woods where naught can reach her,
There are mornings none can borrow,
Love enough for each tomorrow.